MacBook Neo

by Mark L. Chambers

MacBook Neo For Dummies®

Published by: **John Wiley & Sons, Inc.,** 111 River Street, Hoboken, NJ 07030-5774, www.wiley.com

For general information on our other products and services, please contact our Customer Care Department within the U.S. at 877-762-2974, outside the U.S. at 317-572-3993, or fax 317-572-4002. For technical support, please visit https://hub.wiley.com/community/support/dummies.

Wiley publishes in a variety of print and electronic formats and by print-on-demand. Some material included with standard print versions of this book may not be included in e-books or in print-on-demand. If this book refers to media that is not included in the version you purchased, you may download this material at http://booksupport.wiley.com. For more information about Wiley products, visit www.wiley.com.

Library of Congress Control Number: 2026943212

ISBN 978-1-394-45395-5 (pbk); ISBN 978-1-394-45397-9 (ebk); ISBN 978-1-394-45396-2 (ebk)

Printed and bound by CPI Group (UK) Ltd, Croydon, CR0 4YY

C9781394453955_030626

Contents at a Glance

Introduction 1

Part 1: Tie Myself Down with a Desktop? Preposterous! 5
CHAPTER 1: Hey, It Really Does Have Everything I Need 7
CHAPTER 2: Turning On Your Portable Powerhouse 19
CHAPTER 3: The Neo Owner's Introduction to macOS Tahoe 29

Part 2: Shaking Hands with macOS Tahoe 61
CHAPTER 4: A Nerd's Guide to System Settings 63
CHAPTER 5: Searching Amidst Neo Chaos 81
CHAPTER 6: Using Reminders, Notes, Notifications, Maps, and News 89

Part 3: Connecting and Communicating 103
CHAPTER 7: Let's Go on Safari! 105
CHAPTER 8: Expanding Your Horizons with iCloud 119
CHAPTER 9: Creating a Multiuser Neo 127
CHAPTER 10: Working Well with Networks 141
CHAPTER 11: Hooking Up with Your World 157

Part 4: Living the iLife 165
CHAPTER 12: The Multimedia Joys of Music and TV 167
CHAPTER 13: Focusing on Photos 185

Part 5: Getting Productive and Maintaining Your Neo 203
CHAPTER 14: Desktop Publishing with Pages 205
CHAPTER 15: Creating Spreadsheets with Numbers 217
CHAPTER 16: Building Presentations with Keynote 231
CHAPTER 17: When Good Mac Laptops Go Bad 243
CHAPTER 18: Tackling the Housekeeping 255

Part 6: The Part of Tens 263
CHAPTER 19: Ten Neo Rules to Follow 265
CHAPTER 20: Ten Things to Avoid Like the Plague 273

Index 279

Table of Contents

INTRODUCTION 1
   Foolish Assumptions 1
   About This Book 2
   Icons Used in This Book 3
   Beyond the Book 4
   Where to Go from Here 4

PART 1: TIE MYSELF DOWN WITH A DESKTOP? PREPOSTEROUS! 5

CHAPTER 1: **Hey, It Really Does Have Everything I Need** 7
   An Overview of Your Mac Laptop 8
      The parts you probably recognize 8
      The holes called ports 10
      Don't forget the parts you can't see 10
      Whoa! Where's my familiar USB port? 11
   Location, Location, Location! 12
   Unpacking and Connecting Your MacBook Neo 13
      Unpacking for the road warrior 13
      Connecting Cables 101 14
   Great — a Lecture about Handling My Neo 15
   An Overview of Mac Software Goodness 15
      What comes with my Neo? 15
      Connecting to the internet from your lap 16
      Applications that rock 17
   Other Stuff That Nearly Everyone Wants 17

CHAPTER 2: **Turning On Your Portable Powerhouse** 19
   Throwing the Big Leaf Switch 19
   Mark's Favorite Signs of a Healthy Laptop 20
   You Won't Lecture Me about Batteries, Will You? 21
   Harriet, It's Already Asking Me Questions! Setting Up macOS Tahoe 22
   Importing Documents and Data from Your Old Mac 24
   Manually Importing Documents and Data from Windows 26

CHAPTER 3: **The Neo Owner's Introduction to macOS Tahoe** . . . 29
   Your Own Personal Operating System 30
   The Tahoe Desktop 30
      Meet me at the Dock 30
      Check out that Control Center 31

Dig those crazy icons. 32
There's no food on this menu 32
The Finder menu bar is your friend 33
There's always room for one more window 33
Widgets on parade 34
Wait a Second: Where the Heck Are the Mouse Buttons?. 34
Launching and Quitting Apps 36
Performing Tricks with Finder Windows 38
Scrolling in and resizing windows. 38
Minimizing and restoring windows. 39
Moving and zooming windows 39
Closing windows 40
Juggling Folders and Icons 42
A field observer's guide to icons 42
Selecting items. 43
Copying items. 44
Moving things from place to place 45
Duplicating in a jiffy. 45
Using Finder Tabs 46
Keys and Keyboard Shortcuts to Fame and Fortune 46
Special keys on the keyboard 47
Using the Finder and app shortcuts 47
Home, Sweet Home Folder 48
Working with Mission Control. 50
Hiring a Stage Manager 50
Switching Desktops with Spaces 51
Personalizing Your Desktop. 52
Taking Control of Your Neo 53
Customizing the Dock. 54
Adding applications and extras to the Dock 54
Using Desktop widgets. 55
Keeping track with Stacks. 56
Resizing the Dock. 57
What's with the Trash? 57
All You Really Need to Know about Printing 58
And Just in Case You Need Help 60
The Tahoe built-in Help system. 60
The Apple web-based support center 60
Online resources 60

PART 2: SHAKING HANDS WITH MACOS TAHOE 61

CHAPTER 4: **A Nerd's Guide to System Settings** 63
An Explanation — without Jargon, No Less 64
Locating That Certain Special Setting. 65

Popular System Settings Panes Explained. 65
  The Displays pane 65
  The Desktop & Dock pane 66
  The General pane 71
  The Battery pane. 73
  The Menu Bar pane. 74
  The Wallpaper pane 75
  iCloud settings 76
  Appearance pane 77
  Notifications settings 78

CHAPTER 5: **Searching Amidst Neo Chaos**. 81
  Doing a Basic Search. 82
  How Cool Is That? Discovering What Spotlight Can Do 84
  Expanding Your Search Horizons 86
  Customizing Spotlight to Your Taste. 88

CHAPTER 6: **Using Reminders, Notes, Notifications,
Maps, and News** 89
  Remind Me to Use Reminders. 90
  Taking Notes the Neo Way. 92
  Staying Current with Notification Center. .95
  Introducing the Maps Application. 96
  Switching Views in Maps. 97
  Getting Directions Over Yonder 99
  Catching Up on News 100
  Using Favorites and Channels 101

PART 3: CONNECTING AND COMMUNICATING 103

CHAPTER 7: **Let's Go on Safari!**. 105
  Pretend You've Never Used This Thing 105
  Visiting Websites 107
  Navigating the Web. 108
  Organizing with Profiles 110
  Adding and Using Bookmarks 111
  Working with the Reading List 113
  Downloading Files. 113
  Using History 114
  Tabs Are Your Browsing Friends 114
  Printing Web Pages 115

Protecting Your Privacy. 116
        Yes, there are such things as bad cookies 116
        Banishing pesky iCloud Keychain passwords 117
        Setting notifications 117
        Avoiding those @*!^%$ pop-up ads .118

CHAPTER 8: **Expanding Your Horizons with iCloud** 119
    So How Does iCloud Work, Anyway? .120
    Moving, Saving, and Opening iCloud Documents. 121
    Putting Handoff to Work 122
    Expanding Your Horizons with Sidecar 123
    Configuring iCloud. 124
    Managing Your iCloud Storage 125

CHAPTER 9: **Creating a Multiuser Neo** 127
    An Access Fairy Tale 127
    Big-Shot Administrator Stuff 128
        Deciding who needs what access .129
        Adding users. 129
        Modifying user accounts 131
        I banish thee, mischievous user! .132
        Setting up login items and managing access 133
    Tackling Mundane Chores 136
        Logging in and out of Tahoe For Dummies 136
        Interesting stuff about sharing stuff. 138
        Encrypting your Home folder can be fun. 138

CHAPTER 10: **Working Well with Networks** 141
    What Exactly Is the Network Advantage?. 142
    Should You Go Wired or Wireless? 143
    Be a Pal: Share Your Internet! 144
    What Do I Need to Connect? 145
        Wireless connections 145
        Wired connections. 148
    Connecting to the Network 151
        Sharing stuff nicely with others. 152
    Use Your Firewall! 154

CHAPTER 11: **Hooking Up with Your World** 157
    Using Photo Booth 157
    Conversing with FaceTime 159
    Sending and Receiving Instant Messages 160
    Sharing Your Screen 161
    Using Continuity Camera 163

PART 4: LIVING THE iLIFE 165

CHAPTER 12: **The Multimedia Joys of Music and TV** 167

What Can I Play in Music? 168
Playing Digital Audio Files. 168
    Finding songs in your Music library 172
    Removing old music from the library 173
Separating Slim Whitman and Slim Shady: Organizing
with Playlists 173
Knowing Your Songs 175
    Adding song information automatically 176
    Setting the song information manually 176
Ripping Audio Files 177
Tweaking the Audio for Your Ears 178
A New Kind of Radio Station 178
    Tuning in your own stations 179
    Radio stations in your playlists 179
    Creating a custom Music Radio station 179
iSending iStuff to iPhone and iPad 180
Exercising Parental Authority 181
Watching Video with TV 182
Buying Digital Media the Apple Way. 183

CHAPTER 13: **Focusing on Photos** 185

Delving into Photos. 185
Working with Images in Photos 188
    Import images 101 188
    Organize mode: Organizing and sorting your images 190
    Edit mode: Removing and fixing stuff the right way 195
Exploring iCloud Photos 200
Putting iCloud Shared Albums to Work 201
Creating an iCloud Link on the Web 201

PART 5: GETTING PRODUCTIVE AND
MAINTAINING YOUR NEO 203

CHAPTER 14: **Desktop Publishing with Pages** 205

Creating a New Pages Document 206
Opening an Existing Pages Document 206
Saving Your Work 207
Touring the Pages Window 208
Entering and Editing Text 209
Using Text, Shapes, and Graphics Boxes 209

The Three Amigos: Cut, Copy, and Paste 209
    Cutting stuff 209
    Copying text and images 210
    Pasting from the Clipboard 210
Formatting Text the Easy Way 210
Adding a Spiffy Table 211
Adding Alluring Photos 212
Adding a Background Shape 213
Adding 3D Objects 213
Are You Sure about That Spelling? 214
Don't Forget Apple Intelligence 214
Printing Your Pages Documents 215
Sharing That Poster with Others 216

CHAPTER 15: **Creating Spreadsheets with Numbers** 217
Before You Launch Numbers 218
Creating a New Numbers Document 218
Opening an Existing Spreadsheet File 219
Save Those Spreadsheets! 219
Exploring the Numbers Window 220
Navigating and Selecting Cells in a Spreadsheet 221
Entering and Editing Data 222
Selecting a Number Format 223
Aligning Cell Text Just So 224
Formatting with Shading 224
Inserting and Deleting Rows and Columns 225
The Formula Is Your Friend 225
Adding Visual Punch with a Chart 227
Adding Images and 3D Objects 227
Using the Writing Tools 228
Printing Your Spreadsheet 229

CHAPTER 16: **Building Presentations with Keynote** 231
Creating a New Keynote Project 232
Opening a Keynote Presentation 233
Saving Your Presentation 233
Putting Keynote to Work 234
Adding Slides 235
Working with Text, Shapes, and Graphics Boxes 236
Adding and Editing Slide Text 236
Perfecting Your Text with Writing Tools 237
Formatting Slide Text to Perfection 238
Using Presenter's Notes 238
Every Good Presentation Needs Media 239

Adding a Background Shape 239
Adding 3D Objects. 240
Creating Your Keynote Slideshow. 240
Printing Your Slides and Notes 241

CHAPTER 17: **When Good Mac Laptops Go Bad** 243
Repeat after Me: Yes, I Am a Tech! 244
Step-by-Step Laptop Troubleshooting 244
The number-one rule: Reboot! 245
Using Safe mode 246
All hail Disk Utility, the troubleshooter's friend. 247
Disk repair made easy 248
Mark's MacBook Troubleshooting Tree 249
Okay, I Kicked It and It Still Won't Work .253
Local service, at your service 253
The macOS Help Center 254
Apple Help Online 254

CHAPTER 18: **Tackling the Housekeeping** 255
Cleaning Unseemly Data Deposits 255
Managing your storage in macOS (or cleaning the
elegant way) 256
Getting dirty (or cleaning things the manual way) 257
Using a commercial cleanup tool 259
Backing Up Your Treasure 259
Saving Files. 260
Putting Things Right with Time Machine .260
Maintaining Drive Health 262
Updating macOS Automatically. 262

PART 6: THE PART OF TENS. 263

CHAPTER 19: **Ten Neo Rules to Follow** 265
Keep Your Neo in a Bag 265
Opt for That Larger Drive 266
Keep Tabs on Your Neo 267
Keepeth Thy Drive Encrypted 267
Brand Your Neo. 268
Disable Your Wireless 268
Take a Surge Protector with You 269
Don't Consider an Internal Drive Upgrade! 269
Add Storage Space Externally 270
Putting a port to work. 270
Connecting an external drive. 271
Not Again! What Is It with You and Backing Up?. 271

CHAPTER 20: **Ten Things to Avoid Like the Plague** 273

USB 2.0 Storage Devices 274
Phishing Operations 274
The Twin Terrors: Viruses and Malware 275
Submerged Keyboards 276
Antiquated Utility Software 276
Software Piracy 276
The Forbidden Account 277
Unsecured Wireless Connections 277
Refurbished Hardware 278
Dirty Laptops 278

INDEX 279

Introduction

Laptop owners are special people.

You see, a laptop owner demands everything from a computer that a desktop owner does: reliability, performance, expandability, and ease of use. Owners of Mac Studio, Mac mini, and iMac desktop computers can draw the line right there, because their computers are designed for a stationary existence. But you and I are Neo owners. We also need that same Mac to be half an inch thick. We demand that it run for hours on a single battery charge. We require that it be light as a feather. We want to conquer the coffee shop, the library, and even a lecture hall or two!

Today's MacBook Neo delivers all that and more. If you've bought one of these modern masterpieces — or you're thinking about it — I applaud your good taste, common sense, and discerning eye. The Neo has everything: great performance; a top-shelf LED screen; rugged reliability; and a trouble-free, powerful operating system.

I wrote this book for myself — and for every other MacBook Neo owner who wants to become a laptop technowizard. In these pages, you find a guide to both your MacBook's hardware and macOS Tahoe, the latest version of Apple's superb operating system. After I cover the basics that every laptop owner should know, you find out how to accomplish all sorts of cutting-edge productivity, visual, and internet projects. (Oh, and if you already have another of my books, you know that I don't skimp on the power-user tips and tricks that save you time, effort, *and* money.)

Foolish Assumptions

So who is the target audience for this book? As in past editions, I make no assumptions about your previous knowledge of computers and software. I figure that you've just bought a MacBook Neo or are considering buying one. That's the *only* assumption I make. And unlike other books that require a lot of technical expertise to understand, this book's only requirement is your desire to become a Neo *power user* (someone who produces the best work in the least amount of time and has the most fun doing it)!

By the way, if your friends and family predicted that you'll spend half your life savings on software — or that no "decent" software is available for Mac computers — just smile quietly to yourself! A Neo comes complete with more productivity software than any Windows box, and this software is better than anything available on a PC!

About This Book

In writing about the Neo, I've kept one precept firmly in mind: macOS Tahoe, the operating system you'll run, is just as important as the laptop itself. Therefore, you'll find that *MacBook Neo For Dummies* is just as much about familiarizing you with all the software you get as it is with introducing hardware features. After all, it's relatively easy to connect a power cable and turn on *any* new computer. What comes next is the challenging part!

As in my other *For Dummies* titles, I respect and use the same everyday language you do, avoiding jargon, ridiculous computer acronyms, and confusing tech-nobabble whenever possible.

If you're upgrading from a PC running the Windows operating system, I've got tips, tricks, and entire sections devoted to those hardy pioneers called *Switchers*. You discover both the similarities and differences between your Neo running Tahoe and a PC running Windows. I also show you how to make the switch as easily and quickly as possible.

A word about the conventions I use: Even with an absolute minimum amount of technospeak, this book needs to cover the keys you have to press or menu commands you have to choose to make things work. Therefore, please keep in mind this short list of conventions as you read:

>> **Stuff you type:** If I ask you to type (or enter) something, such as in a text box or field, that text appears in bold, like this:

Type me.

You usually have to press Return before anything happens.

>> **Menu commands:** I list menu paths and commands by using another format. This instruction indicates that you should click the Edit menu and then choose the Copy menu item:

Edit ⇨ Copy

» **Web addresses:** No up-to-date book on a computer would be complete without a bag full of web addresses for you to check out. When you see these in the text, they look like this: www.dummies.com. (By the way, that website does exist, and I highly recommend it!)

» **For the technically curious:** Your Neo is an elegant and sophisticated machine, and it's as easy to use as a computer can be. But from time to time, you may be curious about the technical details that surround your hardware and software. (Perhaps you disassembled alarm clocks as a kid, as I did.) Techie stuff is denoted with a margin icon, as discussed in the next section. You don't have to read the technical notes unless you want to know what makes things tick. (Pun by sheer accident.)

Icons Used in This Book

Like other technology authors, I firmly believe that important nuggets of wisdom should *stand out on the page!* With that in mind, this *For Dummies* book includes margin icons for certain situations:

This icon is the most popular icon in the book. You find it parked next to suggestions I make to save you time and effort (and even cash!).

You don't have to know this information, but the technologically curious love high-tech details. (We're great fun at parties, too.)

Always **read this information before you take action!** I'm discussing something that could harm your hardware or throw a plumber's helper into your software.

Consider these nuggets to be highlighter stuff — not quite as universally accepted (or as important to the author) as a Mark's Maxim (described next), but good reminders nonetheless. I use this icon to reinforce what you should remember.

These gold-plated, cream-of-the-crop truisms are *MFRs* (short for My Favorite Recommendations). In fact, I'll bet that just about any Neo power user would tell you the same. **Follow my Maxims to avoid the quicksand and pitfalls I've encountered with all sorts of Macs for almost five decades.**

Beyond the Book

Thanks to my hard-working good friends at Wiley, extra content accompanies this book. Fire up your Safari browser, go to www.dummies.com, and search for **MacBook Neo For Dummies** to find the following:

>> **Cheat Sheet:** I've created Cheat Sheet pages that cover things like common keystrokes and maintenance procedures that every MacBook owner should follow on a regular basis.

>> **Updates for this book, if any.**

Where to Go from Here

Each chapter is a reference for a specific hardware or software topic. Thanks to the fruit of the hard work of my editors, you can begin reading anywhere you like because each chapter is self-contained. If you want to get the most out of this tome (and your MacBook Neo experience), however, there's nothing wrong with reading this book from front to back. I will point out, though, that J. K. Rowling and Stephen King have nothing to fear from my no-frills prose!

Time for the first Mark's Maxim in this book:

Take your time. After all, learning how to use your Neo isn't a race. And don't worry if you're not a graphic artist, professional photographer, or artificial intelligence wizard. With your Neo and its software, you don't have to be!

1

Tie Myself Down with a Desktop? Preposterous!

IN THIS PART . . .

Tour the features of your MacBook Neo and macOS Tahoe.

Unpack and set up your Neo.

Maintain your laptop's battery *the right way*.

Familiarize yourself with the basics of macOS.

Chapter **1**

Hey, It Really Does Have Everything I Need

Most action films have one scene in common: I call it "gearing up," because the good guys strap on their equipment in preparation for battle. The process usually takes a minute or so all told, with whiplash camera work and stirring martial music in the background.

Well, fellow Mac road warrior, it takes only *two seconds* and *one move* — closing the lid — for you to gear up. Your Neo is a self-contained world, providing virtually all the essentials you'll find on a desktop Mac. This is indeed another "decade of the laptop," meshing nicely with your smartphone and that wireless connection at your local coffee shop. Believe me, you've selected the right companion for the open road.

Unlike Apple's other designs, your Neo's exterior looks much like a PC laptop. But your MacBook holds several pleasant surprises that no PC laptop can offer — and you'll save pounds and inches from your chassis!

In this chapter, I introduce you to the hardware and all the major parts of the machine. You even find out how to unpack and connect your Neo. And as frosting on the cake, I preview the software of which Apple is so proud, as well as the accessories you should buy now rather than later.

Welcome to your MacBook Neo, good reader. Gear up!

An Overview of Your Mac Laptop

Sure, your MacBook Neo may be about half an inch thin, but a lot of superb design lives inside. You encounter the same parts you'd find in a desktop machine. In the following sections, I discuss those important parts — both the stuff you can see and the stuff that's shoehorned within.

The parts you probably recognize

Every laptop requires some of the same gizmos. Figure 1-1 helps you track them down. Of course, as you'd expect, a computer has a body of sorts in which all the innards and brains are stored, a display screen, a keyboard, a trackpad or other pointing device, and ports for powering and exchanging data with outside toys.

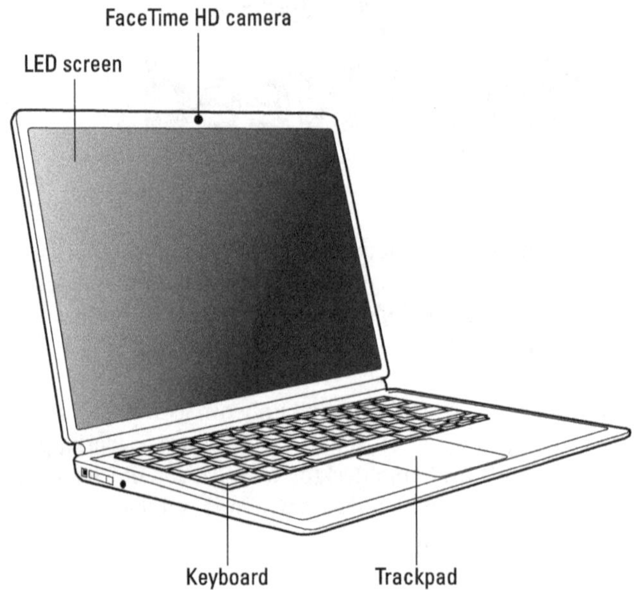

FIGURE 1-1: The charismatic form of a typical Mac laptop.

That magnificent screen

What a view you have! The Neo features a 13-inch LED display. Apple's laptop screens offer a *widescreen* aspect ratio (the screen is considerably wider than it is tall), which augurs well for those who enjoy watching movies.

The keyboard and trackpad

Unlike the external input devices on a standard desktop computer, your Neo has a built-in keyboard and trackpad (which does the job of a mouse). The Neo keyboard is a particular favorite of mine, offering special keys for activating all sorts of features within macOS. The Neo features a great trackpad as well; it's a button-free design that allows you to click any area of the trackpad, as well as perform gestures to control all sorts of macOS functions! (More on gestures later, in Chapter 3.)

The MacBook Neo doesn't have an internal optical drive. Many third-party manufacturers produce external optical drives for MacBooks that connect through your Neo's USB-C ports.

Food for your ears

A machine this nice had better have great sound, and the Neo doesn't disappoint, with built-in stereo speakers and two microphones. You can also use the built-in headphone jack to connect your Mac's audio to a pair of headphones or a more powerful external speaker system. (Of course, portable USB and Bluetooth speaker systems can provide better-quality digital audio as well.)

The power cable

The Neo uses a USB-C port and the included 20-watt power adapter for charging the battery. (Either port can be used for charging.)

Many MacBook owners ask me whether they should disconnect the power after the battery is fully charged or leave it connected. I leave the cable connected. It won't cause any damage to your Neo, and you can continue to use your laptop while it's charging.

The power button

Ready for more convenience? Your MacBook Neo actually powers on whenever you open the lid! To turn the Neo off, you press and hold the Touch ID/Lock button on the upper-right corner of the keyboard.

If the lid is already open, you can also turn on your Neo by pressing the Touch ID/Lock button.

The FaceTime HD camera

The Neo features a built-in FaceTime HD camera, which allows you to chat with others in a videoconferencing environment by using the Messages and FaceTime applications that come with Tahoe. You can even take photos with the camera, using the Photo Booth software that comes with your laptop, or set up a travelin' webcam.

Note that a green light appears in the Finder menu bar or at the upper right corner of the screen — handy information that could prevent visual embarrassment! (Some companies even offer plastic clips especially designed for covering the lens to guarantee privacy.)

The battery

Apple's current laptop computers don't include user-replaceable batteries. The battery is sealed inside the case and can be replaced only by an Apple technician. But you should get several years of trouble-free operation from your Neo's battery, especially if you maintain it properly (as I show you in Chapter 2).

The holes called ports

The next stop on your tour of Planet Neo is Port Central — those two stellar holes on the side of your laptop. Each port connects a USB-C cable or device, allowing you to easily add all sorts of functionality to your road warrior.

Short for *universal serial bus,* the familiar USB port is the jack-of-all-trades in today's world of computer add-ons. Most external devices you want to connect to your laptop (such as portable drives, scanners, and digital cameras) use a USB-C plug.

Luckily, you can also buy an adapter for your USB-C ports that allows you to send the video from your Neo to an external VGA, DVI, or HDMI monitor.

If you need a number of older ports for different legacy hardware (such as the much larger USB-A ports), consider buying a laptop dock that provides multiple ports for your Neo through a single USB-C 3.0 connection. I discuss the laptop dock device in more detail at the end of this chapter.

Don't forget the parts you can't see

When you bought your new digital pride and joy, you probably noticed a number of subtle differences between the MacBook Neo and the pricier MacBook Air and Pro models. I call these differences the *Important Hidden Stuff* (or IHS, if you're addicted to acronyms). They're just as important as the parts and ports you can see.

Internal devices are as follows:

» **CPU:** The Mac Neo features the Apple A18 Pro CPU, while other MacBooks use the Apple M5 line of CPUs.

» **Storage:** Today's MacBook models are equipped with solid-state drives that use memory chips. The drive capacities are different across the entire MacBook product line.

   You'll find no moving parts in a solid-state drive, and it offers better performance than an "antique" magnetic hard drive. The solid-state drive uses RAM chips rather than magnetic platters to hold your data.

Wireless communications devices include the following:

» **Wireless Ethernet:** "Look, Ma, no wires!" As mentioned earlier, you can connect your laptop to an existing wireless Ethernet network. With wireless connectivity, you can share documents with another computer in another room, share a single high-speed internet connection between computers, or enjoy wireless printing. Truly *sassy!*

   Rest assured, you can use your Neo with any standard 802.11b/g/n/ac/ax wireless network. And yes, PCs and Macs can intermingle on the same wireless network without a hitch. (Scandalous, ain't it?)

» **Bluetooth:** Although strangely named, Bluetooth is another form of wireless connectivity. This time, however, the standard was designed for accessories such as your keyboard and mouse and devices like wireless headphones and your smartphone. (The Neo includes version 6 Bluetooth hardware.)

Here's the hidden display device:

» **Video card:** None necessary! That's because all Apple CPUs handle graphics all by themselves, with no additional hardware. Your MacBook Neo is fine for home and business applications, as well as light gaming.

Whoa! Where's my familiar USB port?

It is indeed a bit disconcerting to encounter *anything* electronic these days that doesn't sport a USB 3.0 port, from a smart speaker in your kitchen to your printer in your office. However, don't be hesitant about the USB-C ports on your new Neo: They are versatile performers! Heck, you can do just about everything better and faster with your USB-C ports, including charging your MacBook, connecting an external monitor, joining a wired Ethernet network, or connecting a superfast external drive!

If you do need to connect to an older legacy port — a USB 3.0 device, wired Ethernet port, or a VGA or HDMI display — you will have to invest in the correct USB-C adapter. The entire lineup of Apple connection adapters is available from the Apple website, or you can easily order a third-party adapter online. And rest assured that more and more USB-C devices are on the way, so that external drive you buy in the future will likely use USB-C anyway! These adapters are required only for older technology.

You can use any third-party USB-C DVD drive that's compatible with Apple's laptops and macOS Tahoe.

REMEMBER

Location, Location, Location!

If you choose the wrong spot to park your new Neo, I *guarantee* you'll regret it. Some domiciles and office cubicles don't offer a choice. You have one desk at work, for example, and nobody will hand over another one. But if you can select a home for your MacBook, consider the important placement points in this section:

>> **Keep things cool.** Your Neo is silent, but that super-fast A18 Pro processor generates heat. Make sure that the location you choose is far from heating vents and shielded from direct sunlight. I also recommend a laptop cooling pad, which elevates the base of your laptop to allow air to circulate underneath.

>> **Outlets are key!** Your Neo needs at least one nearby outlet and perhaps as many as two:

- **A standard AC outlet** (using a current adapter if you're traveling abroad, if necessary)

- **A nearby Ethernet jack** (if you use a wired Ethernet network)

  If you prefer to send your data over the airwaves, consider wireless networking for your Mac. I discuss everything you need to know in Chapter 10.

TIP

>> **Don't forget the lighting.** Let me act as your mom. (I know that's *quite* a stretch, but bear with me.) She'd say, "You can't possibly expect to work without decent lighting! You'll go blind!" She's right, you know. You need a desk lamp or floor lamp at minimum if you need to refer to books or documents often in your work. And you do want to look your best during FaceTime calls, right?

>> **Plan to expand.** If your Neo hangs out on a desk, allow an additional foot of space on each side. That way, you have room for external peripherals, more powerful speakers, and an external keyboard and mouse.

If you want to keep an external keyboard handy, consider using a laptop shelf. These Plexiglas or metal stands elevate your laptop several inches above the desk, putting the screen in a better ergonomic position and allowing you to park your keyboard and external mouse below.

Unpacking and Connecting Your MacBook Neo

You'll love the following sections. They're short and sweet because parking a laptop on your desktop is a piece of cake. (Sorry about the cliché overload, but this really *is* easy.)

Unpacking for the road warrior

Follow these guidelines when unpacking your system:

>> **Check for damage.** I've never had a box arrive from Apple with shipping damage, but I've heard horror stories from others (who claim that King Kong must have been working for That Shipping Company).

   Check all sides of the box before you open it. If you find significant damage, take a photograph (just in case).

>> **Search for all the parts.** When you're removing those chunks o' foam, make certain that you've checked all sides of each foam block for parts snuggled therein or taped for shipment.

>> **Keep all packing materials.** Do *not* put the box and packing materials in the trash. Keep the box and all packing materials for at least a year, until the standard Apple warranty runs out. If you have to ship your Neo to an Apple service center, the box and the original packing are the only way for your machine to fly.

And now, a dramatic Mark's Maxim about cardboard containers:

Smart computer owners keep their boxes far longer than a year. If you sell your Neo or move across the country, for example, you'll want that box. *Trust me on this one.*

>> **Store the invoice for safekeeping.** Your invoice is a valuable piece of paper.

Save your original invoice in a plastic bag, along with your computer's documentation. Keep the bag on a shelf or stored safely in your desk, and enjoy a little peace of mind.

>> **Read the manual.** "Hey, wait a minute, Mark. Why do I have to read the manual from Apple along with this tome?" Good question, and here's the answer: The documentation from Apple for the latest version of the Neo may contain new and updated instructions that override what I tell you here. (Say, "*Never* cut the red wire. Cut the blue wire instead." Or something to that effect.) Besides, Apple manuals are rarely thicker than a restaurant menu.

Connecting Cables 101

Your MacBook makes all its connections simple, but your computer depends on you to get the outside wires and thingamabobs where they go.

The absolutely essential connection

After your new Neo is resting comfortably in its assigned spot (I assume that's a desktop or a lap), you need to make just one required connection: the power cable. First, plug the cable into the corresponding USB-C port on the MacBook; and then plug 'er into that handy AC outlet. After your battery is completely charged, you can go mobile at a moment's notice.

Adding the internet to the mix

If you have high-speed wired internet service, or if you're in an office or school with a wired network, you can probably connect by using an Ethernet adapter with your USB-C port. You make two connections:

1. **Plug one end of the Ethernet cable into the USB-C–to–Ethernet adapter on your Neo (or a handy laptop dock).**

2. **Plug the other end of the Ethernet cable into the Ethernet port from your network.**

    Your network port is probably one of the following: an Ethernet wall jack, an Ethernet hub or switch, or a cable, fiber, or DSL internet router (or sharing device).

Will you be joining a wireless network? If so, you can find the information you need about configuring Tahoe for wireless networking in Chapter 10.

Great — a Lecture about Handling My Neo

Proper handling of your Neo is important, so take a moment to read the Rules of Proper Laptop Deportment. Okay, perhaps I'm lecturing a bit, but a little common sense goes a **long** way when you're handling *any* computer equipment, and your MacBook is no different. (Scolding mode off.)

Keep these rules in mind while opening and carrying your Neo:

>> **The cover is your friend.** Open your laptop's lid slowly, without jerking or bending it.

>> **Close it before you move it.** By closing your laptop, you put your macOS operating system into sleep mode. The laptop is still on; it will spring back to life when you open the lid.

>> **Don't stack stuff on your laptop.** You'd be surprised how many horror stories I've heard about laptop owners piling a stack of books or other heavy stuff on their computers. Remember that LED display? Made of glass?

>> **Be nice to your keyboard.** Don't press those keys too hard! Use the same amount of pressure you use on a desktop computer's keyboard. (And use an external keyboard whenever possible.)

>> **Keep food and drinks far away.** Care to turn your MacBook into an expensive doorstop? Go ahead and park your soda next to it. (Oh, and crumbs are perfect if you're interested in buying replacement keyboards.)

An Overview of Mac Software Goodness

The following sections answer the most common novice computer question: "What the heck will I *do* with this thing?" You find additional details and exciting factoids about the software you get for free, software you'll want to buy, and stuff you can do on the internet.

What comes with my Neo?

Currently, Apple laptops ship with the following major software applications installed and ready to use:

>> **macOS Tahoe:** Naturally, your MacBook comes preloaded with Tahoe.

>> **Apple's digital lifestyle suite:** You know you want these applications! They turn your Mac into a digital hub for practically all kinds of high-tech devices, including camcorders, digital cameras, tablets, portable music players, and smartphones.

Chapters 12 and 13 focus on the major applications that will appeal to MacBook owners: Music, TV and Photos.

>> **Apple's digital productivity suite:** Owners of new MacBooks can download all three of Apple's great productivity applications — Pages, Numbers, and Keynote — for free in the App Store. Pages is a desktop publishing jewel, Numbers is a great spreadsheet tool, and Keynote is a superb slideshow/presentation application. Chapters 14 through 16 are your guides to the basic functions of all three applications. 'Nuff said.

The installed software on your Neo may change as new programs become available.

Connecting to the internet from your lap

What's a modern laptop without the internet? Apple gives you great tools to take full advantage of every road sign and off ramp on the Information Superhighway right out of the box:

>> **Web surfing:** I use Apple's Safari web browser every day. It's fast and well designed, with features such as tabbed browsing and a customizable Start page.

If *tabbed browsing* sounds like ancient Aztec to you, don't worry. Chapter 7 is devoted to Safari.

>> **Instant messaging and video chat:** *Messages* lets you use your Neo to chat with others around the world for free on the internet. You can also use the FaceTime application to video-chat with folks who have an iPhone or iPad, as well as another Mac. Chapter 11 introduces you to both Messages and FaceTime.

Always wear a shirt when videoconferencing.

>> **Email:** Soldier, Apple has you covered. The Apple Mail application is a full-featured email system complete with defenses against the torrent of junk mail awaiting you. Send pictures and attached files to everyone on the planet, and look doggone good doing it.

Applications that rock

Dozens of small applications are also supplied with macOS Tahoe. I mention many of them in later chapters, but here are three good examples to whet your appetite:

>> **Calendar:** Regulate your days throughout the year with this fully featured calendar application. (And yes, you can share your calendar events with others.)

>> **Contacts:** Throw away that well-thumbed collection of fading addresses on paper. Use the Tahoe Contacts application to store, search, and recall just about any piece of information on your friends, family, and acquaintances.

>> **Chess:** This isn't the chessboard your dad used! Play the game of kings against a tough (and configurable) opponent — your Neo — on a beautiful 3D board. Heck, your Mac even narrates the game by speaking the moves!

TIP

You can use the data you store in your Contacts in other Apple applications included with Tahoe, such as Apple Mail and Messages.

Other Stuff That Nearly Everyone Wants

No man is an island, and no computer is either. I always recommend the same set of stuff for new Windows and Mac laptop owners. These extras help keep your new MacBook clean and healthy (and some make sure *you're* happy as well):

>> **A laptop sleeve or case:** Most laptop owners eschew the traditional bulky laptop bag because a bag broadcasts the fact that you're carrying a valuable laptop (and adds yet another item to carry on your trip). On the other hand, if you pack your MacBook in a briefcase, book bag, or backpack, you need to provide protection from bumps and scratches. (Make sure that any sleeve or case you buy provides padding around the entire computer, not just on the top surface.) That's where a laptop sleeve or thin case comes in.

>> **An external camera:** Your Neo has a built-in FaceTime camera, but many folks prefer a standalone external camera that they can pan, tilt, and point where they like (especially moviemakers or podcasters who need high-resolution video clips of whatever's happening around them). With the Continuity Camera feature in macOS, you can even use your iPhone as an external camera! (See Chapter 11 for more details on Continuity Camera.)

>> **Surge suppressor:** Even an all-in-one computer like your laptop can fall prey to a power surge. I recommend using one of these:

- **A basic surge suppressor** with a fuse can help protect your MacBook from an overload.

- **A UPS (uninterruptible power supply)** costs a little more but does a better job of filtering your AC line voltage to prevent brownouts or line interference from reaching your computer.

  Your Neo's battery immediately kicks in if you experience a blackout, of course, so a UPS is less important for your MacBook. But a UPS can also provide backup power for external devices that *don't* have a battery.

>> **A laptop docking station:** Will your MacBook Neo often do double duty as both a desktop computer *and* a mobile powerhouse? If so, a laptop docking station will prevent you from disconnecting USB-C cables each time you hit the road. In essence, you need to unplug only one connection between your Neo and the docking station. *All* your external desktop peripherals — monitor, backup drive, USB trackball, and such — remain blissfully in place. When your Neo returns to the desktop, you simply reconnect that one USB-C cable, and you're back in business. Most docking stations also sport a wired Ethernet port, an HDMI port and at least one or two USB-A ports, so you won't need to use adapters to make these connections.

>> **Screen wipes:** Invest in a box of premoistened screen wipes to keep your screen pristine. Your MacBook's screen can pick up dirt, fingerprints, and other unmentionables faster than you think.

>> **Cables:** Depending on the external devices and wired network connectivity you'll be using, these are:

- **A standard Ethernet cable** (for wired networks or high-speed internet)

- **USB-C cables and adapters** for devices you already have

>> **Wrist rest:** You may have many reasons to buy a new Mac Neo, but I know that a bad case of carpal tunnel syndrome isn't one of them. Take care of your wrists by carrying a keyboard wrist rest in your laptop bag or backpack.

IN THIS CHAPTER

» **Turning on your Neo**

» **Checking your MacBook for proper operation**

» **Setting up macOS Tahoe**

» **Getting your Neo set up**

» **Copying information from a Windows PC**

Chapter **2**

Turning On Your Portable Powerhouse

f you've already been through Chapter 1, you got as far as unpacking your Neo (and connecting at least one cable to it). And unless you bought this computer solely as a work of modern art, it's time to actually turn on your MacBook and begin living The Good iLife. (Plus you still get to admire that Apple design whilst using TV.) After you get your new beauty powered on, I help you here with an initial checkup on your Neo's health, including that all-important battery.

I also familiarize you with the initial chores you need to complete before settling in with your favorite applications, like setting up macOS and moving the data and settings from your existing computer to your MacBook.

Throwing the Big Leaf Switch

The power switch on most MacBook models is located in the top-right corner of the keyboard. Your Touch ID or Lock button acts as the power button. To turn on your laptop when it's open, simply press the key. If your Neo is closed, all you have to do is open your laptop to power up!

You hear the pleasant startup tone that's been a hallmark of Apple computers for many years now. Don't be alarmed if you don't immediately see anything onscreen because it takes a few seconds for the initial Apple logo to appear.

If your Neo ever locks up tight and you can't quit an application (I discuss quitting in Chapter 3), the power button gives you another option: Hold the Touch ID/Lock button down for five seconds or so, and your MacBook shuts off *completely*, even if your laptop is locked up tight.

While the Apple logo appears, you see the familiar "moving bar" progress indicator appear. That's the sign that your MacBook is loading Tahoe. Sometimes the bar can take a bit to disappear. As long as it's moving, though, something Good is Happening. At last, your patience is rewarded, and you see the Tahoe Setup Assistant appear.

Mark's Favorite Signs of a Healthy Laptop

Before you jump into the fun stuff, don't forget an important step: a quick preliminary check of the signs that your new mobile Mac survived shipment intact and happy.

If you can answer yes to each of these questions, your Neo likely made the trip without serious damage:

1. **Does the laptop's chassis appear undamaged?**

   It's pretty easy to spot damage to your Neo's svelte metal and glass design. Look for scratches, dents, and puncture damage.

2. **Does the LED screen work, and is it undamaged?**

   Does the cover open smoothly? Are any individual dots (or *pixels*) on the LED screen obviously malfunctioning? Malfunctioning pixels appear black or in a different color from everything surrounding them.

3. **Do the keyboard and mouse work?**

   Check your MacBook's built-in trackpad by moving your finger across its surface; the pointer should move onscreen. To check the keyboard, press the Caps Lock key on the left side, and observe whether the Caps Lock light turns on and off. (Don't forget to check for good batteries in all your wireless input devices and make sure they're turned on.)

If you do notice a problem with your MacBook Neo (and you can still use your Safari browser and reach the web), you can make the connection to an Apple support technician at www.apple.com. If your Neo remains dead — like a hi-tech paperweight — and you can't get to the internet, proceed to a local Apple service center, or call the AppleCare toll-free number at (800) 275-2273. Chapter 17 also offers troubleshooting information.

You Won't Lecture Me about Batteries, Will You?

No, this isn't a lecture. In fact, the only lecture I put you through in this book concerns backing up (which, naturally, *you should do*). Instead, consider these as tips for monitoring and charging your battery:

TIP

>> **Recharge your Neo in sleep mode or when powered off.** The battery recharges faster when your laptop is off or in sleep mode. (I go into more detail on sleep mode in Chapter 4.)

>> **Keep your Neo plugged into an AC socket whenever possible.** I take every opportunity to top off my laptop's battery, and so should you.

If you don't have much time to charge your battery before you're away from an AC socket — say, half an hour — don't use your Neo while it's plugged in and charging. That way, your battery will gain the maximum benefit from the charge time. (When you're using your MacBook while it's charging, the charging process takes much longer.)

>> **Save your juice.** To get the most juice you can scavenge, here are some easy tricks:

- **Turn off your Neo when possible,** or close it to enter sleep mode.

- **Open the Battery pane in System Settings** and change your Low Power Mode to Always.

- **Turn off unnecessary hardware.** To conserve battery power as much as possible, disconnect any unnecessary external devices. Also turn off your Wi-Fi wireless hardware if you're not connected to a network. (I cover Wi-Fi wireless networking in Chapter 10.)

- **Avoid using processor-intensive applications** (such as Adobe Photoshop or iMovie).

- **Monitor your battery level.** I love the battery-monitoring system built into macOS. Your Neo's battery life can be displayed in the Finder menu as a simple battery icon, or you can add it to your Desktop or the Control Center display within System Settings.

TIP

Here's a MacBook power-user trick: Click the battery icon in the Finder menu to display the most power-hungry applications that you're currently running! If you're low on power and you need to conserve your precious charge, quit those apps (if possible) to extend your computing time.

Keep in mind that the charge percentage shown with the battery icon is an estimate based on your current System Settings and power use. If you change your Battery settings or remove a USB device that draws power from your laptop, you see that change reflected in the battery meter.

macOS Tahoe provides even more detailed information on battery usage in the Battery pane within System Settings, featuring the Usage History display, where you can see your Battery Level, Energy Usage, and Screen On Usage for the last 24 hours or the last 10 days.

» **Calibrate your battery.** You can "train" your battery to provide the maximum charge by calibrating it, which Apple recommends doing monthly. The process is a snap:

1. **Charge your battery until the menu bar's battery meter indicates that the unit is fully charged, at 100%.**

2. **Keep your Neo connected to an AC socket for another two hours to ensure a maximum charge.**

3. **Disconnect the power cord, and use your laptop on battery power until it's fully discharged and automatically switches to sleep mode.**

   Make sure that you close all your applications when you see the low-battery warning dialog box so that you don't lose anything.

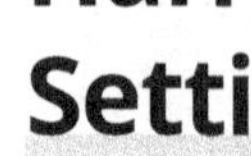

WARNING

4. **Allow your laptop to sleep (or turn it off) for a full five hours.**

5. **Reconnect the AC cord, and fully charge your battery.**

» **Invest in an external battery.** If you often find yourself running out of battery power on the road without an AC socket handy, consider buying an external battery that's specially designed to charge your MacBook and other USB-powered devices. A rechargeable battery can power and charge your MacBook, as well as an iPhone and iPad.

Harriet, It's Already Asking Me Questions! Setting Up macOS Tahoe

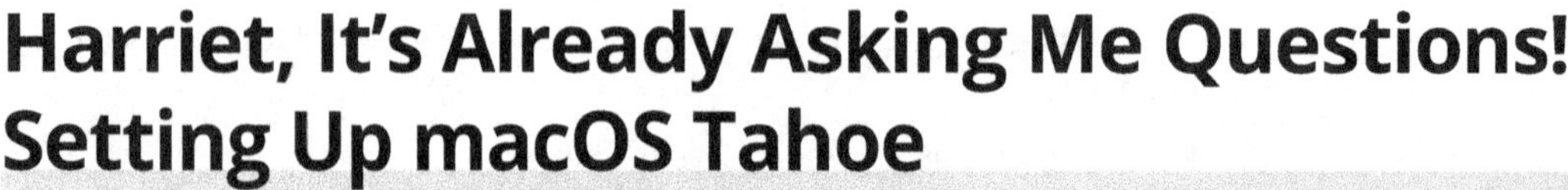

After your Neo is running and you've given it the once-over for obvious shipping damage, your next chore is to set up your laptop. Unlike most other tasks in this book, I don't cover the setup process step by step. Apple "tweaks" the questions

that you see during setup on a regular basis, and the questions are really very easy to answer. Everything is explained onscreen, complete with onscreen Help if you need it.

However, I do want you to know what to expect as well as what information you need to have at hand. I also want you to know about support opportunities, such as the AppleCare Protection Plan and Apple's iCloud internet services — hence, this section. Consider it a study guide for whatever your Neo's setup procedure has to throw at you.

After you start your MacBook Neo for the first time, it will automatically launch the Tahoe setup procedure. The setup process takes care of several tasks:

>> **Setup provides Tahoe your personal information.**

As I mention in Chapter 1, your MacBook ships with a bathtub full of applications, and many of those use your personal data (like your address and telephone number) to automatically fill out your documents.

Apple has recently strengthened its efforts to guard your privacy online. If personal stored information starts you worrying about identity theft, I congratulate you. If you're using your common sense, it *should*. However, Apple doesn't disseminate this information anywhere else, and the applications that use your personal data won't send it anywhere, either. And the Safari web browser fills out forms on a web page automatically *only* if you give your permission. I applaud Apple's decades-long commitment to privacy and security, and I trust them with my personal data.

>> **Setup creates your user account.** You're prompted for a username and password, which Setup uses to create your administrator-level account.

>> **Setup configures your language and keyboard choices.**

macOS Tahoe is a truly international operating system, so you have a chance to configure your Neo for a specific language and keyboard layout.

>> **Setup configures your email accounts within Apple Mail.**

If you already have an email account set up with your Internet service provider (ISP), keep that email account information handy to answer these questions. (The list should include the incoming POP3/IMAP and outgoing SMTP mail servers you'll be using, your email address, and your login name and password. Don't worry about those crazy acronyms, though, because your ISP will know exactly what you mean when you ask for this information.) Tahoe can even automatically configure many email accounts for you — including web-based services such as Google Mail — if you supply your account ID and password. *Sweet.*

>> **Setup allows you to sign up for an iCloud ID and Apple's iCloud service.**

iCloud makes it easy to share data automatically between your Neo and other iOS devices, along with Apple email accounts. I go into all these in more detail in Chapter 8. For now, just create your iCloud ID (also often called an Apple ID), sign up for iCloud, and take the opportunity to feel smug about owning an Apple computer.

All sorts of macOS applications hinge on your iCloud account, including the App Store, Messages, the iTunes Store, and FaceTime. Without an iCloud account, these applications will either offer limited features or may not allow you to use them at all! If you skip the iCloud account-creation process during setup, you can take care of that chore at any time. It's free and painless, and makes you one of the "in crowd."

>> **Setup sends your registration information to Apple.**

As a proud owner of a Neo, take advantage of the year of hardware warranty support and the free 90 days of telephone support. Rest assured that Apple is not one of those companies that constantly pesters you with email advertisements and near-spam. I've registered every Apple computer I've owned, and I've never felt pestered. (And I have an *extremely* low tolerance for pester.)

>> **Setup launches Migration Assistant.**

This assistant guides you through the process of *migrating* (an engineer's term for *copying*) your existing user data from your old Mac or PC to your new MacBook. Naturally, if your MacBook is your first computer, you can skip this step with a song in your heart! (Read more on Migration Assistant in the section "Importing Documents and Data from Your Old Mac.")

I heartily advocate the purchase of an AppleCare+ Protection Plan extended warranty with your new MacBook Neo for the ultimate in peace of mind. If you can invest a little over a hundred dollars more with Apple, you'll have a full three years of service coverage from the purchase date.

Importing Documents and Data from Your Old Mac

If you're upgrading from an older Mac computer to your new Neo, I have great news for you: Apple includes the Migration Assistant utility application that can help you copy (whoops, I mean, *migrate*) all sorts of data from your old Mac to your new machine. It does so via your laptop's wired or wireless Ethernet network connection or an existing Time Machine backup on an external drive. The list of stuff that gets migrated includes:

>> **User accounts:** If you set up multiple user accounts (so that more than one person can share the computer), the utility ports them all to your new MacBook.

>> **Network settings:** Boy howdy, this is a real treat for those with manual network settings provided by an ISP or network administrator! Migration Assistant can re-create the entire network environment of your old Mac on your Neo.

>> **System Preferences settings:** If you're a fan of tweaking and customizing macOS to fit you like a glove, rejoice. Migration Assistant actually copies over all the changes that you've made within System Preferences (now called System Settings) on your old Mac!

>> **Documents, Photos, and Music:** The files in these folders are copied to your MacBook.

>> **Applications:** Migration Assistant tries its best to copy over the third-party applications that you've installed in your Applications folder on the older Mac. I say *tries its best* because you might have to reinstall some applications, anyway. Some developers create applications that spread out all sorts of files across your internal drive, and Migration Assistant just can't keep track of those nomadic files. Also, some other applications make the trek just fine, but you might have to re-enter their serial numbers.

If you're migrating from an Intel Mac to a Neo, you may also find that some applications can no longer be launched — unfortunately, these apps are not compatible with macOS Tahoe. I recommend checking with the software developer to see whether a new version of the app is available.

REMEMBER

Setup launches Migration Assistant automatically if you indicate that you need to transfer stuff during the setup process, but you can also launch Migration Assistant manually at any time. Hold down the Command key and press the spacebar to display the Spotlight search box, type **Migration,** and press Return when you see the Migration Assistant app appear in the results list. Note that Migration Assistant will close any running applications, so make sure to save and close any open documents.

TIP

To use Migration Assistant to copy your system from your older Mac, you need one of the following:

>> **Wired or wireless network connection between the computers:** If you've already hooked up your Neo to your wired or wireless Ethernet network while

using Setup Assistant, eschew cables completely! (Note, however, that a Wi-Fi migration will be much slower than migrating with either a direct cable connection or a wired network connection.) Of course, the other Mac must be connected to the same network you're using on your MacBook.

>> **Time Machine external drive:** If you're using Time Machine on the older Mac with an external drive, you can migrate directly from your most recent backup — just plug your external Time Machine drive into your new Neo.

If the source computer is a PC, you'll use a free Windows program called Windows Migration Assistant, which you can download directly from www.apple.com.

After the two computers are connected, simply follow the onscreen instructions displayed within the Migration Assistant window. The application will lead you through the process step by step. If you need to return to the previous step at any time, click the Back button that appears at the bottom of the screen.

Manually Importing Documents and Data from Windows

If you're a classic Windows-to-Mac *Switcher*, you made a wise choice, especially if you're interested in the creative applications supplied by Apple. Although you can choose to start your Apple computing life anew, you probably want to migrate some of your existing documents and files from that tired PC to your bright, shiny new citrus Neo!

If you're switching from a PC to the Neo, you can run the Windows version of the Migration Assistant on your PC (available from Apple's website) to automatically handle most of your migration tasks for you, and you should witness the miracle of your PC's photos, video, music, and documents suddenly appearing on your MacBook. Unfortunately, you'll have some exceptions. Some stuff won't make the move because the Windows Migration Assistant simply can't recognize and transfer files and folders from some nonstandard locations — and naturally, your Windows programs won't run under macOS. Owners of the MacBook Neo can buy a virtual PC application like Parallels Desktop from Parallels International (www.parallels.com) to run Windows. (However, you'll still have to move those Windows applications manually to your Neo.)

Here's the good news, though: You can easily copy those files that weren't transferred by moving items manually from a USB flash drive or over a network.

The macOS Help system contains an entire subsection on specific tricks that you can use when switching from Windows to Mac, including how to connect to a Windows network and how to directly connect the two computers.

In general, you can move documents, movies, photos, and music without a problem. Table 2-1 illustrates what can be moved between Windows (versions 7, 8, 8.1, 10, and 11) and macOS, as well as the application that you use in Tahoe to open those files and documents.

TABLE 2-1   **Moving Media and Documents betwixt Computers**

File Type	Windows Location	macOS Location	Mac Application
Music files	Music folder	Music folder	Music
Video and movie files	Videos folder	Movies folder	QuickTime/DVD Player/TV
Digital photos	Pictures folder	Pictures folder	Photos
Office documents	Documents folder	Documents folder	Mac Office/Open Office/Pages, Numbers, and Keynote

Chapter **3**

The Neo Owner's Introduction to macOS Tahoe

Ah, the Finder. Many admire its scenic beauty. But don't ignore its unsurpassed power or its many moods. Send a postcard while you're there!

Okay, so the Tahoe Finder might not be *quite* as majestic as the region it's named after, but it's the toolbox you use every day while piloting your Neo. The Finder includes the most common elements of macOS: window controls, menus, icons, keyboard shortcuts, and even the Trash. If you master the Finder, you're a step closer to becoming a power user!

This chapter is your Finder tour guide, and we're ready to roll. I satisfy your curiosity about your new playground and introduce you to the basic elements of the Tahoe Desktop. I also outline the resources available if you need help with macOS. (Oh, and I promise to use honest-to-goodness English in my explanations, with a minimum of engineerspeak and indecipherable acronyms.)

Your Own Personal Operating System

Tahoe is a special type of software called an *operating system* (or *OS,* as in *macOS*). Tahoe essentially runs your Neo and allows you to use your other apps, such as Music. It's the most important *software* that you run. Think of a pyramid, with Tahoe as the foundation and other apps running on top.

You're using the OS when you aren't using a specific app. It controls actions like copying files from one location to another, or navigating through files and folders. Sometimes, Tahoe even peeks through an app while it's running: macOS controls actions such as the Open and Save As dialogs you see in Keynote, or the Print dialog you use in Pages.

In the following sections, I escort you around the most important hotspots in Tahoe, and you meet the most interesting onscreen thingamabobs you use to control your Neo. (I told you I wouldn't talk like an engineer!)

The Tahoe Desktop

The Tahoe Desktop isn't made of wood, and you can't stick your gum underneath it. But this digital desktop does work much like the surface of a traditional desk. You can store things there, organize things into folders, and take care of important tasks such as writing and drawing (using tools called *applications,* or *apps* for short). Heck, you even have a trash can.

Gaze upon Figure 3-1, and follow along as you explore macOS Tahoe. I discuss these Desktop elements in more detail later in this chapter.

Meet me at the Dock

The Dock is a versatile combination: one part organizer, one part application launcher, and one part system monitor. From the Dock, you can launch apps. The postage-stamp icon represents the Apple Mail app, for example, and clicking the spiffy compass icon launches your Safari web browser. Icons on the Dock also allow you to see what's running and to display or hide the windows displayed by your applications.

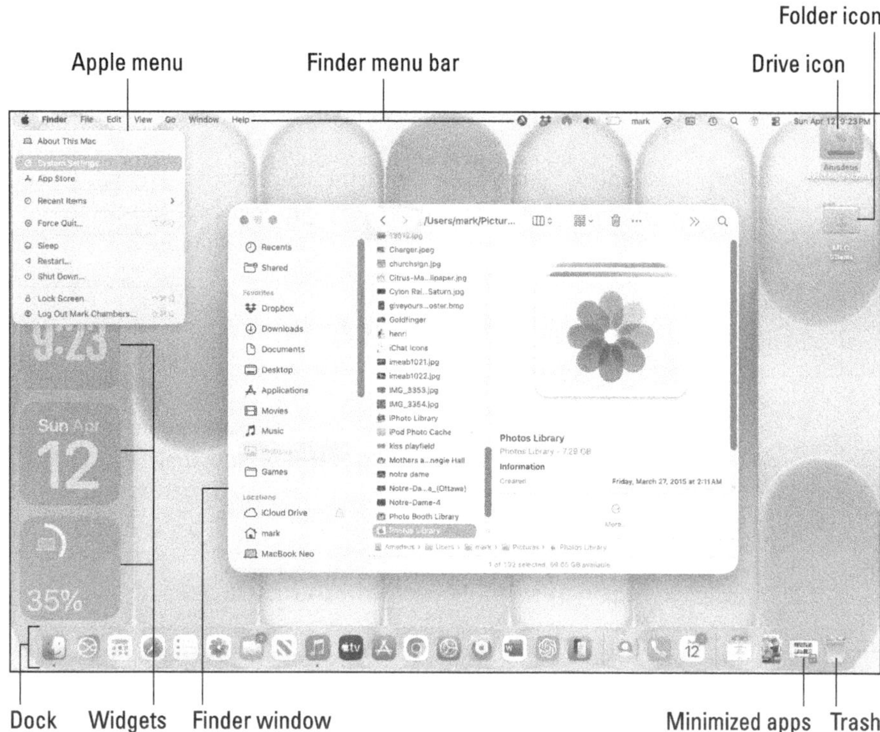

Each icon on the Dock represents one of the following (refer to Figure 3-1):

>> An application you can run (or that's running)

>> An application window that's *minimized* (shrunk)

>> A web page's URL link

>> A document or folder on your system

>> A network server, shared document, or shared folder

>> Your Trash

The Dock is highly configurable — it can appear at different edges of the screen, and it can disappear until you move the pointer to the edge to call it forth. You can also resize it.

Check out that Control Center

Let's face it: Even with more than two decades of excellent design behind it, your macOS Desktop can be a somewhat confusing landscape! A Neo often needs a quick settings change around campus, at the airport, or the coffee shop. With Tahoe, Apple's designers devised the macOS Control Center to present all these options in a single, convenient spot.

The Control Center is easily customized, too — after all, this is macOS — so you can decide what goes where! You can learn all the details in the section titled "Taking Control of Your Neo," later in this chapter.

Dig those crazy icons

By default, Tahoe typically displays at least one icon on your Desktop: your Neo's internal drive. (If your drive icon doesn't appear on the Desktop, choose Finder⇨Settings, click the General tab, and then enable the Hard Disks check box.) To open a drive and view or use the contents, double-click the icon. Each icon represents something, including:

>> External drives, USB flash drives, CDs, and DVDs

>> Applications and documents

>> Files and folders

>> Network servers you access

Note that an icon can represent apps you run and documents you create. Sometimes, you *single*-click an icon to watch it do its thing (as on the Dock), but usually you *double*-click an icon to make something happen.

There's no food on this menu

The menu bar resides at the top of the Desktop, where you can use it to control your apps. Virtually every app you run on your Neo has a menu bar.

To use a menu command, follow these steps:

1. **Click the menu title (such as File or Edit).**

2. **Choose the desired command from the menu (refer to Figure 3-1).**

When you click a menu, it extends down so that you can see the commands it includes. While the menu is extended, you can choose any enabled menu item (just click it) to perform that action. You can tell that an item is enabled if its name appears in black and white. Conversely, a menu command is disabled if it's grayed-out. Clicking it does nothing.

When you see a menu path printed in this book (such as File⇨Save), it's just a visual shortcut that tells you to click the File menu and then choose Save from the menu that appears.

Virtually every Mac app has menus, such as File, Edit, and Window. You're likely to find similar commands on these menus. But only two menus are in *every* macOS app:

>> The *Apple menu,* identified by that jaunty Apple Corporation icon (). This menu is special because it appears on both the Finder menu bar and the menu bar in *every* app you run. Whether you're in Music or Microsoft Word doesn't matter: If you see a menu bar, the menu is there. The menu contains commands to use throughout Tahoe, such as Restart, Shut Down, and System Settings. Figure 3-1, shown previously, proudly displays the Apple icon and menu.

>> The *Application menu,* which always bears the name of the active app. The TV menu group appears when you run the Tahoe TV app, for example, and the Word menu group appears when you launch Microsoft Word.

You can also display a contextual menu — which regular human beings call a *shortcut* or *right-click menu* — by right-clicking the Tahoe Desktop or an icon. (Because your Neo is equipped with a trackpad, you can right-click by tapping the trackpad with two fingertips. I explain tapping later, in the section titled "Wait a Second: Where the Heck Are the Mouse Buttons?")

The Finder menu bar is your friend

Whenever the Finder itself is ready to be used (or, in Macspeak, whenever the Finder is the *active* application), the Finder menu bar appears at the top of the screen. You know that the Finder is active and ready when the word *Finder* appears at the left end of the menu bar.

There's always room for one more window

You're probably familiar with the ubiquitous window itself. Both Tahoe and the apps you run use windows to display things such as the documents you create and the contents of your drive.

The window shown in Figure 3-1 earlier in this chapter is a Finder window, where Tahoe gives you access to the apps, documents, and folders on your system. You use Finder windows to launch apps, perform chores such as copying and moving files, and navigate your drive.

Widgets on parade

Widget. What a ridiculous word — it reminds me of the browser cookie, another modern computing term that I find hilarious. Anyway, after using your macOS widgets for a few weeks, you'll find yourself a huge fan of these tiles, just like me. Widgets are modules that you add to your Control Center and your Desktop (as shown earlier, in Figure 3-1) that constantly display specific information (and, in some cases, allow you to interact with them). I describe how to add them to your system later in this chapter.

Wait a Second: Where the Heck Are the Mouse Buttons?

Tahoe takes a visual approach to everything. What you see in Figure 3-1, earlier in this chapter, is designed for point-and-click convenience, because the *trackpad* is your primary navigational tool while you're using your Neo. You move your finger over the surface of the trackpad, and the *pointer* (also called the *cursor*) follows like an obedient pup. The faster you move your finger, the farther the pointer goes. When your pointer is over the desired item, you tap it (or *click* it, if you prefer the more familiar term); it opens; you do your thing; Life is Good.

Never use any object other than your finger on the trackpad! No pencils (not even the eraser end) or chopsticks; they'll damage the trackpad in no time.

WARNING

If you've grazed on the other side of the fence — if you're one of Those Who Were Once Windows Users — you're probably accustomed to using a mouse with at least two buttons. This brings up the nagging question: "Hey, Mark, where the heck *are* the buttons?"

In a nutshell, the buttons simply ain't there if you're using your Neo's trackpad. The entire surface of the trackpad can act as both buttons. To customize how the trackpad operates, click the menu on the Finder menu bar, click System Settings, and then click the Trackpad entry in the sidebar at the left of the window. The Trackpad pane appears, and from the Point & Click settings there, for example, you can:

>> **Enable the Tap to Click switch.** Now when you tap anywhere on the trackpad, your Neo counts that as a click. Tap twice quickly, and your Neo recognizes a double-click.

>> **Click the Secondary Click pop-up menu.** A single tap with two fingers displays the right-click menu (which I cover later), or you can choose to click in either bottom corner.

>> **Adjust your tracking speed.** Click and drag the Tracking speed slider to speed or slow the rate at which the pointer moves.

Apple illustrates each gesture available from the Trackpad pane in System Settings. A short video clip shows you both the gesture itself and its effect.

DOING THE MULTI-TOUCH THING

Today's crop of MacBooks has the smartest trackpads on the planet because the *Multi-Touch* feature allows you to control the view of a document by using specific finger motions on the trackpad surface. Here's the rundown:

- **Two-finger scrolling:** Move two fingers over the surface of the trackpad to scroll the contents of the active Finder window or application in the same direction. You can use the scroll function to move up and down through the pages of a document, for example, or to move up and down through a long web page.

- **Two-finger zooming:** Pinching your thumb and forefinger together on the trackpad zooms out on a document or image. The reverse (moving your thumb and fingertip away from each other) zooms in. (iPhone and iPad owners are grinning broadly right now because they use the same motions.)

- **Two-finger Smart Zoom:** Tap twice with two fingers to zoom in, and double-tap again with two fingers to zoom out.

- **Two-finger rotating:** Move your thumb and forefinger in a circle on the trackpad to rotate in the corresponding direction.

- **Two-finger paging:** Swipe your thumb and forefinger to the left or right across the trackpad to page through a document or to move to the next or previous image in a set.

- **Three-finger full-screen switching:** Swipe your thumb and first two fingertips to the left or right across the trackpad to move among open applications in full-screen mode.

- **Two-finger Notification Center display:** Swipe to the left with two fingers from the right edge of the trackpad, and Tahoe displays the Notification Center. To hide the panel, reverse the gesture and swipe from the left edge using two fingers.

- **Action in Mission Control:** Using the combination of thumb and fingers you specify, you can configure the display and operation of these features within Tahoe.

I'll be honest: When my Neo is on my desk at home, I plug in a Logitech optical trackball. This neat device has two buttons and a scroll wheel, saving me wear and tear on my trackpad and offering even finer control in my apps.

If you can afford a wireless Bluetooth mouse, trackpad, or trackball for your Neo, *buy it.*

If you tap the trackpad with two fingertips (or click the right mouse button on a mouse), Tahoe performs the same function that a right click does in Windows. When you right-click most items — icons, documents, even your Desktop — you get a *contextual menu* of commands specific to that item.

If you're using a mouse, don't forget to visit the System Settings Mouse pane to configure it.

Launching and Quitting Apps

Now you can pair your new trackpad acumen with the Finder window. Move the pointer over the Music icon in the Dock. (Look for the symbol of a musical note.) Then tap the trackpad once. (See the preceding section for details on how to configure it.) Whoosh! Tahoe *launches,* or starts, the Music app, and you see the Music window appear on your Desktop.

If an app or document icon is already selected (which I discuss later in the chapter), you can simply press ⌘+O to launch or open it.

Besides the Dock, you have a plethora of ways to launch an app or open a document in Tahoe:

>> **From the menu:** You can launch several apps from anywhere in Tahoe by using the menu. Choose System Settings to change all sorts of macOS settings. Choose App Store to launch the macOS App Store and display software that you can download.

>> **From Apps:** This window arranges all your application icons in a single scrolling list display. (The Apps icon on the Dock is a grid of colored squares.) Click a category button at the top of the window to display apps that match that category. To launch an app, just click the desired icon.

>> **From the Desktop:** If you have a document you created or an app icon on your Desktop, you can launch or open it by rapidly tapping the trackpad twice with one finger when the pointer is on top of the icon.

Double-clicking a device or network connection on your Desktop opens the contents in a Finder window. This method works for external drives and USB flash drives.

>> **From the Recent Items selection:** When you click the menu and hover the pointer over Recent Items, the Finder displays the apps and documents you've used over past few sessions. Click an item to open it.

>> **From the Login Items list:** Login items are apps that Tahoe launches automatically each time you log in. I cover login items in Chapter 9.

>> **From the Finder window:** You can also double-click an icon within the confines of a Finder window to open it (documents), launch it (apps), or display the contents (folders).

The macOS Quick Look feature can display the contents of just about any document or file — but without actually opening the corresponding app! *Sweet.* From a Finder window, click a file to select it and press the spacebar.

After you finish using an app, you can quit that app to close its window and return to the Desktop. Here are several ways to quit an app:

>> **Press ⌘+Q.** This keyboard shortcut quits virtually every Mac app. Just make sure that the app you want to quit is currently active first. (The app name should appear immediately to the right of the menu.)

>> **Choose the Quit command from the app's menu.** To use the Quit command, click the app's named menu on the menu bar. As I mentioned, this menu is always to the immediate right of the menu.

>> **Choose Quit from the Dock.** You can right-click an app's icon on the Dock and then choose Quit from the menu that appears.

A running app displays a small dot below its icon on the Dock.

>> **Click the Close button in the application window.** Some apps quit entirely when you close their window, such as the System Settings window. Other apps might continue running without any window, such as Safari or Music; to close these apps, you have to use another method in this list. (More on window controls such as Close in the next section.)

>> **Choose Force Quit from the menu. *This is a last-resort measure!*** Use this method **only** if an app has frozen and you can't use another method to quit. (It should be marked as unresponsive in the Force Quit dialog.) *Force-quitting an app doesn't save any open documents!*

Performing Tricks with Finder Windows

In the following sections, I describe basic windows management in Tahoe: how to move things around, how to close windows, and how to make windows disappear and reappear like magic.

Scrolling in and resizing windows

Can you imagine what life would be like if you couldn't see more than a single window's worth of stuff? Shopping would be curtailed quite a bit — and so would the contents of the folders on your system! That's why Tahoe includes *scroll bars* that you can click and drag to move through the window's contents. (By default, scroll bars don't appear in Tahoe until you move the pointer close to them.) You can:

- >> Click the scroll box and drag it. For the uninitiated, that means clicking the darker portion of the bar and holding your finger on the trackpad while you move your finger in the desired direction.

- >> Click anywhere in the area above or below the scroll box to scroll pages one at a time.

- >> Hold down the Option key and click anywhere in the empty area above or below the bar to scroll to that spot in the document.

You can also drag two fingertips across the trackpad to scroll a window's contents (both vertically and horizontally). To control trackpad behavior, open System Settings and click the Trackpad pane. You can read all about configuring trackpad settings in the earlier section, "Wait a Second: Where the Heck Are the Mouse Buttons?"

Figure 3-2 shows two vertical scroll bars in a typical Finder window, as well as the Sidebar and three Finder Tabs.

Often, pressing the Page Up and Page Down keys moves you through a document one page at a time, whereas pressing the arrow keys moves the insertion pointer one line or one character in the four compass directions.

You can resize Finder and app windows by enlarging or reducing the window frame itself. Move the pointer over any window corner or edge and then drag the edge in any direction. (More on dragging is coming up.)

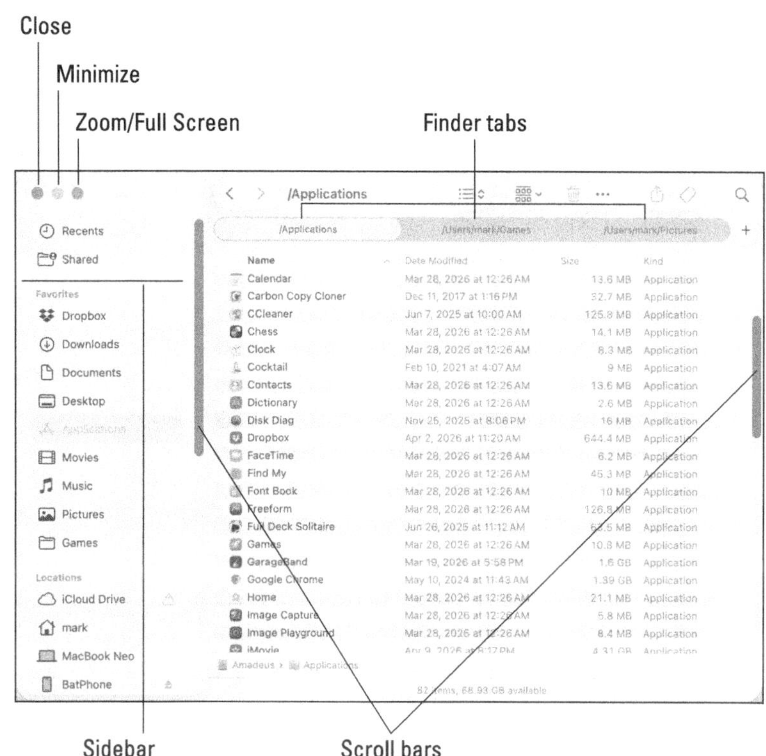

FIGURE 3-2: A plethora of helpful window controls.

Minimizing and restoring windows

Resizing a window is indeed helpful, but maybe you simply want to banish it until you need it again. That calls for the Minimize button, which also appears in Figure 3-2, shown previously. A *minimized* window disappears from the Desktop but isn't closed; it reappears on the Dock as an icon.

Minimizing a window is easy: Move the pointer over the Minimize button (the second of the three buttons in the top-left corner of the window). Click when you see the minus sign appear on the button. Double-clicking the window's *title bar* (the top frame of the window, which usually includes a document or application name) also minimizes the window.

To restore the window to its full size (and its original position on the Desktop), just click its window icon on the Dock.

Moving and zooming windows

Perhaps you want to move a window to another location on the Desktop so that you can see the contents of multiple windows at the same time. Click the window's title bar and drag the window anywhere you like; then release the hold.

Many apps can automatically arrange multiple windows (such as Microsoft Word). Choose Window ⇨ Arrange All if this option appears.

You can use Zoom to expand any Finder or app window to its maximum practical size. (Zooming a Finder window is different from zooming with the Multi-Touch feature, because you're expanding only the size of the Finder window, not an image or document.) A zoomed window can fill the entire screen, but if that extra space isn't applicable for the app, the window might expand to only a larger part of the Desktop.

To zoom a window, move your pointer over the third button in the top-left corner of the window. Again, refer to Figure 3-2, which illustrates the position. (Man, that is one versatile figure.) A double-arrow icon appears on the Zoom/Full-Screen button. Click to expand your horizons to full-screen, or hold down the Option key while clicking (the icon changes to a plus sign) to zoom the window to maximum size.

Speaking of *full-screen* mode, it comes in handy: A single app fills the screen without displaying a window frame or traditional Finder menu bar. The method you use to switch to full-screen mode varies depending on the app. Most of the apps included with macOS use View ⇨ Enter Full Screen. A click of the Zoom/Full-Screen button (*without* holding down the Option key) switches most Apple apps (and Finder windows) into full-screen mode. To exit full-screen mode, just press Esc.

So how do you switch among apps if they're all in full-screen mode?

>> Move your pointer to the bottom of the screen to display the Dock, where you can click another application to switch to it.

>> Swipe three fingers to the left or right across the trackpad surface.

>> Press the ⌘+Tab shortcut to cycle through your open apps.

Closing windows

When you're finished with an app, or you no longer need a window open, move the pointer over the Close button in the top-left corner of the window (the first of the three buttons). When the X appears on the button, click it. And yes, I can make *one more* reference to Figure 3-2, shown earlier and which I'm thinking of nominating as Figure of the Year.

TOGGLING TOOLBARS THE TAHOE WAY

It's time to define a window control that's actually *inside* the window for a change. A *toolbar* is a strip of icons that generally appears below the window's title bar. These icons typically perform the most common actions in an app; the effect is the same as choosing a menu command or pressing a keyboard shortcut. Toolbars are popular these days. You see 'em in everything from the Finder window to most app windows.

You can usually banish a window's toolbar to make extra room for icons, or whatever the window happens to be holding. Just choose View ⇨ Hide Toolbar. To restore the toolbar to its original position, choose View ⇨ Show Toolbar.

If you haven't saved a document and you try to close that application's window, the app gets downright surly and prompts you for confirmation: "Hey, human, you don't *really* want to do this, do you?" If you answer in the affirmative — "Why, yes, Neo, I do want to throw this away and not save it" — the app discards the open document. If you decide to keep your document (thereby saving your posterior from harm), you can cancel the action and then save the document within the application.

MARK'S
MAXIM

ONLY ONE CAN BE ACTIVE AT A TIME

Here's a very special Mark's Maxim in the macOS universe:

Only one application window can be active in Tahoe at any time.

You can always tell which window is active:

- The active window is on top of other windows. (You can still use a window's Close, Minimize, and Zoom buttons when the window is inactive.)

- Any input you make by typing or by moving your finger on the trackpad appears in the active window.

- macOS *dims* the title bars of inactive windows you haven't minimized.

Juggling Folders and Icons

Finder windows aren't just for launching apps and opening files and documents. You can also use the icons in a Finder window to select specific items or to copy and move items from place to place.

A field observer's guide to icons

Not all icons are created equal. Earlier in this chapter, I introduce you to your Neo's drive icon on the Desktop. Here's a little background on the other types of icons you might encounter during your mobile Mac travels:

- » **Hardware:** These icons include your drive as well as external peripherals, such as an external optical drive, a backup drive, or a USB flash drive.

- » **Applications:** These icons represent the apps you can launch. Most apps have a custom icon that incorporates the company's logo or the specific app logo. Double-clicking an app usually doesn't load a document; you typically get an Open dialog, where you can select a file to open.

- » **Documents:** Many of the files on your system are documents that can be opened in the corresponding app; the icon usually looks similar to the app's icon, so documents are easy to recognize. Double-clicking a document automatically launches the associated app.

- » **Files:** Most of the file icons on your system are mundane things such as settings files, text files, log files, and miscellaneous data files. Yet most icons are identified by at least some type of recognizable image that lets you guess what purpose the file serves. You'll also see generic file icons that look like a blank sheet of paper (used when Tahoe has no earthly idea what the file type is).

- » **Aliases:** An *alias* acts as a link to another item elsewhere on your system. To launch Adobe Acrobat, for example, you can click an Adobe Acrobat alias icon that you can create on your Desktop instead of clicking the actual Acrobat app icon. The alias essentially acts the same way as the original icon, but it doesn't take up the same amount of space — only a few bytes for the icon itself compared with the size of the actual app. (Windows switchers know an alias as a Windows *shortcut.* The idea is the same, although Macs had it first.) You can always identify an alias by the small curved arrow at the base of the icon, and the icon might also sport the tag alias at the end of its name.

    You have two ways to create an alias. First, you can select the item (more on selecting items in the next section) and choose File ⇨ Make Alias. Using a trackpad or mouse, you can hold down ⌘+Option while you drag the original icon to the location where you want the alias.

So why bother to use an alias? Two good reasons:

>> **You can open an app or a document from anywhere on your drive.** If you occasionally need to use Photoshop while working on a Pages project, for example, you can add an alias and launch Photoshop directly from the folder in which you store those Pages documents.

>> **You can send an alias to the Trash without affecting the original item.** When that Pages project is finished, you can safely delete the entire folder without worrying about whether Photoshop will run the next time you double-click its application icon!

Selecting items

Often, the menu or keyboard commands you perform in the Finder need to be performed *on* something (perhaps you're moving an item to the Trash or getting information on the item). To identify the target of your action to the Finder, you need to select items on your Desktop or in a Finder window.

Selecting one thing

Tahoe gives you a couple of options for selecting just one item for an upcoming action:

>> **Move the pointer over the item and click.** A dark border (or *highlight*) appears around the icon, indicating that it's selected.

>> **If an icon is already highlighted on your Desktop or in a window, move the highlight to another icon in the same location by using the arrow keys.** To shift the selection highlight alphabetically, press Tab (to move in order) or press Shift+Tab (to move in reverse order).

Selecting items in the Finder doesn't actually *do* anything by itself. You must perform an action on the selected items to make something happen.

Selecting a whole bunch of things

You can also select multiple items by using one of these methods:

>> **Adjacent items:**

- **Drag a box around them.** Click a spot above and to the left of the first item. Keep holding down your finger on the trackpad surface (or the mouse button), and drag down and to the right. (This is called *dragging* in Macspeak.)

A box appears, indicating what you're selecting. Any icons that touch or appear within the box outline are selected when you release the button.

- **Click the first item to select it, and then hold down the Shift key while you click the last item.** Tahoe selects both items and everything between them.

>> **Nonadjacent items:** Select these by holding down the ⌘ key while you click each item.

Check out the Finder window status bar (which can appear at the top or bottom, depending on whether the toolbar is hidden). It tells you how much space is available on the drive you're working in, as well as how many items are displayed in the current Finder window. When you select items, it shows you how many you highlighted. (If you don't see a status bar, choose View ⇨ Show Status Bar.)

Copying items

Want to copy items from one Finder window to another or from one location (like a flash drive) to another (like your Desktop)? Très easy. Just use one of these methods:

>> **On the same drive:**

- **To copy one item to another location:** Hold down the Option key (no need to select the icon first) and click and drag the item from its current home to the new location.

  To put a copy of an item in a folder, just drop the item on top of the receiving folder. If you hold the item you're dragging over the destination folder for a second or two, Tahoe opens a new window so that you can see the target's contents.

- **To copy multiple items to another location:** Select them all (see the preceding section), hold down the Option key, and then drag and drop one of the selected items where you want it. All the items you selected follow the item you drag.

  To help indicate your target when you're copying files, Tahoe highlights the location to show you where the items will end up. If the target is a window, Tahoe adds a highlight to the window border.

>> **On a different drive:**

- **To copy one or multiple items:** Click and drag the item (or the selected items if you have more than one) from the original window to a window you open on the target drive. (No need to hold down the Option key while copying to a different drive.)

If you try to move or copy something to a location that already has an item with the same name, you see a dialog that prompts you to decide whether to replace the file or to stop the copy/move procedure and leave the existing file alone. Heck, you can even keep *both*. (macOS performs the copy or move but also appends the word *copy* to the item being copied. Good insurance indeed.)

Moving things from place to place

Moving things from one location to another location on the same drive is a breeze. Just drag the selected item or items to the new location. The item disappears from the original spot and reappears in the new spot.

Duplicating in a jiffy

If you need more than one copy of the same item in a folder, use the Tahoe Duplicate command. I use Duplicate often when I want to edit a document but want to ensure that the original document stays pristine, no matter what. I just create a duplicate and edit that file instead.

MY, WHAT AN ATTRACTIVE SIDEBAR!

Have you noticed the Sidebar that typically occupies the left side of a Finder window? It's a pane of links to common locations and devices that you can use to jump to a specific spot on your system. You can click the Applications link below the Favorites heading, for example, and you're instantly transported to your Applications folder.

Here's a great example of Sidebar magic: I make a point of adding my current book project folder to my Finder window Sidebar so that it's available immediately from any Finder window. To do this, just drag the folder into the column at the left side of the Finder window and drop it on top of the Favorites heading in the Sidebar's list.

You can configure the items that will appear in your Sidebar: Choose Finder ⇨ Settings and then click the Sidebar tab of the Settings dialog to display the list. Then you can select and deselect check boxes to configure your Sidebar to your liking.

To use Duplicate, you can click an item to select it and then choose File⇨ Duplicate, or right-click the item and choose Duplicate.

The duplicate item has the word *copy* appended to its name. A second copy is named copy2, a third is copy3, and so on.

Duplicating a folder also duplicates *all* the contents of that folder. Therefore, creating a duplicate folder can take some time if the original folder was stuffed full. The duplicate folder has copy appended to its name, but the contents of the duplicate folder keep their original names.

Using Finder Tabs

Tahoe includes a powerful feature you can use to display multiple locations in the same window. *Finder Tabs* work just like the tabs in Safari, allowing you to switch among multiple locations on your Neo *instantly* by clicking a tab. You can even drag files and folders from tab to tab!

To open a new tab in a Finder window, you can click the location and press ⌘+T, or right-click the location and choose Open in New Tab. The location appears as a new tab below the toolbar. You can open as many tabs as you like, and you can drag the Finder Tabs themselves to reorder them. To close a tab, hover the pointer over it and then click the X button that appears. That hard-working Figure 3-2 earlier in the chapter shows three Finder Tabs at work.

You can also set new folders to open in tabs instead of windows. Click the Finder menu, choose Settings, click the General tab, and then click the Open Folders in Tabs Instead of New Windows check box to enable it.

Keys and Keyboard Shortcuts to Fame and Fortune

Your Neo's keyboard might not be as glamorous as the trackpad, but any Mac power user will tell you that using keyboard shortcuts is the fastest method of performing tasks in the Finder (and in your apps). I recommend committing these shortcuts to memory and putting them to work as soon as you begin using your Neo so that they become second nature.

Special keys on the keyboard

Your Neo's keyboard has special keys that you might not recognize — especially if you've made the smart move and decided to migrate from Windows to macOS! Table 3-1 lists the keys that bear strange hieroglyphics on the Apple keyboard and describes what they do.

TABLE 3-1   **Too-Cool Function Keys**

Action/Key Name	Symbol	Purpose
Audio Mute	F10	Mutes (and restores) all sound produced by your Neo
Volume Down	F11	Decreases the sound volume
Volume Up	F12	Increases the sound volume
Control	Ctrl	Displays the right-click menu when clicking
Command	⌘	Primary modifier for menus and keyboard shortcuts
Option	Option	Modifier for shortcuts

Using the Finder and app shortcuts

The Finder is chock-full of keyboard shortcuts that you can use to take care of common tasks. Some of the handiest shortcuts are listed in Table 3-2.

TABLE 3-2   **Tahoe Keyboard Shortcuts of Distinction**

Key Combination	Location	Action
⌘+A	Edit menu	Selects all items (works in the Finder too)
⌘+C	Edit menu	Copies the selected items to the Clipboard
⌘+H	Application menu	Hides the current application window
⌘+M	Window menu	Minimizes the active window to the Dock (also works in the Finder)
⌘+O	File menu	Opens or launches an existing document, file, or folder (also works in the Finder)
⌘+P	File menu	Prints the current document
⌘+Q	Application menu	Exits (quits) the application and prompts you to save any changes

(continued)

TABLE 3-2 *(continued)*

Key Combination	Location	Action
⌘+T	Finder	Opens a new Finder tab in a Finder window with the selected location
⌘+V	Edit menu	Pastes the contents of the Clipboard at the current pointer position
⌘+X	Edit menu	Cuts the highlighted item to the Clipboard
⌘+Z	Edit menu	Reverses (undoes) the effect of the last action you took
⌘+Tab	Finder	Switches between open applications
⌘+Option+M	Finder	Minimizes all Finder windows to the Dock
⌘+Option+Esc	Apple	Opens the Force Quit dialog
⌘+Option+W	Finder	Closes all Finder windows

TIP

But wait — there's more! Most of your apps also provide their own set of keyboard shortcuts. While you're working with a new app, display its Help file and print a copy of the keyboard shortcuts as a handy cheat sheet.

If you've used a PC before, you're certainly familiar with three-key shortcuts. The most infamous is Ctrl+Alt+Delete, the beloved reboot/Task Manager shortcut nicknamed the *Windows three-finger salute.* Three-key shortcuts work the same way in Tahoe. To use a three-key shortcut, hold down the first two keys and then press the third key.

Home, Sweet Home Folder

Each user account you create in Tahoe is actually a self-contained universe. Each user has unique characteristics devoted to them, and Tahoe keeps track of everything that the user changes. (In Chapter 9, I describe the innate loveliness of multiple users living in harmony on your Neo.)

This unique universe includes a different system of folders for each user account on your system. The top-level folder uses the short username that Tahoe assigns when that user account is created. Naturally, the actual folder name is different for each person. Mac techno types typically call this folder your *Home folder.* (On the Sidebar, look for the teeny house icon below the Locations heading, marked with your account name.)

When you're on the hunt for your Home folder, don't look for a folder that's actually named *Home.* Instead, look for the short username.

Each account's Home folder contains a set of subfolders, including:

>> Movies

>> Music

>> Pictures

>> Desktop (the contents of your Tahoe Desktop)

>> Downloads (for files you download by using Safari or through Apple Mail attachments)

>> Public (for files you want to share with others on your network)

>> Documents (for files created by the user)

Although you can store your stuff on your Desktop, that gaggle of items can get crowded and confusing quickly. Here's a Mark's Maxim to live by:

Your Home folder is where you hang out and where you store your stuff. Use it to make your computing life *much* **easier!**

Create subfolders within your Documents folder to organize your files and folders even further. I create a subfolder in my Documents folder for every book I write so that I can quickly locate all the files for that book project.

I discuss security for your Home folder, as well as what gets stored where, in Chapter 9. For now, remember that you can reach your Home folder easily because it appears in the Finder window's Sidebar. (If your Home folder doesn't appear in the Sidebar, that's easy to fix: Choose Finder ⇨ Settings, click the Sidebar tab of the Settings dialog, and then select the check box to display your Home folder.)

In addition to using the Finder window's Sidebar, you can reach your Home folder by choosing Go ⇨ Home, or by pressing ⌘+Shift+H. From within most apps, the standard File Open and File Save dialogs include the Home location.

Here's another reason to use your Home folder to store your stuff: *default locations!* Tahoe expects your stuff to be there when you migrate your files from an older Mac to a new Mac.

Working with Mission Control

For those power users who often work with a passel of applications, allow me to turn your attention to one of the sassiest features in Tahoe: Mission Control. You can activate Mission Control from your keyboard:

>> **Press F3** to show *all* open windows using Mission Control, grouped by app. Move the pointer on top of the window to actvate — the window border turns blue when selected — and click to switch to that window.

>> **Press Ctrl+F3** to show all open windows of just the app that you're currently using; click the one you want to activate.

From the trackpad, display the Mission Control screen by swiping up with three fingers.

Besides the F3 and Control+F3 hot keys that I just discussed, Mission Control provides one more nifty function: Press ⌘+F3, and all your open windows scurry to the side of the screen. Now you can use drives, files, and aliases on your Desktop! When you're ready to confront those dozen app windows again, press the keyboard shortcut a second time.

Naturally, these key shortcuts can be customized! Open the Desktop & Dock pane in System Settings and click the Shortcuts button at the bottom of the pane to specify what key sequence does what.

Hiring a Stage Manager

macOS Tahoe includes another feature, Stage Manager, that allows you to focus on a single app window while enjoying quick access to other recent apps. I like to think of Stage Manager as an enhancement to the familiar ⌘+Tab keyboard shortcut, which can cycle through the open application windows on your Desktop. You can turn Stage Manager on from the Desktop & Dock pane in System Settings.

With Stage Manager on, you'll notice that the active app window appears at the center of your Desktop, while all other recent app windows are displayed at the left side of the Desktop as thumbnails. To switch to another open app, click the desired thumbnail. The thumbnail expands as the active window, and the app you were using joins the thumbnail list.

You can toggle the thumbnail display off from the Desktop & Dock pane to save Desktop space, but the thumbnails are still available: Move your pointer to the left edge of the screen and they'll appear. To open even more space, disable the Show Items in Stage Manager check box (you can click directly on the Desktop to display its icons if you need them).

Switching Desktops with Spaces

What if you want to switch to a different *set* of apps? Suppose that you're slaving away at your pixel-pushing job — say, designing a magazine cover with Pages. Your Desktop includes Adobe's Photoshop and InDesign, which you switch among by using one of the techniques I just described. Suddenly you realize that you need to schedule a meeting using Calendar, and you want to send email to the participants in Apple Mail. What to do?

Well, you could certainly open Apps and launch those two applications on top of your graphics apps and then minimize them. But with Mission Control's *Spaces* feature, you can press the Control+← or Control+→ sequences to switch to a different "communications" Desktop, with Calendar and Apple Mail windows already open and in your favorite positions. *Whoa!*

After you set up your meeting and send that important email, simply press Control+← or Control+→ again to switch back to your "graphics" Desktop, where all your work is exactly as you left it. (And yes, Virginia, Spaces does indeed work with full-screen applications.)

To create a new Desktop for use in Spaces, press the Control+↑ shortcut for Mission Control. Move your pointer to the top right of the Mission Control screen and click the Add button (with the plus sign) that appears. Spaces creates a new empty Desktop thumbnail. Switch to the new Desktop by clicking the label at the top of the Mission Control screen and then open those apps that you want to include. That's all there is to it!

To switch an app window between Spaces Desktops, drag the window to the edge of the Desktop and hold it there. Spaces automatically moves the window to the next Desktop. (Apps can also be dragged between Desktops within the Mission Control screen.) To delete a Desktop from the Mission Control screen, hover your pointer over the offending Spaces thumbnail; then click the Delete button (with the X) that appears.

You can jump directly to a specific Spaces Desktop by clicking its thumbnail in your Mission Control screen or by holding down the Control key and pressing the number corresponding to that desktop. Finally, you can always use the Control+← or Control+→ shortcuts to move between Desktops and full-screen applications.

Personalizing Your Desktop

Many folks put all their documents, pictures, and videos on their Tahoe Desktop because the file icons are easy to locate! Your computing stuff is right in front of you . . . or *is* it?

Call me a finicky, stubborn techno-oldster — go ahead, it's true — but I prefer a clean macOS Desktop without all the iconic clutter. In fact, my Desktop usually has just three or four icons even though I use my Neo several hours every day. It's an organizational thing; I work with literally hundreds of apps, documents and assorted knickknacks daily. Sooner or later, you'll find that you're using that many, too. When you keep your stuff crammed on your Desktop, you have to laboriously scan your screen for a particular file, and you end up taking more time to locate it on your Desktop than in your Documents folder! And don't forget: Open windows hang out on your Desktop, too. To find anything, you have to close or move those windows!

Besides keeping things clean, I can recommend other favorite tweaks that you can make to your Desktop:

>> **Keep Desktop icons arranged as you like.**

1. **Right-click any open spot on your Desktop and choose Sort By.**

2. **Choose the criteria that Tahoe uses to automatically arrange your Desktop icons, including name, modification date, or size.**

   I personally like things organized by name, but many Neo owners prefer to see things organized by date (putting the most recently modified item at the top, for example).

>> **Choose a favorite background.**

1. **Right-click any open spot on your Desktop and choose Change Wallpaper.**

2. **Browse the various folders of background images that Apple provides, open a folder of your own images, or use an image from your Photos library.**

>> **Display all the peripherals and network connections on your system.**

   1. **Choose Finder ⇨ Settings.**

   2. **Make sure that all four of the top check boxes on the Settings dialog are selected: Hard Disks; External Disks; CDs, DVDs, and iPods; and Connected Servers.**

   If you're connected to an external network, or if you've loaded an external drive or device, these external storage locations will now show up on your Desktop. You can double-click that Desktop icon to view your external stuff.

Taking Control of Your Neo

Another source of "customization glee" (yes, I am honestly that much of a computer nerd) is the macOS Control Center, which adds a welcome level of convenience when changing system settings. To display the Control Center anywhere within Tahoe, click the Control Center icon in the Finder menu bar. (It looks like two horizontal sliding switches.) The Center appears as in Figure 3-3, at the right side of the Desktop.

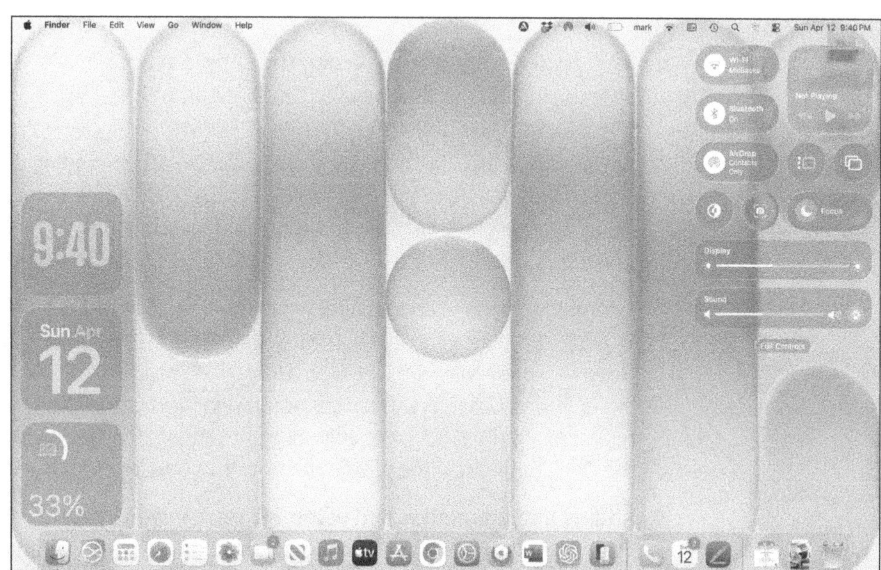

FIGURE 3-3: The Control Center makes it easy to quickly change global settings.

Most of the tiles you see displayed in the Control Center are simple switches for macOS features, like the Display and Sound sliders — you can click and drag them directly to adjust the levels. The Wi-Fi tile is different (offering a submenu of multiple settings), allowing you to not only enable or disable your Neo's Wi-Fi but also switch networks or display the full Network pane within System Settings.

You can specify what features are shown within the Control Center and which features remain on the Finder menu bar. Click the System Settings icon on the Dock; then click the Menu Bar entry in the sidebar. This pane displays the available features for the menu bar in a list. Click the switches next to a module to toggle the display of the module in the menu bar. Click the Add Controls button to drag the tiles you want to the Control Center.

Customizing the Dock

In terms of importance, the *Dock* — the quick-access strip for apps and documents that appears on your Desktop — ranks at the top of macOS features, so it had better be easy to customize!

Adding applications and extras to the Dock

Why be satisfied with just the icons that Apple places on the Dock? You can add your own apps, files, and folders to the Dock as well:

>> **Adding apps:** You can add any app to your Dock by dragging its icon into the area to the *left* side of the vertical line on the Dock. You'll know when you're in the proper territory because the existing Dock icons obligingly move aside to make space for it.

Attempting to place an app directly on the right side of the Dock sends it to the Trash (if the Trash icon is highlighted when you release the button), so beware. Note, however, that you can drop an app icon inside a Stack (more on that in a bit) or a folder that already exists at the right end of the Dock. (If you've repositioned the Dock on the left or right side of the screen, consider the top of the Dock to be the left side and the bottom of the Dock to be the right side.)

>> **Adding individual files and volumes:** You can add individual files and volume icons to the Dock by dragging the icon into the area at the *right* end of the Dock. (Attempting to place icons on the left end of the Dock opens the app associated with the contents instead.) Again, the existing Dock icons move aside to create a space when you're in the right area.

>> **Adding several files or a folder:** Tahoe uses a feature called *Stacks,* which I discuss in a page or two, to handle multiple files or add an entire folder to the Dock.

>> **Adding websites:** You can drag any URL from Safari directly to the right end of the Dock. Clicking that Dock icon automatically opens your browser and displays that page.

REMEMBER

If you see *two* vertical lines in the Dock, you've turned on the Dock's Recent Applications feature, which displays icons for the last apps you've recently launched. (You can find this setting in the System Settings Dock & Menu Bar pane.) Consider the vertical line farthest to the right to be the right side of the Dock when adding items to the Dock.

To remove an icon from the Dock, just click and drag it off the Dock. Note, however, that the original app, folder, or volume is *not* deleted; only the Dock icon itself is permanently excused. If you like, you can delete almost any of the default icons that macOS installs on the Dock; only the Finder and Trash icons must remain on the Dock.

Using Desktop widgets

As I mention earlier in the chapter, you can easily add widgets to your Control Center, Notification Center, and Desktop, but they especially capture my fancy on the Desktop. By default, Desktop widgets are always visible, providing information like the current time, date, and weather without requiring a single click.

To add one or more widgets to your Desktop, follow these steps:

1. **Click the Time/Date display in the Finder menu bar.**

   macOS displays Notification Center.

2. **Click the Edit Widgets button at the bottom of Notification Center.**

   The Edit Widgets sheet appears, complete with suggestions on modules you may want to add. However, you're not limited to the suggestions; you can click any of the categories in the sidebar to see what's available.

3. **Drag a module to the desired location on the Desktop.**

   Alternatively, of course, you can drag the module to the upper-right of the Desktop to add the widget to your Notification Center instead.

4. **Click the Done button to save your changes.**

You can configure all widgets as a group from the Desktop & Dock pane in System Settings.

Keeping track with Stacks

Tahoe offers *Stacks*, which are groups of items (documents, applications, and folders) that you want to place on the Dock for convenience — perhaps the files needed for a project you're working on or your favorite game apps. I have a Stack named Wiley on my Dock that holds all the project files I need for the book I'm currently writing, for example.

To create a Stack, select a folder containing the items and drag the folder to the right side of the Dock. Again, the Dock opens a spot at the right end of the Dock to indicate that you're in the zone.

To display the items in a Stack, just click it:

>> **If the Stack holds relatively few items,** they're displayed in a really cool-looking arc that Apple calls a *fan,* and you can click the item you want to open or launch. Figure 3-4 illustrates a typical Stack unfurled as a fan.

>> **If the Stack is stuffed full of many items,** the Stack opens in a grid display, allowing you to scroll the contents to find what you need.

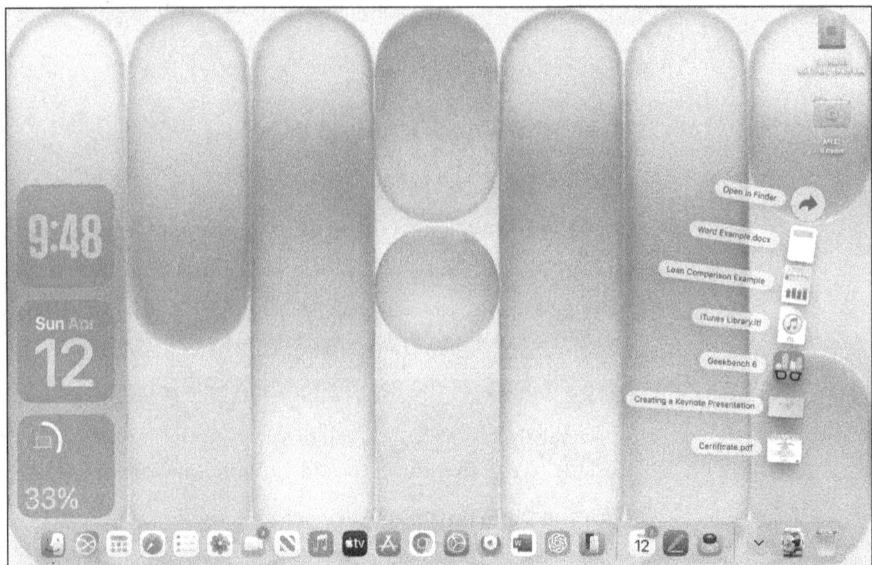

FIGURE 3-4: Stacks make it easy to access your stuff from the Dock.

Right-click the Stack icon and you can choose to sort the contents by name, date created or added, date modified, or file type. If you prefer a grid display (no matter how many items the Stack contains), you can choose Grid mode. Choose List to display the Stack's contents in much the same way as List view mode in a Finder window. List view mode also allows you to view folders in a Stack as nested menu items. Choose Automatic to return to the default view mode.

When set to Display as Stack, the Stack icon is displayed with icon images from the contents of the folder; if security is an issue, however, choose Display as Folder from the shortcut menu to display the Stack as a plain folder icon instead.

You can remove a Stack from the Dock by right-clicking the Stack icon and choosing Options; then choose Remove from Dock from the submenu that appears. Alternatively, just drag that sucker right off the Dock.

You can also display the contents of a Stack in a Finder window. Right-click the Stack icon and choose the Open item at the bottom of the pop-up shortcut menu.

Apple provides a Stack that's already set up for you. The Downloads folder, situated next to the Trash, is the default location for any new files that you download with Safari or receive in your email. Tahoe bounces the Download Stack icon to indicate that you've received a new item.

Resizing the Dock

You can change the size of the Dock from the Desktop & Dock settings — but here's a simpler way to resize the Dock right from the Desktop.

Move your pointer over the vertical solid line that separates the left end of the Dock from the right end; the pointer turns into a funky vertical line with arrows pointing up and down. This is your cue to click and drag while moving up and down, expanding and shrinking the Dock, respectively. Right-click when the funky line pointer is visible to display a shortcut menu of Dock settings.

What's with the Trash?

Another sign of a Neo power user is a well-maintained Trash can. It's a breeze to empty the discarded items you no longer need, and you can even rescue something that you suddenly discover you *do* still need!

The translucent Tahoe Trash icon resides on the Dock, and it works just like the Trash has always worked in macOS. Simply drag selected items to the Trash to delete them.

Note one *very* important exception: If you drag a Desktop icon for an external device or a removable media drive to the Trash (such as a USB flash drive), the Trash icon turns into a giant Eject icon, and the removable device or medium is ejected or shut down — not erased. Repeat, *not erased.* (That's why the Trash icon changes to the Eject icon — to remind you that you're not doing anything destructive.)

Here are other ways to chuck items you select to go to the wastebasket:

>> Choose File ⇨ Move to Trash.

>> Click the Action button on the Finder toolbar and choose Move to Trash from the list that appears.

>> Press ⌘+Delete.

>> Right-click the item and choose Move to Trash from the shortcut menu.

You can always tell when the Trash contains at least one item, because the icon is full of colorful waste. To display the contents of the Trash, just click the Trash icon on the Dock. To rescue something from the Trash, drag the item(s) from the Trash folder to the Desktop or any other folder in a Finder window. (Remember to act as though the task was a lot of work.)

When you're sure that you want to permanently delete the contents of the Trash, choose Finder ⇨ Empty Trash or right-click the Trash icon on the Dock and choose Empty Trash.

All You Really Need to Know about Printing

Because I'm near the end of this chapter, I turn now to a task that most Neo owners need to tackle soon after buying their MacBook: printing documents. Because basic printing is so important (and in most cases, so simple), allow me to demonstrate how to print a document.

Most of us have a USB printer — USB being the favored hardware connection in macOS. As long as your printer is supported by macOS, setting it up is as easy as plugging it into one of your MacBook's USB-C ports. (Note that a USB 2.0 or 3.0 printer will require an adapter to connect to your Neo's USB-C ports.) Naturally, a Wi-Fi printer needs no adapter.

Before you print, *preview!* Would you jump from an airplane without a parachute? Then why would you print a document without double-checking it first? Most apps now have their own built-in Preview thumbnails in the Print sheet. This feature is definitely A Good Thing, because you see what the printed document will look like, possibly saving you both paper and some of that hideously expensive ink or toner.

To print from any app with the default page characteristics (standard 8½" × 11" paper, portrait mode, no scaling), follow these steps:

1. **In your application, choose File ⇨ Print or press ⌘+P.**

   In most applications, macOS displays the simple version of the Print sheet. (To display all the fields under a specific heading, click the disclosure triangle next to the heading.) Some apps use their own custom Print dialogs, but you should see similar general settings.

2. **Click the Copies field and enter the number of copies you need.**

3. **Decide what you want to print.**

   - **The whole shootin' match:** To print the entire document, use the default Pages radio button setting of All.

   - **Anything less:** To print a range of selected pages, select the Range From radio button and enter the starting and ending pages (or, if the application allows it, click the Selection radio button to choose a selection of individual pages).

4. **(Optional) Choose application-specific printing parameters.**

   Each macOS app provides different headings so that you can configure settings specific to that application. You don't have to display any of these extra settings to print a default document, but the power is there to change the look dramatically. If you're printing from Contacts, for example, you can display the Contacts section and elect to print a list, an envelope, or mailing labels from the Style pop-up menu.

5. **When everything is a go for launch, click the Print button.**

   The printing system in macOS offers more settings and more functionality, of course. But I can tell you from my experiences that this short introduction to printing will likely suffice for 90 percent of the Neo owners on Earth. 'Nuff said.

And Just in Case You Need Help . . .

You can call on the resources described in this section if you need additional help while you're discovering how to tame Tahoe.

Some of the help resources are located on the internet, so your Safari web browser will come in handy when you search for answers.

The Tahoe built-in Help system

Sometimes the help you need is as close as the Help menu on the Finder menu bar. You can get help for either of the following:

>> **A specific application:** From the menu bar, choose Help and then click in the search box and type a short phrase that sums up your query (such as *keyboard shortcuts*). You see a list of help topics on the menu. Just click a topic to display more information.

>> **General topics:** Click a Finder window and then click Help on the menu bar. Again, you see the search box, and you can enter a word or phrase to find in the Help system.

The Apple web-based support center

Apple has online product support areas for every hardware and software product it manufactures. Visit `https://www.apple.com` and click the Support link at the top of the web page.

The search box on the Apple Support site works just like the macOS Help system, but the Apple online knowledge base has *a lot* more answers.

Online resources

Many online publications offer tips and tricks on using and maintaining macOS Tahoe. My personal online favorites are Macworld (`https://www.macworld.com`) and the Wiley For Dummies website (`https://www.dummies.com`).

2

Shaking Hands with macOS Tahoe

Chapter **4**

A Nerd's Guide to System Settings

Remember the old TV series *Voyage to the Bottom of the Sea*? You always knew you were on the bridge of the submarine *Seaview* because it had an entire wall made up of randomly blinking lights, crewmen darting about, and all sorts of exotic-looking controls on every surface. You could fix just about anything by looking into the camera with grim determination and barking an order. After all, you were *On the Bridge.* That's why virtually all the dialogue and action took place on that one (expensive) set: It was the nerve center of the ship, and a truly happenin' place to be.

In the same vein, I devote this chapter to the System Settings window and the most commonly used settings within it. After all, if you want to change how Tahoe works, you should head toward System Settings. This one window is the nerve center of macOS and a truly happenin' place to be. Sorry, no wall of blinking lights — but you *do* find exotic controls just about everywhere.

An Explanation — without Jargon, No Less

The System Settings window, shown in Figure 4-1, is a self-contained beast. You can reach it by clicking the Apple menu ( ) and choosing System Settings, or by clicking the System Settings icon on the Dock (it looks like two gears).

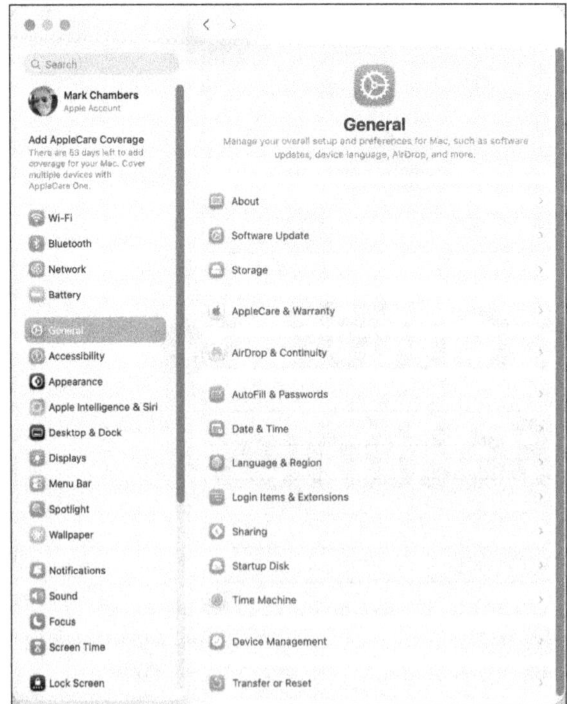

FIGURE 4-1:
The powerhouse of settings and switches: System Settings.

When the System Settings window is open, you can click any of the entries in the sidebar to switch to that *pane*. The right side of the window morphs to display the settings for the selected pane. Many panes also include a number of entries that display additional settings, easily distinguished by their snazzy right-arrow icons at the far right of the pane. You can click these entries to switch to another section in the same pane. (Figure 4-1 illustrates the General pane, which is populated completely by these section entries.) This design allows our friends at Apple to group a large number of related settings in the same pane without confusion.

You can also click the familiar Back and Forward icons at the top of the window to move backward through panes you've already visited and then forward again, in sequence. (Yep, just like the browser controls in Safari.)

REMEMBER

Right-click the System Settings icon on the Dock to jump to any pane.

You won't find an OK button that you have to click to apply any System Settings changes. Apple's developers do things the right way. Your changes to the settings in a pane are *automatically* saved when you click Back and exit a pane, or when you click the Close button in the System Settings window. You can also press ⌘+Q to exit and save all your changes.

Locating That Certain Special Setting

Wouldn't it be great if you could search through all the different panes in System Settings — with those countless radio buttons and slider controls — from one place, even when you're not sure what you're looking for?

It's Tahoe to the rescue! Just click in the System Settings Spotlight search box (located at the top of the Settings sidebar, with the magnifying glass icon) and type just about anything. For example, if you know part of the name of a particular setting you need to change, type that. Tahoe proudly displays panes that might contain matching settings. And if you're a *switcher* from the Windows world, you can even type what you might have called the same setting in Windows. (This also works in the Spotlight search box. Find more on this cool feature in Chapter 5.)

Popular System Settings Panes Explained

It's time to get down to brass tacks. In this section, I take you through the most often-used panes in System Settings to show what magic you can perform. I don't discuss every pane, because I cover many of them in other chapters. In fact, you might never need to open some System Settings panes, such as the Language & Region pane. This chapter covers just about all the settings you're likely to use on a regular basis.

The Displays pane

If you're a heavy-duty gamer, you have an external monitor, or you work with applications such as Keynote or Photoshop, you probably switch your monitor's characteristics regularly. To tweak your visuals, visit the Displays pane, shown in Figure 4-2. It includes these settings:

>> **Display:** To allow Tahoe to choose the best resolution for your display, select the resolution from the list that includes the label (Default). To manually select a resolution, click the Advanced button and click the Show All Resolutions switch to turn it on, and then click the resolution you want to use from the full list that appears. Note that many of the resolutions displayed in the full list will look "stretched" on your Neo's screen.

>> **Brightness:** Move the Brightness slider to adjust the brightness level of your MacBook's display. If you like, you can enable the Automatically Adjust Brightness switch to allow your Neo to select a brightness level.

>> **Color Profile:** Click a display ColorSync profile from the pop-up menu to control the colors on your screen (typically Color LCD for the Neo). To create a custom ColorSync profile and calibrate the colors that you see, click the Customize item at the bottom of the menu, and then click the Add button to launch the Display Calibrator. This easy-to-use assistant walks you step by step through the process.

>> **When Connected to TV:** If your Neo is connected to a TV via an HDMI adapter, this menu allows you to control what the TV will display (including mirroring the Neo's screen or acting as an extended screen).

>> **Night Shift:** This feature allows Tahoe to automatically adjust your display to provide warmer colors during the nighttime. Click the Night Shift button; then click Schedule to choose either Sunset to Sunrise operation or create your own custom schedule. To turn on Night Shift manually, use the Turn On Until Tomorrow switch. Adjust the Color Temperature slider to change the warmth of colors on your display.

If you connect your Neo to an external monitor, don't be surprised to see additional settings appear as well! You can drag the output to a different monitor, or drag the menu bar to another screen; or you can choose to mirror the same output to all connected displays.

The Desktop & Dock pane

As you discover in Chapter 3, the macOS Tahoe Desktop is a truly wondrous place — and therefore this pane is chock-full of cool stuff.

Dock settings

I'll come clean: I think the Dock is the best thing since sliced bread. (What did people refer to before sliced bread was invented?) You can use the settings shown in Figure 4-3 to configure the Dock's behavior:

>> **Size:** Pretty self-explanatory. Drag the slider to change the Dock's scale.

>> **Magnification:** When you select this check box, each icon in the Dock swells like a puffer fish when you move the pointer over it. (The Magnification slider determines just how much it magnifies.)

>> **Dock Position on Screen:** Select a radio button here to position the Dock on the left, bottom, or right edge of the Desktop.

>> **Minimize Windows Animations:** Tahoe includes two cool animations that you can choose from when shrinking a window to the Dock (and expanding it back to the Desktop).

>> **Window Title Bar Double-Click Action:** Select this check box to minimize or zoom a Finder or app window by double-clicking the window's title bar.

>> **Minimize Windows into Application Icon:** If this check box is not enabled, minimized app windows appear as thumbnail icons on the Dock. To minimize application windows into the application icon on the Dock, select this check box. (To restore a window that's been minimized into the application icon, right-click the icon on the Dock and choose Restore.)

>> **Automatically Hide and Show the Dock:** Select this switch, and the Dock disappears until you need it. (Depending on the size of your Dock, the Desktop real estate you gain can be significant.) To display a hidden Dock, move the pointer over the corresponding edge of the Desktop.

>> **Animate Opening Applications:** Active souls who like animation probably get a kick out of the bouncing application icons in the Dock, which indicate that you've launched an application and that it's loading.

>> **Show Indicators for Open Applications:** macOS indicates which applications are running on the Dock with a small gray dot in front of the icon. To disable these indicators, deselect this check box.

>> **Show Suggested and Recent Apps in Dock:** Enable this check box to park the icons for the three applications you used last at the right side of the Dock (a real boon for those of us who use the same group of applications often). macOS automatically updates the three icons as you use your Neo.

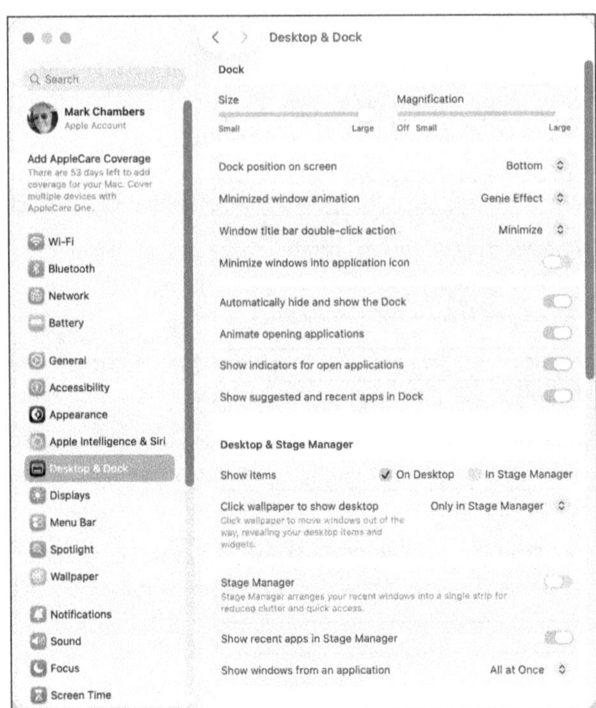

FIGURE 4-3:
The Dock, Desktop, and Stage Manager settings.

Desktop & Stage Manager settings

The settings in this section are:

>> **Show Items:** This setting determines when items you've located on the Desktop will appear, like drive, file and folder icons. You can choose to show items only on the Desktop, only within Stage Manager, or both. (If you disable both check boxes, the items are hidden.)

>> **Click Wallpaper to Show Desktop:** With a single click anywhere on your wallpaper, macOS can temporarily move all open windows to the edges of the Desktop, allowing you easy access to both your Desktop items and widgets. Choose Always from this pop-up menu to activate this feature at any time, or choose Only in Stage Manager to reveal the Desktop only when you're using Stage Manager.

>> **Stage Manager:** Click this switch to turn Stage Manager off and on. (I describe Stage Manager in detail in Chapter 3.)

>> **Show Recent Apps in Stage Manager:** To display thumbnails for recent apps in Stage Manager, turn this switch on. Disabling the switch hides the thumbnails until your pointer moves to the left edge of the Desktop.

>> **Show Windows From An Application:** This pop-up menu determines whether Stage Manager will display all open windows for an application when you select it (All at Once), or just the last window you used (One at a Time). If you choose the One at a Time option, you must click the app thumbnail to cycle through all its open windows.

Widgets settings

Since widgets can comfortably reside on your Desktop, Tahoe provides three settings to fine-tune their operation. These settings are:

>> **Show Widgets:** Widgets can always appear on your Desktop, or they can appear only while you're using Stage Manager. Disable both check boxes to hide widgets altogether.

>> **Dim Widgets on Desktop:** Click this pop-up menu to specify whether widgets should switch automatically between color and monochrome, or whether they should always remain color or monochrome.

>> **Use iPhone Widgets:** Turn this switch on to allow widgets you've used in the past on your iPhone to appear in the Edit Widgets sheet.

Although it seems a bit out of place, this section also includes a pop-up menu that allows you to set your default web browser. By default, macOS uses Safari, which I cover like a blanket in Chapter 7.

Windows settings

The settings in this section have nothing to do with That Other Operating System — instead, they control the behavior of macOS app windows when you're opening and closing documents. The settings include:

>> **Prefer Tabs When Opening Documents:** You can specify when applications open documents in a new tab instead of a new window (either Never, Always, or when viewing in Full Screen).

>> **Ask to Keep Changes When Closing Documents:** Turn this switch on and macOS will specifically request your approval to save changes when closing a document. If turned off, the application will automatically save your changes when you close the document.

>> **Close Windows When Quitting an Application:** Turn this switch on to force Tahoe to close all windows when you quit an app.

Mission Control settings

The Mission Control and Spaces settings that you can configure in this section are described in Chapter 3. The settings are as follows:

>> **Automatically Rearrange Spaces Based on Most Recent Use:** If this switch is set to On, Mission Control presents your most recently used Spaces first in the thumbnails at the top of the screen.

>> **When Switching to an Application:** When enabled, this setting allows you to switch apps between Spaces desktops by using the ⌘+Tab shortcut. Tahoe jumps to the Desktop that has an open window for the application you choose, even if that Desktop is not currently active.

>> **Group Windows by Application:** When selected, this switch arranges windows in the Mission Control screen by the app that created them.

>> **Displays Have Separate Spaces:** If you have multiple monitors connected to your Neo, select this switch to create a Spaces display for each monitor.

>> **Drag Windows to Top of Screen:** When selected, this switch displays the Mission Control screen when you drag a window to the top of the display.

>> **Shortcuts:** Click this button to specify keyboard and mouse shortcuts. From each pop-up menu, set the key sequences (and mouse settings) for Mission Control, Application Windows, and Show Desktop. You're not limited to keyboard and mouse shortcuts in the pop-up menus; press the Shift, Control, Option, and ⌘ keys while a pop-up menu is open, and you see these modifiers appear as menu choices!

>> **Hot Corners:** Click this button to specify your hot-corner settings. These pop-up menus allow you to control the operation of the screen management features within Tahoe. Click one to designate that corner as one of the following:

- **A Mission Control corner** displays the Mission Control screen.

- **An Application Windows corner** displays only the windows from the active application.

- **A Desktop corner** moves all windows to the outside of the screen to uncover your Desktop.

- **An App corner** displays your apps in a convenient Spotlight window.

- **A Quick Note corner** opens the Notes app.

- **A Notification Center corner** displays Notification Center.

Note that you can also set the Screen Saver Start and Disable corners from here, as well as put your display to sleep or lock your Neo.

The General pane

The talented General pane (refer to Figure 4–1) includes a number of sections that control a range of macOS features. (If you've used an iPhone or iPad, you'll be right at home.)

The entries are:

>> **About:** Click this entry to display details about your Neo's hardware (like your serial number, memory, processor, and display) and your macOS Tahoe system, including the status of your warranty coverage.

>> **Software Update:** This entry allows you to check for macOS updates and apply them. To set macOS to automatically apply updates, click the Info icon that appears to the right of the Automatic Updates item, and enable all the switches on the Automatically sheet that appears.

- >> **Storage:** Click the Storage entry to locate unnecessary files, applications and documents and easily delete them. (I cover these settings and how to use them in Chapter 18.)

- >> **AppleCare & Warranty:** Click this entry to display a list of all your Apple devices and their current warranty status. Click any device in the list for specific support information.

- >> **AirDrop & Continuity:** These controls allow you to enable or disable the macOS Handoff feature (which I cover in Chapter 8), as well as specify who can make an AirDrop or AirPlay connection (as I discuss in Chapter 10).

- >> **Login Items & Extensions:** In this section, you can specify what applications Tahoe will launch automatically when you first start your MacBook. For the full story, visit Chapter 9.

- >> **AutoFill & Passwords:** This section allows you to open the Passwords app to manage your system passwords. You can also control how Safari and your apps use your passwords for the AutoFill feature.

- >> **Date & Time:** Click this entry to control whether macOS sets the time and date automatically, as well as toggling between 12- and 24-hour formats and selecting a time zone. If you're an experienced traveler, you can also click the Set Time Zone Automatically Using Your Current Location to ensure your MacBook's clock is always correct with the local time!

- >> **Language & Region:** This section allows you to select the primary language macOS uses, as well as a number of regional standards (such as temperature in Celsius or Fahrenheit, measurements in Metric/US/UK format, and the format for displaying dates and numbers).

- >> **Sharing:** From this section, you can determine what type of hardware and software connections can be made to your Neo. Each entry in the services list controls a specific type of sharing, including File Sharing (with other Macs and PCs running Windows, covered in Chapter 10), Internet Sharing with other devices, Printer Sharing and file sharing over Bluetooth. To turn on any of these services, click the switch for that service to enable it. To turn off a service, click the switch to disable it. Click the Info icon at the far right of an entry to configure any additional settings. Finally, click the Edit button to change the default network name assigned to your Neo.

Leave the Advanced Sharing features turned off. You should enable Remote Management, Remote Login, and Remote Application Scripting *only* if instructed to by an Apple technician or your network administrator. (Sharing control of your Neo is a hacker's dream come true.)

» **Startup Disk:** This entry is for folks like me who have an external drive with a bootable macOS partition installed. Tahoe displays the bootable drives it finds connected to your Neo, and you can select which partition your laptop should use. After you've selected a partition, click Restart to boot your MacBook using that version of macOS.

» **Time Machine:** Here's how you configure one of my favorite macOS features, the backup miracle that is Time Machine! To add a Time Machine drive to your system, connect an external drive and click the Add button (which carries a plus sign) — select an external drive that has at least twice the capacity of your internal drive. Click the Options button, click the Backup Frequency pop-up menu, and choose Automatically Every Hour. You should leave the Time Machine backup drive connected to your Neo — but if you can't, choose Manually from the Backup Frequency menu. When your Time Machine backup drive is connected, click the Time Machine icon in the Finder menu bar (which looks like a clock face with a circular arrow) and choose Back Up Now.

By default, Time Machine backs up all the files and folders on your system; however, you may not need to back up some locations on your drive. To save time and backup drive space, Time Machine allows you to exclude specific folders from the backup process. Click Options, and then click the Add button (with the plus sign) to select the drives or folders you want to exclude. They appear in the Exclude From Backups list.

» **Device Management:** From this section, you can apply or remove device configurations assigned to you by a work or school network system administrator. Note that you'll need to sign in to your work or school account before adding or deleting profiles.

» **Transfer or Reset:** This section allows you to launch the Migration Assistant to transfer data between Macs (and even between your Neo and a PC running Windows). Chapter 2 provides more details on Migration Assistant. You can also elect to completely reset your Neo, erasing *all* of its contents and settings and returning it to factory-fresh condition. (Of course, this is A Good Idea if you're selling or donating it, but you should give the Erase Assistant a wide berth otherwise.)

The Battery pane

I'm an environmentalist, so I can attest that the controls on this pane are pretty doggone important — they can help conserve power and extend your Neo's battery life.

You can easily optimize your energy use automatically with the Low Power Mode pop-up menu! I usually recommend that you choose the Only on Battery setting, which reduces the drain on your battery to extend its charge, but you can choose Always (which reduces power consumption even if your Neo is plugged in and charging).

The Battery Level and Screen On Usage graphs can help you track the amount of time you've used your Neo and the battery's charge level for both the last 24 hours and the last 10 days.

Click the Options button to dim your laptop's display — slightly reducing the brightness — while running on battery, which saves energy.

The Menu Bar pane

As I discuss in Chapter 3, the Finder menu bar and the Control Center are both powerful and convenient, allowing you to monitor and manage important features in macOS with a single click. Fine-tune the contents of both the Control Center and the Finder menu bar with these settings:

- **Modules:** This series of check boxes and pop-up menus allow you to determine whether each of the modules should appear in the Finder menu bar, the Control Center or both.

- **Allow in the Menu Bar:** These modules can appear only in the Finder menu bar, but you can still hide them if desired. Click the Clock Options button to choose the format of the clock display, and even set Tahoe to announce the time with a voice of your choosing!

- **Automatically Hide and Show the Menu Bar:** Similar to the Automatically Hide and Show the Dock switch I describe earlier in this chapter, you can click this menu to banish the Finder menu bar (either on the Desktop or in full screen view). To display the hidden menu bar, move your pointer to the top edge of your screen.

- **Show Menu Bar Background:** Click this switch to display either your wallpaper or a solid color behind the Finder menu bar.

- **Recent Documents, Applications and Servers:** If you're a fan of the Apple menu's Recent Items submenu that I mention in Chapter 3, here's where you can specify how many recent items are displayed.

The Wallpaper pane

No offense to the iconic Neo wallpaper, but what if you want to choose your own background? Change your Neo's mood with these options:

>> **Current Desktop picture:** You can click a picture in the thumbnail list in the right half of the screen to select it. The Desktop is immediately updated, and the thumbnail appears in the *well* (the box at the top of the pane). To display a different image or open a folder of images, click the Add Photo button in the Your Photos section. A click on Choose Folder or an album from your Photos library allows you to add multiple images.

Click the Show All link in a section to display all the images it contains in a single list.

>> **Layout:** Click this pop-up menu by the well to fit your background image to your screen (without cropping it), center it, fill the screen with it (cropping the edges if necessary), and stretch it to fill the screen (without cropping). Note that filling the screen in either case may distort the image. If you select Fit to Screen or Center, you can click the color swatch that appears to change the color of any "empty" areas on the Desktop.

The layout pop-up menu appears only when you're using your own pictures; you won't see it if you're using a wallpaper image from Apple.

>> **Show on All Spaces:** If you use the macOS Spaces feature that I describe in Chapter 3 (or if you have an external monitor connected to your Neo), you can enable the Show On All Spaces switch to use the same wallpaper on each Space and screen.

To display your photos in sequence, click the thumbnail in the Your Photos section with the two circular arrows. The wallpaper images are displayed in the sequence in which they appear in the thumbnail list, but you can also randomize the sequence and specify the duration for each image with the settings that appear next to the well.

The Dynamic Wallpaper selections automatically change the brightness of your wallpaper image based on the local time of day! You can also force only the Light or Dark versions of these dynamic wallpapers.

If a thumbnail carries a tiny Play icon in the lower-left corner, it indicates that the wallpaper is animated, and that it can also be used as a screen saver. (Typically these animated wallpapers are quite large, so if an arrow appears next to a thumbnail name, it will take a few moments to download from Apple.)

>> **Colors:** Do you prefer a soothing, solid-color wallpaper? Pick a color or choose a custom color from the palette (by clicking the icon bearing the plus sign). You can choose to rotate between colors by clicking the icon with the two circular arrows.

Click the Screen Saver button to specify a delay before your screen saver starts. You can also choose whether Tahoe will select a saver (Automatic) or you will choose your own (Custom). The Custom screen saver selection list works similarly to the Wallpaper pane, with the thumbnail at the top of the pane displaying the current screen saver. To try out the screen saver in full-screen mode, hover your pointer over the thumbnail and click the Preview button that appears. (End the test by moving the pointer.)

iCloud settings

To configure your iCloud settings, click your account entry at the top of the System Settings sidebar and then click the iCloud entry. From this pane, you can specify which types of data are automatically pushed to your Neo and iOS devices.

The sections are as follows:

>> **iCloud Storage Graph:** This graph displays the amount of space remaining for iCloud.

>> **Account Storage:** Click the Manage button to display the individual apps using iCloud and the amount of space they're taking up, sorted in order of the worst offenders first. You can click any of these app entries to display actions you may be able to take to recover space, including deleting the data used by that application from your iCloud account.

>> **Apps Using iCloud:** Enable and disable iCloud access for specific apps, like Photos, Mail, Notes, and your iCloud Drive. To toggle iCloud access on for a specific app, click the entry. Note that only the most often-used apps are visible — display the entire list by clicking the See All button.

>> **Get More with iCloud+:** Apple provides you with 5GB of iCloud storage for free, but if you need additional elbow room for more photos or files, you can upgrade to iCloud+ with a click of the Upgrade button. For 99 cents a month, you'll expand your iCloud territory to 50GB. (If you actually need up to 12TB [yes, that's *terabytes*!] of storage, Apple can do it!)

Turn on Advanced Data Protection to enable the highest security for your iCloud data. Click the Turn On button at the top of the sheet to enable Advanced Data Protection and begin creating a recovery key.

I recommend that you enable the Data Access on `iCloud.com` switch at the very bottom of the pane — this feature allows you to use the tools provided online at `www.icloud.com` to access all of your iCloud data from any web browser, even without your Neo!

Appearance pane

Aesop said, "Appearances are often deceiving." Not so with macOS Tahoe! These settings guarantee that your Finder menu and Finder windows are pleasing to your eye (and that your scroll bars work the way you want).

The Appearance settings are the following:

>> **Appearance:** Click the Light, Dark or Auto option to switch between Light or Dark mode for your Finder menu bar, window buttons and window background, and your Dock. The Auto option cycles between the Light and Dark modes based on the local time.

>> **Liquid Glass:** Choose a clear look for screen controls, windows and dialogs, or specify a tinted look instead.

>> **Color:** Click an accent color to use for buttons and menus.

>> **Text Highlight Color:** Choose a color to highlight selected text in fields and pop-up menus.

>> **Icon & Widget Style:** Choose the color scheme for Dock and Desktop icons and any widgets you add to the Desktop.

>> **Folder Color:** Folders in Tahoe can use your color selection (Automatic) or you can specify a color.

>> **Sidebar Icon Size:** Select the size of the icons in the Finder window Sidebar (the strip to the left of the Finder window that displays your devices and favorite locations on your system). If you have a large number of devices, or if you've added several folders to the Sidebar, reducing the size of the icons allows you to display more without scrolling.

>> **Tint Window Background with Wallpaper Color:** When this switch is on, macOS displays open windows with a tinted background when you're using Dark mode.

>> **Show Scroll Bars:** Specify when Tahoe should display scroll bars in a window. By default, they're placed automatically when necessary, but you can choose to display scroll bars always or only when you're actually scrolling through a document.

- **Click in the Scroll Bar To:** By default, macOS jumps to the next or previous page when you click in an empty portion of the scroll bar. Select the Jump to the Spot That's Clicked radio button to scroll to the approximate position in relation to where you click.

Notifications settings

Although I discuss Notification Center in Chapter 6, I'll take a moment here to cover the settings that control which notifications you receive and how they're displayed. They include:

- **Show Previews:** This pop-up menu controls the default action for notification previews. If set to Always, notifications for all applications will include a preview of the content (like a preview of the contents of a text message); if set to Never, previews will never appear with notifications. For additional privacy, you can also specify that previews will appear only if your Neo display is not locked.

- **Show Notifications When the Display Is Sleeping:** If enabled, notifications are shown if your Neo's display is asleep. If disabled, notifications are paused until the Neo awakes from sleep mode.

- **Show Notifications When the Screen Is Locked:** Turn this option on to display notifications by default even when your laptop is locked (personally, I don't use this feature — if it's enabled, a locked Neo could still display sensitive information in a notification).

- **Show Notifications When Mirroring or Sharing the Display:** If enabled, this option allows notifications to be displayed if you're mirroring or sharing a display, such as a projector. Again, if you're security conscious, you may want to disable this feature. Don't forget to disable this switch if you're holding a Keynote presentation (your audience likely won't appreciate distracting notifications from News appearing on the screen)!

The Applications Notifications section lists each application that can display notifications in macOS, allowing you to individually configure each one. If you click an application entry, the following settings appear:

- **Allow Notifications:** Consider this the "main switch" that completely turns notifications on or off for this application.

- **Alert Style:** These check boxes specify whether alerts should appear on the Desktop, Notification Center or the Lock Screen. Persistent notifications remain onscreen until you click the confirmation button in the Alert dialog, while Temporary notifications will close automatically.

>> **Time Sensitive Notifications:** When enabled, apps can display notifications for events that require your immediate attention.

>> **Badge Application Icon:** This switch toggles on and off the display of this application's icon in alert boxes and in Notification Center. It also activates the numeric display of pending items on the icon itself (for example, unread mail and messages).

>> **Play Sound for Notifications:** Enable this switch to play a sound when alerts appear.

>> **Show Previews:** Click this menu to specify whether notifications for this application will include a preview of the content. You can also control whether the preview will appear while your Neo's display is locked.

>> **Notification Grouping:** From this drop-down list, you can specify that multiple notifications from the same source are displayed by application or by automatic arrangement, or turn off grouping altogether.

>> **Summarize Notifications:** Enable this switch to allow Apple Intelligence to automatically condense notification text for easier reading.

Chapter **5**

Searching Amidst Neo Chaos

What would you say if I told you that you could search your entire system for *all* the data connected with a person — and in only the short time it takes to type that person's name? And I'm not just talking about files and folders that might include that person's name. I mean *every* email message and *every* Calendar event that references that person. Heck, how about if that search could dig up every occurrence of the person's name *inside* your PDF documents? What if it could even search folders shared on other Macs across your network?

You'd probably say, "That makes for good future tech. I'll bet I can do that in five or ten years. It'll take Apple at least that long to do it — and just in time for me to buy a new MacBook! (Harrumph.)"

Don't be so hasty. You can do all this right now. (In fact, this functionality has been part of macOS for a number of years.) The technology is the macOS feature named *Spotlight,* built into Tahoe. In this chapter, I show you how to use it like a fearsome MacBook Neo power guru.

Doing a Basic Search

Figure 5-1 shows the Spotlight search box, which is always available from the Finder menu bar. Click the magnifying glass icon once (or press ⌘+spacebar), and the search box appears on your Desktop.

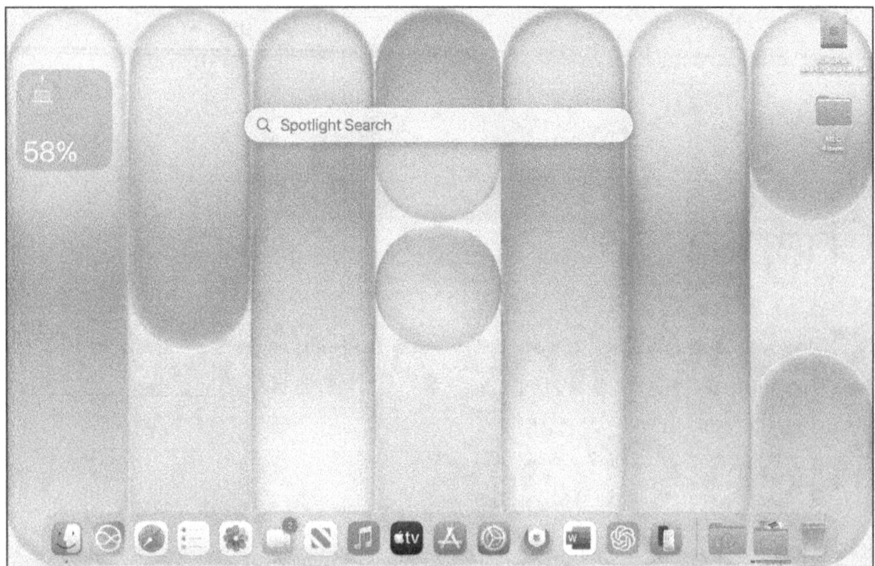

FIGURE 5-1:
An unbelievable amount of power purrs behind this single Spotlight search box.

To run a search, simply begin typing. (The words you type that you want to match are called *keywords*.) Matching items appear as soon as you type, and the search results are continually refined while you type the rest of your search keywords. You don't need to press Return to begin the search. If Spotlight recognizes an app by name, it displays that app instantly, and you can launch it by pressing Return. (This is how I usually launch apps that aren't on the Dock.)

After a second or two, the Spotlight search box expands to display the results of your search, and the list is updated automatically in real time while you continue to type. The most relevant items are grouped into categories — such as Messages, Websites, and Documents — right in the Spotlight search box. Spotlight Search takes a guess at the item that's most likely the match you're looking for and presents it first. To open the top item like a true Tahoe power user, just press Return.

TIP

Although one or two keywords are typically enough to do the job, you can also type phrases, such as **emails from Mark Chambers**.

Ready for a real time-saver? You can single-click many items in the list and press the spacebar to display them using Quick Look! If Quick Look is supported by that document type, Spotlight displays the contents (such as a preview image of a document or an album cover) or information on the item. For example, if the item is a News article, the story appears in the Quick Look window. A Microsoft Word document? It's displayed just as if you had opened it! (Yep, it's another "I'm glad I bought a Neo!" moment.)

When you click an item in the list, Spotlight indicates which application will be used to open the item by displaying the icon for that application in the upper-right corner of the Spotlight box. For example, you'll see the Music icon for a song. If you right-click an item and choose Share, Spotlight can share the item through Messages, Mail, Notes, or AirDrop.

Any text string is acceptable as a Spotlight search. However, here's a short list of the common search criteria I use every day:

>> **Names and addresses:** Because Spotlight has access to the Contacts application in Tahoe, you can immediately display contact information using any portion of a name or an address.

>> **Email message text:** Need to open a specific message, but you'd rather not launch Mail and spend time digging through the message list? Enter the person's email address or any text string contained in the message.

>> **File and folder names:** A simple item name is the classic search favorite. Spotlight searches your entire system for that one file or folder in the blink of an eye.

>> **Events and Reminder items:** Yep, Spotlight gives you access to your Calendar events and those all-important Reminders you've created.

>> **Specific songs and playlists:** Itching to hear "Rock Me Amadeus" by Falco? With the power of Spotlight and your Music library, you can satisfy your musical needs in seconds!

>> **System Settings:** Try typing the word **wallpaper** in the Spotlight field. At least one of the results in the list will be a System Settings pane! That's right: Every setting in System Settings is referenced in Spotlight.

>> **Weather, stocks, news, and sports scores:** Get instant displays of current weather (type **weather** followed by a town name), stock figures (type the desired abbreviation), and sports scores (type your team name).

>> **Web pages:** *Whoa.* Stand back, Google. You can use Spotlight to search the web — and, if necessary, the pages you've recently displayed in Safari!

>> **Metadata:** This category is pretty broad, but it fits like a glove. Think of the information stored by your iPhone each time you take a photo (time, date, and even the location where the photo was taken, which are also transferred to Photos when you import). Here's another example: I like to locate Word documents on my system using the same metadata that's stored in the file, such as the contents of the Comments field. Other supported applications include Adobe Photoshop, Microsoft Excel, Keynote, Music, and other third-party apps that offer a Spotlight plug-in.

>> **Airline flight information:** Type a flight number, and let Spotlight provide you information such as the flight's status, points of departure and arrival, and even gate numbers.

To reset the Spotlight Search and try another text string, press ⌘+A to select the entire contents and then press Delete.

After you find the item you're looking for in the list, you can *double*-click the entry in the list to launch it (for applications), open it in System Settings (if it's a Settings field or pane), open it in the corresponding app (for documents) or display it in a Finder window (if the item is a folder).

Here's another time-saver: You can display all the files of a particular type on your system by using the file type as the keyword. To provide a list of all photos with the word *horse* in the title on your system, for example, use *images horse* as your keywords. The same goes for *movies* and *audio*.

How Cool Is That? Discovering What Spotlight Can Do

Don't get fooled into simply using Spotlight as another file-'n'-folder-name search tool. Sure, it can do that, but Spotlight can also search *inside* PDFs, Pages and Word documents, and HTML files, finding matching text that doesn't appear in the name of the file! To wit: A search for *Tahoe* on my system pulls up all sorts of items, not only files with *Tahoe* in their names, but also files with the text *Tahoe* within the documents themselves:

>> **Apple Store SF.ppt** is a PowerPoint presentation with several slides containing the text *Tahoe.*

>> **new ch03.doc** is a Microsoft Word file chapter of this book that mentions Tahoe in several spots.

>> **Conference Call with Wiley** is a Calendar event pointing to a conference call with my publisher about my Tahoe book projects.

Not one of these three examples has the word *Tahoe* occurring anywhere in the title or filename, yet Spotlight found them because they all contain the text *Tahoe* therein. That, dear reader, is the *true* power of Spotlight; you'll never lose another piece of information in the hundreds of thousands of files and folders on your Neo's drive.

Heck, suppose that all you remember about a file is that you received it in your mail last week or last month. To find it, you can type time periods, such as *yesterday, last week,* or *last month,* to see every item that you saved or received within that period.

By default, Spotlight matches only those items that have *all* the words you enter in the Spotlight box. To return the highest number of matches, use the fewest number of words that will identify the item. For example, use *horse* rather than *horse image,* and you're certain to be rewarded with more hits. On the other hand, if you're looking specifically for a picture of a knight on horseback, using a series of keywords — such as *horse knight image* — shortens your search. It all depends on what you're looking for and how widely you want to cast your Spotlight net.

IS SPOTLIGHT SECURE?

So how about all those files, folders, and events that you *don't* want to appear in Spotlight? What if you're sharing your Neo as a multiuser computer? Can others search for your personal information through Spotlight?

Definitely not! The results displayed by Spotlight are controlled by file and folder permissions as well as your account login, just as the apps that create and display your personal data are. For example, you can't access other users' calendars using Calendar, and they can't see your Mail messages. Only *you* have access to your data, and only after you've logged in with your username and password. Spotlight works the same way. If a user doesn't normally have access to an item, the item simply doesn't appear when that user performs a Spotlight search.

However, you can hide certain folders and disks from your own Spotlight searches if necessary. Check out the final section of this chapter for details on setting private locations on your system.

To allow greater flexibility in searches, Apple also includes those helpful Boolean friends that you may already be familiar with: AND, OR, and NOT. For example, you can perform Spotlight searches such as these:

>> **Horse AND cow:** Collects all references to both those barnyard animals into one search

>> **Batman OR Robin:** Returns all references to either Batman or Robin

>> **Apple NOT PC:** Displays all references to Apple that don't include any information about dastardly PCs

Expanding Your Search Horizons

I can just hear the announcer's voice now: "But wait, there's more! If you scroll to the end of the search results and double-click the Search in Finder button, we'll expand your Spotlight search box into the Finder Search window!"

Keyboard mavens will appreciate the Finder Search window shortcut key, and I show you where to specify this shortcut in the final section of this chapter.

Figure 5-2 illustrates the Finder Search window. To further filter the search, click one of the buttons on the search criteria bar under the toolbar to create your own custom filter. Click the button with the + (plus) on the search criteria bar and then click the pop-up menus to choose criteria, such as the type of file, the text content, or the location on your system (for example, your internal drive, your Home folder, or a network server). You can also filter your results listing by the date when the items were created or last saved. To add new criteria, click the + (plus sign) button at the right end of the search criteria bar; to delete existing criteria, click the − (minus sign) button to the left of the + button for the offending criteria. To save a custom filter that you've created, click the Save button.

As you can see in Figure 5-2, some documents and images appear as thumbnail icons, so you can use that most sophisticated search tool — the human eye — to find the picture you're looking for. (If you don't see thumbnail images, click the View button on the toolbar and choose Show as Icons.) Don't forget that you can increase or decrease the size of the icons by dragging the slider at the bottom right of the window.

To display the contents of an item in the list using Quick Look, click the item to select it, and press the spacebar. Note that Tahoe must recognize the format of the file, and it must be supported by at least one application.

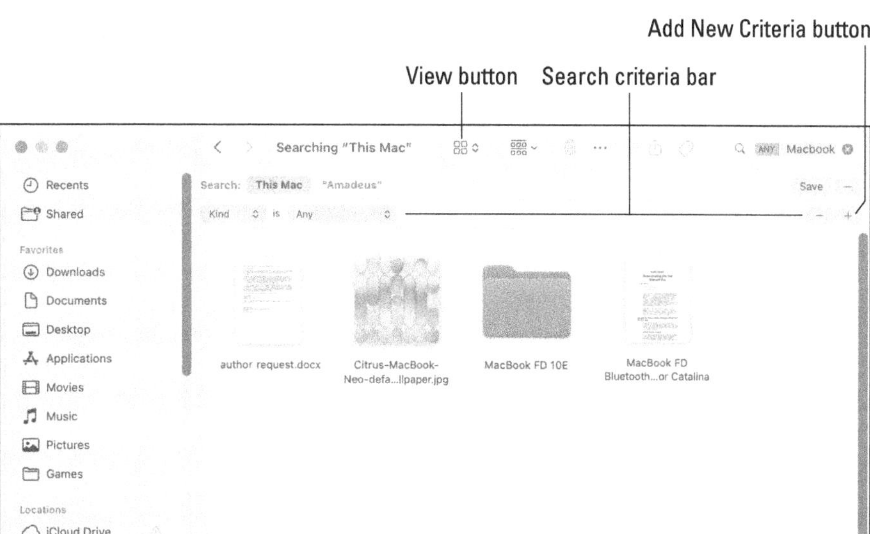

FIGURE 5-2: The spacious borders of the Finder Search window.

Again, when you're ready to open an item, just double-click it in the Finder Search window.

As I mention earlier, Spotlight can look for matching items on other Macs on your network *only* if those remote Macs are configured correctly. To allow another Mac to be visible to Spotlight on your system, enable File Sharing on the other Mac. (Oh, and remember that you need an admin-level account on that Mac.)

Follow these steps to enable file sharing on other Macs running Tahoe:

1. **On the Dock, click the System Settings icon (the one with the gears), or display the Spotlight search box, type** System Settings, **and press Return.**

2. **Click the General pane and click the Sharing entry.**

3. **In the Content & Media list on the right side of the Sharing pane, click the File Sharing switch to turn it on.**

4. **Click the Close button in the System Settings window (or, if you're a keyboard power user, simply press the ⌘+Q shortcut).**

You can search only those items that you have rights and permissions to view on the remote Mac (such as the contents of the Public folders on that computer). I discuss these limitations earlier in this chapter, in the sidebar "Is Spotlight secure?"

Customizing Spotlight to Your Taste

You might be thinking that such an awesome macOS feature must have its own pane in System Settings — and you'd be right again. Click the System Settings icon on the Dock and click the Spotlight entry in the sidebar to see these settings.

Click the switches in the Results from Apps section to determine which applications can appear in the Spotlight search box. For example, if you don't listen to podcasts on your Neo, you can deselect the switch next to Podcasts to disable it (thereby making more room to display other app results that you *will* use). In a similar fashion, you can fine-tune results from macOS using the categories in the Results from System section.

Click the Search Privacy button at the bottom of the pane to specify disks and folders that should *never* be listed as results in a Spotlight search. I know, I know — I say earlier that Spotlight respects your security, and it does. However, the disks and folders that you add here won't appear even if *you* are performing the search — a great idea for folders and removable drives that you use to store sensitive information, such as medical records.

To add locations that you want to keep private, click the Add button (+) and navigate to the desired location. Click the location to select it and then click Choose. Alternatively, you can drag folders or disks directly from a Finder window and drop them onto the pane.

IN THIS CHAPTER

» **Setting reminders**

» **Making notes**

» **Using Notification Center**

» **Navigating with Maps**

» **Staying current with News**

Chapter **6**

Using Reminders, Notes, Notifications, Maps, and News

As I've said many times before in my books, "If it works in one place, it's likely to show up in another." In this case, five popular time-saving apps have crossed over from the world of iOS devices — the iPhone and iPad — and landed securely on your Tahoe Desktop. These apps are Reminders, Notes, Notification Center, Maps, and News, all taken from the iOS world.

And here's more good news: These five apps work seamlessly with an iCloud account! So if you also use an iOS device (with the same Apple ID), much of the data you store — such as the notes you take and the reminders you make — is automatically synchronized among all your devices.

Because all five of these applications have a similar goal — keeping you in touch with the information, tasks, locations, and digital events that matter to you — I decided to cover them in one shiny chapter. Consider this chapter a guide to organizing your world like a true Neo power user.

Remind Me to Use Reminders

In its simplest form, a *reminder* is just a short phrase or sentence. You don't need to look far to find the Reminders application on your Neo. Click the Reminders icon on the Dock to open the app, shown in Figure 6-1.

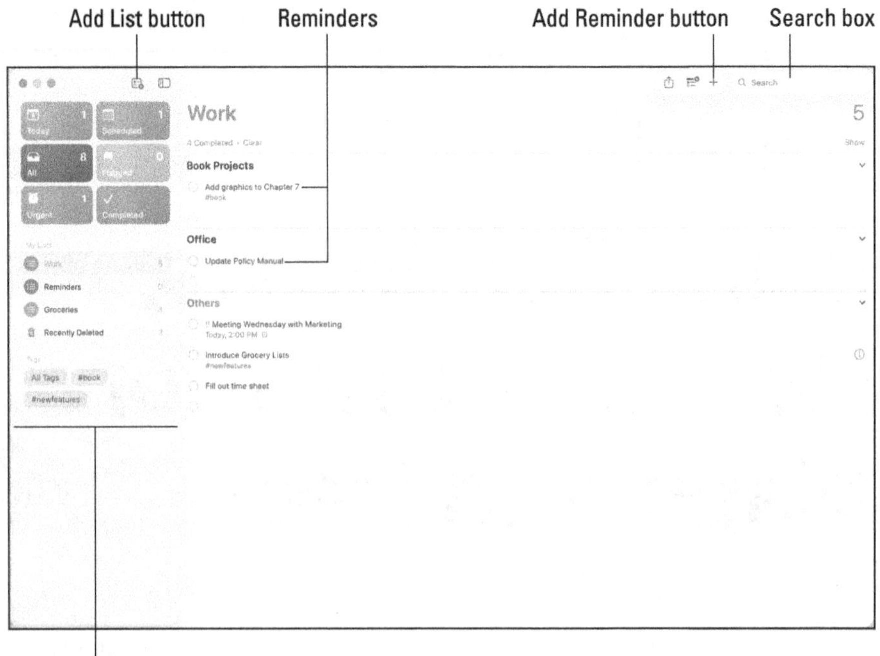

FIGURE 6-1: The main Reminders window in action.

These are the highlights of the Reminders window:

>> **Search box:** Click here and type a phrase or name to search through your reminders.

>> **Reminders sidebar:** You can add as many separate reminder lists as you like in the application (one for work, for example, and another for your Mac user group). In the sidebar, you can switch quickly among your lists.

You can hide or show the Reminders sidebar at any time using the View menu or by pressing ⌘+Control+S.

>> **Add List button:** Click this button (or press ⌘+Shift+N) to add a new reminder list to the sidebar. The list name is highlighted in a text box, so you can simply type the new name and press Return.

- **» Reminders:** These entries are the reminders themselves. Each reminder is prefaced by a radio button; select the radio button when the reminder is complete, thereby moving that reminder to the Completed list. And yes, if you click the Completed button in the sidebar and deselect the radio button for a reminder, it returns (like a bad penny) to the original list.

- **» Add Reminder button:** Click this button (or press ⌘+N) to add a reminder to the selected list. Press Return to save the reminder.

Adding a reminder is straightforward. First, click an entry in the My Lists display or click the Today group and then click the Add Reminder button. (You can also click the blank reminder radio button under a section heading.) Type a few words, and press Return to create a basic reminder.

Naturally, you're not limited to a simple text message! When you create a reminder, the application allows you to add notes, add a tag, link a location, flag it as important, or add a date to display a message. You can also hover your pointer over any existing reminder to display an Info button (the lowercase *i*-in-a-circle icon that appears at the right of the entry). Click the Info button to display the Edit sheet.

These fields are on the Edit sheet:

- **» Reminder text:** Click this text at the top of the sheet to edit the reminder text itself.

- **» Notes:** Click the Notes label to enter a free-form text note along with the reminder text.

- **» URL:** Click this field and enter a web page to associate with the reminder. When the reminder is displayed, you can click this address to launch Safari and display that page.

- **» Date & Time:** Select these switches if the reminder should appear in Notification Center on a particular day and/or a specific time. By default, the date is the one selected when you created the reminder.

- **» Urgent:** Enable this switch to sound an alarm on your iPhone or iPad when the reminder is due.

- **» List:** Click this drop-down list box to assign the reminder to a different list.

- **» Tags:** Click in this field to add one-word keywords that you can search on later, like "taxes" or "schoolproject." Reminders adds the "#" symbol in front of the tag, and you can choose from existing tags in future reminders.

- **» Flag:** Click this button (bearing a flag icon) to add this reminder to your Flagged group. This button allows you to display just the flagged reminders you've created.

>> **Priority:** You can assign one of four priorities to the reminder: Low, Medium, High, or None. Assigning a priority prefaces the reminder text with one (Low), two (Medium), or three (High) blue exclamation points so that the reminder stands out from the crowd.

>> **Location:** This feature is powerful. Select the Location switch and you can type an address in the Enter a Location field. Reminders monitor your current location on your iPad or iPhone by using Location Services. They notify you when you're leaving or arriving at that approximate location (and, optionally, on the date you specify in the Date field). You could create a reminder that appears on your iPhone when you arrive at the mall on September 15 to pick up the watch that's being repaired.

>> **When Messaging:** Enable this switch to display a reminder notification when you chat with a contact that you specify.

>> **Images:** Click the Add Image button to select a photo for this reminder.

Click anywhere outside the Edit sheet when you've finished making changes. You can edit a reminder as often as you like (I sometimes need to change the date on a reminder multiple times as my schedule changes).

To delete a reminder from the list, right-click it and choose Delete.

iCloud connectivity allows the Reminders app to share information with other Macs and iOS devices, as well as Microsoft Outlook on both PCs and macOS. To share reminders, click the System Settings icon on the Dock, click the Internet Accounts icon, and then click one of the accounts on the right side of the pane. If an account allows you to share data — such as the iCloud account — you'll see a Reminders entry on the right side. (You may have to click the See All button to see the Reminders entry.)

The Reminders application can even create an interactive grocery list! Add a new list using the button at the bottom of the Reminders sidebar and select Groceries from the List Type pop-up menu. Reminders will automatically create sections for you, like Produce and Household Items.

Taking Notes the Neo Way

Imagine a notepad of unlimited pages that's always available whenever you're around your Neo, iPhone, or iPad. That's the idea behind Notes, and it's superbly simple. To open the macOS version of the app, click the Notes icon on the Dock. The window shown in Figure 6-2 appears.

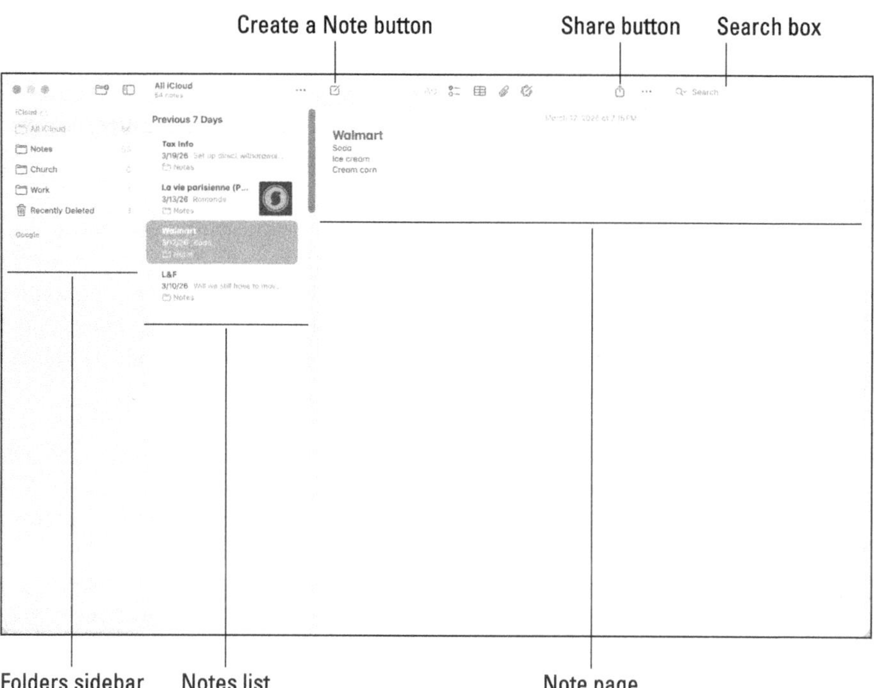

FIGURE 6-2:
The notable
Notes
application
window.

The salient stuff in the Notes window includes these items:

>> **Search box:** If you're hunting for a specific note, click this box and type a phrase or name to search for it.

>> **Folders sidebar:** You can create new folders to hold specific kinds of notes. In Figure 6-2, I added two folders: Work and Church. To add a new folder, choose File ⇨ New Folder or press ⌘+Shift+N and type the new folder name. To switch between folders, click the desired folder in the sidebar. You can display the Folders sidebar by clicking the Show Folders button on the far-left side of the toolbar.

>> **Notes list:** Each note you create appears as a separate entry in the list. You can click a note in the list to switch to it immediately.

>> **Create a Note button:** Click this button to add a new note. Notes uses the first line of text as the title of the note, which appears in the list.

>> **Note page:** This free-form pane is where you type the body of your note. You can also drag images from a Finder window to include them in the body of the note, or embed PDF and audio files by dragging them from a Finder window as well. The Photos Browser, available from the Notes toolbar, makes it easy to add images from your Photos library.

>> **Share button:** Got a shopping list to distribute? Click this button to share the contents of the current note. Sharing options can include a new email message, a new message in the Messages application, and exchanging information with another device via AirDrop.

To edit a note, click it to select it in the Notes list and then simply make your changes or additions on the note page. You can format the text from the Format menu, choosing everything from fonts and colors to bulleted and numbered lists. Toolbar buttons make it simple to add a checklist (complete with fancy controls that you can click to mark something completed), add a table or lock specific notes with a password. If you've used the Apple Intelligence Writing Tools in Pages already, you'll be happy to see them included on the toolbar as well. You can compose new text or rewrite existing text in a note, proofread selected text, change the writing tone, summarize or create a list using selected text, or generate a table. It's neat to use your Neo's artificial intelligence features!

To delete a note, right-click it in the list and choose Delete. The note is moved to the Recently Deleted folder, where it can be retrieved for 30 days.

You can pin a note to the top of the Notes list to make it more visible; the note stays anchored to the top of the list whenever it's visible. Right-click the desired note in the list and choose Pin Note (or choose Unpin Note to return the note to regular status).

As mentioned earlier, a note can include tables to help organize your data, much like the Pages app! Click the Table button on the Notes toolbar to create a default table (two columns and two rows); then click the first field and begin typing. Press Tab to continue to the next field in the table. Click within a cell (or select the table as a whole) and click the row and column controls that appear to specify the number of rows and columns.

Like Reminders, the Notes application can share information with Macs and iOS devices, as well as with Microsoft Outlook on both Macs and PCs. The process is the same as the Reminders app: Open System Settings and click the Internet Accounts icon; then click the desired account on the right side of the pane. Accounts that support Notes display a Notes check box on the right side (although you may have to click the See All button to see it). Imagine all the sundry things you include in a class project — notes, photos, charts, and tables — all in one convenient location!

Need an extra layer of security for your notes? The application allows you to lock your notes to keep them private, requiring a password to view them. Click Notes ⇨ Settings and click Set Password; then enter your password twice and click the Set Password button. (Neo keyboards with a Touch ID sensor can unlock notes with a fingerprint! Click Use Touch ID to start the ball rolling.) Now you can select a note in the list and click the three dots icon that appears in the Notes toolbar; then choose Lock Note to lock it, which places a tiny lock icon next to the note's title. You can also right-click the note in the Notes list and choose Lock Note or click the Lock icon that appears in the toolbar to unlock the selected note.

Staying Current with Notification Center

Unlike Reminders and Notes, Notification Center isn't an app that you launch. Instead, Notification Center appears at the far-right end of the Tahoe Desktop. It's always running, and you can display or hide Notification Center at will.

Click the clock display (or, if you're using the trackpad, swipe with two fingers from the right edge to the left) to display your notifications. These notifications can be generated by a host of Tahoe apps and functions, including Calendar, Mail, FaceTime, Reminders, Messages, Safari, and even the Mac App Store. Third-party apps can also generate notifications.

Notification Center displays all sorts of information that specifically applies to today's date, including Calendar events, Reminders, the current weather, News events and the latest stock figures. (In fact, Notification Center actually scrolls vertically to show you more content.) You can specify what information is displayed by clicking the Edit Widgets button at the bottom of Notification Center and dragging desired widgets to the Center. To switch back to Notifications view, click the Done button that appears at the bottom of the Edit Widgets view.

I love how Notification Center doesn't interfere with open apps; it simply muscles the entire Desktop to the left!. You can close Notification Center at any time by clicking the clock display on the Finder menu bar again, or swiping two fingers across the trackpad from left to right.

Notification entries that appear in Notification view are grouped below the app that created them. You can delete many entries by hovering your pointer over the entry and clicking the Delete button that appears next to the app heading (which bears an *X* symbol). Other entries, such as Calendar alerts, remain in Notification Center until the event has passed.

Depending on the settings you choose, notifications can also appear without Notification Center's being open at all. These notifications are displayed as pop-up *banners* (which disappear in a few seconds) and *alerts* (which you must dismiss by clicking a button).

One of the best features in macOS Tahoe is the ability to drag widgets from your Notification Center (or from the Edit Widgets sheet) directly to your macOS Desktop! Tahoe automatically groups the widgets you've chosen and displays them whenever your Desktop is visible. Naturally, if you maximize an app window or switch to full screen, your Desktop widgets obligingly give up that screen real estate until you close the application.

Tahoe can also allow *actions* in notifications. Depending on the application or function that generates the notification, you may see buttons on a banner or an alert that allow you to take care of business (without requiring the application to be running). If a new email message is received in Apple Mail, for example, you can choose to reply to or delete the message. Websites can display updates as notifications, and you can answer a FaceTime or an iPhone call directly from the notification.

You can configure the notifications for all your apps from the Notifications pane in System Settings (which I cover in Chapter 4).

Introducing the Maps Application

If you own an iPad or iPhone, prepare yourself for great news: Your beloved iOS Maps app also resides on your Dock! As long as you have a connection to the internet, Maps is ready to display locations, provide directions, and even supply informal views of important sites worldwide. (Recognize the grand dame in Figure 6-3?)

FIGURE 6-3:
The Statue of Liberty shines in the Maps application.

Displaying an overhead view of an address is one of the simplest chores in all of macOS. In the Maps window, click the search box at the top of the Maps sidebar, type the address, and choose the correct entry from the results list. Maps displays the address with a red pushpin!

Depending on the location you've chosen, you may also see an Info dialog that provides additional information, including buttons that display the directions to that spot from your current location.

Ah, but why stop with a simple address? You can also enter the following types of information:

>> The name of a landmark or building (such as *Statue of Liberty*).

>> The name of a business or restaurant (or even a genre of food, such as *Chinese*) followed by the city name. Maps displays matching sites with icons, complete with reviews, and you can click any of the locations to display more information, complete with corresponding links. (Note that multiple locations in the same general area will display a number icon.)

>> Attractions and services, followed by the city name. You can search for a gas station, movie theater, or local park.

If you need to zoom in or zoom out on a Maps display, click the plus and minus buttons at the right side of the Maps window or press the ⌘+plus and ⌘+minus shortcuts. To move around the Maps window, click and drag the map in the desired direction.

Teachers and parents, take note: A virtual flyby of a famous site in Maps is a valuable (and cool) resource. Look for a Flyover Tour option in the Info panel when you're viewing famous tourist sites!

Switching Views in Maps

A printed map offers you only one view, which may be perfectly fine for determining a route but lacks visual interest. Maps, on the other hand, offers four types of views, each of which offers certain advantages:

>> **Explore mode** is a familiar line map with streets and highways marked, including major buildings and landmarks.

>> **Driving mode** is best for planning a road trip, with real-time indicators of current traffic density.

>> **Satellite mode** is a photographic overhead view without streets or highways marked, which is great for getting panoramic views of your neighborhood or a location and its surroundings.

>> **Transit mode** displays public-transportation routes and bus, subway, and train schedules. Note, however, that Transit information isn't available in every location.

To select your view, click the Map Mode Menu button in the toolbar (it resembles a folded map) or press ⌘+1 for Explore mode, ⌘+2 for Driving mode, ⌘+3 for Transit mode, or ⌘+4 for Satellite mode. Figure 6-3, shown earlier, illustrates Satellite view, whereas Figure 6-4 shows off the same location in Explore view.

FIGURE 6-4: Explore view reminds me of an auto GPS unit.

Have I mentioned the 3D map yet? No special glasses are required! For a visual thrill, you can angle the Maps display with a slight 3D effect — nothing as grand as a 3D TV, but it does help add depth to Satellite view. To toggle 3D, press ⌘+D or choose View ➪ Show 3D Map.

TIP

By default, Maps is oriented with north at the top of the screen, but if you need to change the orientation, click the compass icon at the right side of the screen and drag it in the desired direction. To return to having north at the top of the screen, choose View ➪ Snap to North.

TIP

Getting Directions Over Yonder

My primary use for a map is to get directions from one point to another, and Maps doesn't disappoint when it comes to navigation. Press ⌘+R or choose View ➪ Show Directions to plot your course.

Follow these steps to get directions between two addresses:

1. **In the From box, type the starting address.**

   As you type, Maps provides a pop-up list of suggestions taken from your recent locations, as well as addresses from your Contacts database and matching streets from around the globe. To choose one of these suggestions, just click it. To clear the contents of the field, click the *X* button that appears on the right side of the box.

2. **Click in the To box and type the destination address.**

   Note that your destination doesn't have to be a specific address. **Memphis, TN**, for example, works just fine. Maps displays a list of possible locations as you type, and you can click any suggestion to select it. If you enter the destination manually, press Return.

3. **Maps displays the suggested route.** Note the four buttons at the top of the panel; you can click the Drive button for road directions, click the Walk button for walking directions, click the bicycle icon for cycling directions, or display mass-transit information by clicking the Transit button.

Maps usually offers more than one route for your trip. The first route provided is typically the fastest or shortest, and it appears in bright blue. To view one of the other routes, click a light-blue line, which turns bright blue to indicate that now it's the selected route, or click the alternate route in the results list. (You can see the approximate mileage and time for the selected route in the Directions panel.) Click the Info button next to an option to see a turn-by-turn list that provides the approximate mileage for each leg of the journey.

You can easily print the route map and directions by choosing File ➪ Print (or pressing ⌘+P) and then clicking the Show Details button at the bottom of the Print sheet to display all the options. If you'd rather create a PDF document with your map and directions, choose File ➪ Export As PDF.

Finally, Maps allows you to share your maps and directions by using Mail, Messages, Notes, Reminders, or AirDrop. Choose File ➪ Share and then choose the desired sharing method.

Catching Up on News

Are you a current events junkie like I am? Before the arrival of the internet, I used to remain glued to my TV, absorbing the latest information from the news channels — heck, I even subscribed to an old-fashioned *newspaper!* If news is your passion, you'll love Tahoe's News app, shown in Figure 6-5.

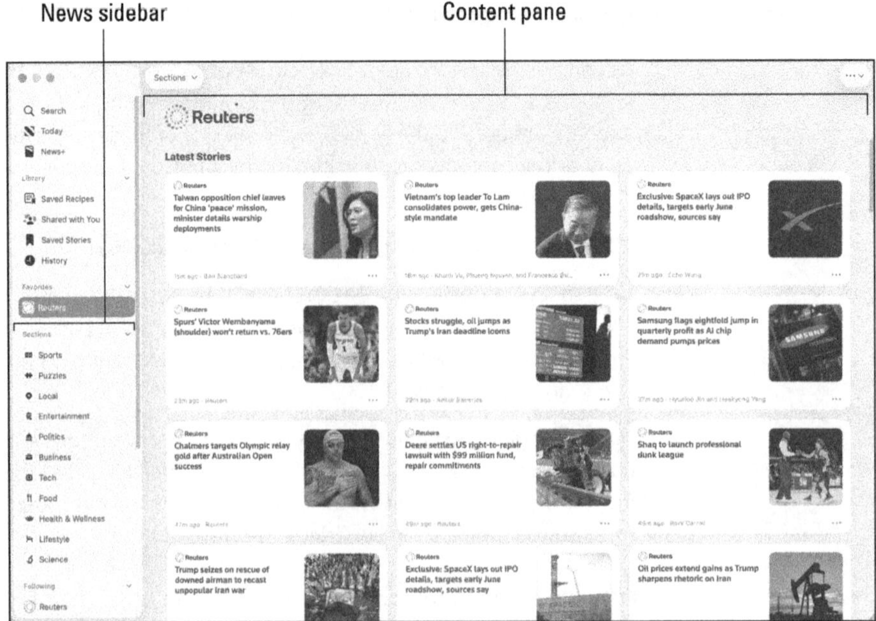

FIGURE 6-5: All the news that fits, News displays!

The News window includes a number of items to help in your perusal:

TIP

>> **Sidebar:** The News sidebar makes it easy to navigate among topics, news sources, and stories you've saved. You can display or hide the sidebar from the View menu.

Although the items in the sidebar change over time (as News "learns" your preferences and you add channels), you can right-click most of the entries and choose Unfollow Channel to remove items. (Note that some items are included by News automatically and can't be removed.)

>> **Content pane:** Here's where News displays its content. Similarly to a web page in Safari, you can click an item title or accompanying image to load the entire story. When a single story occupies the Content pane, you can click the

left arrow icon at the far-left side of the Content pane to return to the item list. (Note that when you're viewing a story, News displays a toolbar with additional icons.)

>> **Share button:** If you'd like to share a link to the displayed story within a Mail message, social media post, or a Message, click the Share button to display the pop-up menu. You can also create a new Reminder or Note from the story. (The Share button appears only when you're reading a story, so you don't see it in Figure 6-5.)

Rushed for time? To save a story you're reading for later, press ⌘+S. News adds the story under the Saved Stories heading in the sidebar.

Using Favorites and Channels

As I mention earlier, News actually "learns" what type of stories you like as you use it and will present stories that it thinks will interest you in the sidebar (under the "Suggested" heading). However, there are two News features that help you focus even more on certain topics and news sources: *favorites* and *channels.*

Many channels require that you pay a subscription fee (either through Apple or the provider themselves) before you can view the content — for example, *The Wall Street Journal* and *Wired* magazine. Of course, you can always find plenty of free content within News, but don't be surprised if a premium channel is off-limits unless you subscribe!

Within News, you can specify a news source as a channel, such as *Bloomberg* or *BBC News* — they will appear in the News sidebar. To choose channels, click File on the News menu bar and click Discover Channels. If you see a news source or a topic you'd like to monitor, click the Add button (which bears a plus sign) to change it to a red check mark. After you click Done, your channel selections are added to the sidebar under the "Following" heading. To stop following a channel, right-click the channel entry in the sidebar and choose Unfollow Channel.

News allows you to mark a channel as a favorite, indicating that you'd like to see more stories covering similar subjects. To mark a channel as a favorite, right-click that channel in the News sidebar and choose Add to Favorites; the channel appears under the Favorites heading in the sidebar.

If you'd like to block all the stories from a specific channel, right-click that channel's entry in the sidebar and choose Block Channel. You can manage your Block list from the File menu.

3

Connecting and Communicating

IN THIS PART . . .

Surf the web with ease using Apple's Safari browser.

Sync documents and data automatically using iCloud.

Share your Neo with other users safely.

Join or create a wireless network with your Neo.

Use snazzy features like Photo Booth, FaceTime, instant messaging, and screen sharing.

Chapter **7**

Let's Go on Safari!

proudly surf the web via a lean, mean — and *fast* — browser application. That's Safari, of course, and it keeps getting better with each new version of macOS. Safari delivers the web the right way, without the wait. You'll find that Safari includes features that no other browser offers, such as the Reading List, which saves selected articles and pages for later perusal.

Within these pages, I show you how to use those other controls and toolbar buttons in Safari — you know, the ones in addition to the Forward and Back buttons. You discover how to keep track of where you've been and where you'd like to go.

Pretend You've Never Used This Thing

Figure 7-1 illustrates the Safari window. You can launch Safari directly from the Dock, or you can open the Spotlight search box and type *Safari*.

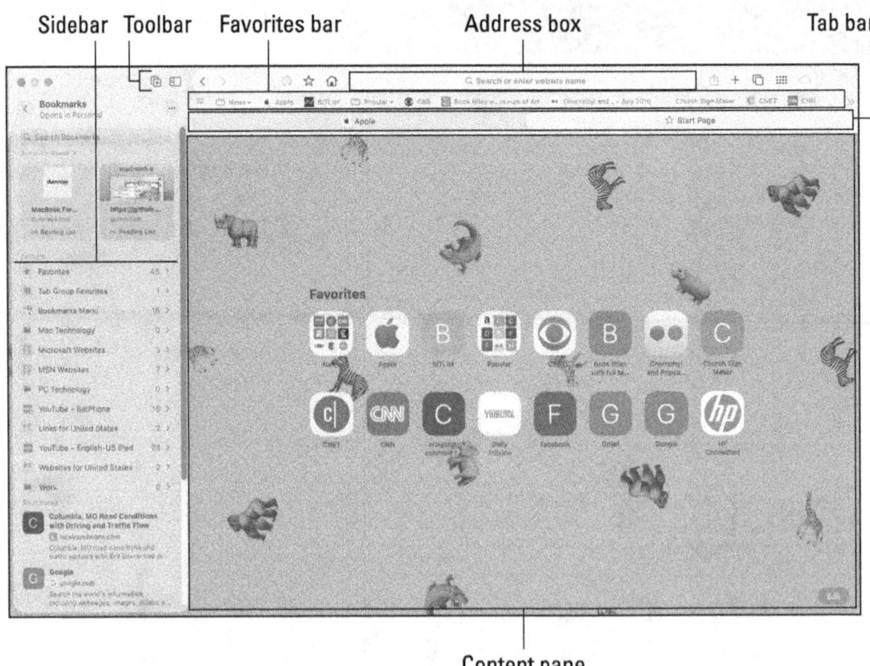

FIGURE 7-1:
Safari at a glance.

These are the major sections of the Safari window:

>> **The toolbar:** Here are the most-often-used commands for tasks such as navigation, sharing content, and searching. Also, the toolbar includes the Address box, where you can type or paste the addresses of websites that you'd like to visit. (Note that the toolbar can be easily customized, so your toolbar icons will likely differ from those I use, shown in Figure 7-1.)

>> **The Favorites bar:** This toolbar allows you to jump directly to your favorite websites with a single click. I show you later, in the section "Adding and Using Bookmarks," how to add sites to and remove sites from your Favorites bar. You hide or display the Favorites bar by choosing View ⇨ Hide/Show Favorites Bar or pressing ⌘+Shift+B.

>> **The Tab bar:** This toolbar allows you to quickly switch among multiple web pages that you've loaded, using what appear to be old-fashioned file-folder tabs. You can pin sites to the Tab bar permanently (see the sidebar "Power users pin sites," later in this chapter).

>> **The sidebar:** The sidebar pane allows you to use your bookmarks, Reading List, and shared links. To hide or display the sidebar, click the Show/Hide Sidebar button at the far left side of the toolbar. (You can also choose View ⇨ Hide/Show Sidebar or press ⌘+Shift+L.)

» **The Content pane:** Congratulations! At last, you've waded through the pregame show and reached the area where web pages are displayed. The Content pane can be scrolled, and when you minimize the Safari window to the Dock, you get a *thumbnail* (minimized) image of the Content pane.

The Content pane often contains underlined text and graphics that transport you to other pages when you click them. These underlined words and icons are *links,* and they zip you right from one area of a website to another area (or to a different site altogether). You can tell when your pointer is resting on a link because it changes to that reassuring pointing-finger hand. *Handy!* (Sorry about that.)

» **The Status bar:** The Status bar displays information at the bottom of the Safari window about what the pointer is resting on, such as the address of a link or the name of an image. To hide or display the Status bar, choose View ⇨ Hide/Show Status Bar or press ⌘+/ (forward slash).

Visiting Websites

Here's the stuff that virtually everyone over the age of five knows how to do . . . but I get paid by the word, and some folks might not be aware of the many ways to visit a site. Visit a web page by using any of these methods:

» **Type (or paste) a website address in the Address box on the toolbar and press Return.** If you're typing an address, and Safari recognizes the site as one that you've visited in the past, it "helps" by autocompleting the address for you. Press Return if you want to accept the suggested site. If the site is a new one, just keep typing.

» **Click a Bookmarks or Favorites entry.** Bookmarks appear in the sidebar and on the Bookmarks menu, whereas Favorites appear in the sidebar and on the Favorites bar.

» **Click a tab for a pinned site.** Pinned tabs appear at the left end of the Tab bar.

» **If the Start Page button appears on the toolbar, click it to open the Start Page display.** Safari displays page icons from your Favorites, your most frequently visited sites, your Reading List, and your iOS shared bookmarks. You can jump to a site by clicking the desired icon.

» **Click an item in the Reading List.** To display items in your Reading List, click the left arrow at the top of the sidebar and click Reading List.

» **Click a page link on another web page.** By default, Safari opens the new page in a separate tab.

>> **Type a search term in the Address box.** By default, Safari uses Google as a search engine, but you can also use Yahoo!, Bing, DuckDuckGo or Ecosia if you prefer. To set the default search engine, choose Safari ⇨ Settings; then, on the Search tab of the Settings dialog, make a choice from the Search Engine drop-down list. Click the Address box, type the contents that you want to find, and press Return.

If you minimize Safari to the Dock, you'll see a thumbnail of the page with the Safari logo superimposed on it. Click this thumbnail on the Dock to restore the page to its full glory.

Speaking of full glory, Safari supports full-screen mode. Click the Zoom/Full Screen button in the top-left corner of the Safari window to switch to full-screen mode, or press the Fn +F shortcut (a good shortcut to memorize because it works with virtually all Tahoe-compatible apps). To exit full-screen mode, press Esc or the Fn +F shortcut again.

Navigating the Web

A typical web-surfing session is a linear experience. You bop from one page to the next, absorbing the content you want and discarding the rest. Sometimes, however, you may need to return to where you've been or head to your home page. These navigational controls include:

>> **Back:** Click the Back button (the left-facing arrow) on the toolbar to return to the last page you visited. Additional clicks take you to previous pages, in reverse order.

>> **Forward:** If you've clicked the Back button at least once, clicking the Forward button (the right-facing arrow) takes you to the next page (or through the pages) where you originally were, in forward order.

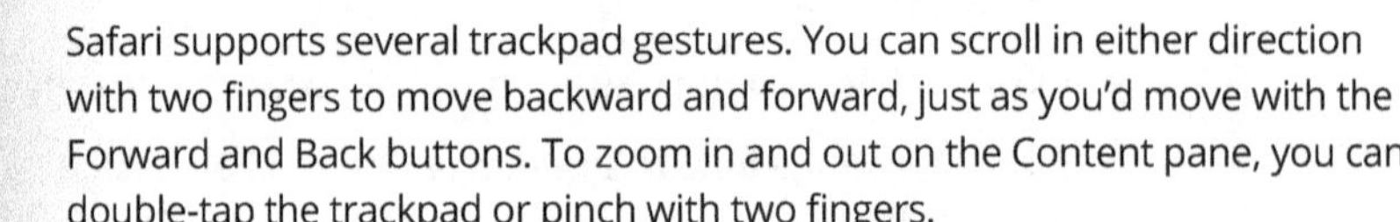

Safari supports several trackpad gestures. You can scroll in either direction with two fingers to move backward and forward, just as you'd move with the Forward and Back buttons. To zoom in and out on the Content pane, you can double-tap the trackpad or pinch with two fingers.

>> **Home:** Click the button with the house icon to return to your home page.

Not all these buttons and controls may appear on your toolbar; you may not see many of these toolbar controls unless you add them yourself. To display or hide toolbar controls, choose View ⇨ Customize Toolbar. Drag the control you want from the sheet to your Safari toolbar, or drag a control that you don't want from the toolbar to the sheet. (To return to the default toolbar configuration, drag the default set into the toolbar.) As with most controls in Mac apps, if you hover your pointer over an unfamiliar button, Safari displays a tooltip to identify the button for you.

- » **Show/Exit Tab Overview:** A click of this toolbar button displays all the tabbed sites you've opened, as well as the iCloud tabs from Safari on your other Macs, PCs, and iOS devices.

- » **AutoFill:** Click the AutoFill button (which looks like a little text box and a pen) to complete online forms automatically. You can set what information is used for AutoFill by choosing Safari ⇨ Settings and clicking the AutoFill tab at the top of the Settings dialog.

WARNING

I'm not a big fan of *automatically* releasing *any* of my personal data to *any* website, so I don't use AutoFill. If you do decide to use it, make sure that Safari doesn't display a *Not Secure* message in the Address box. *Never* enter credit-card numbers or personal data without a secure connection!

- » **Start Page:** Click this button to display the Start Page screen.

- » **Zoom:** Shrink or expand the text on the page by clicking one of the Zoom buttons, which are labeled with a small and large letter *A*, respectively. (Press ⌘+= (equal sign) to expand and ⌘+- (hyphen) to shrink.) To reset to the actual size, press ⌘+0.

- » **Bookmarks:** Click this button (which carries the star icon/Favorites symbol) to display or hide the Favorites bar.

- » **Stop/Reload:** Click the circular Reload icon in the Address box to reload the contents of the current page. Although most pages remain static, some pages change their content at regular intervals. By clicking Reload, you can see what's changed on these pages. While a page is loading, the Reload button turns into the Stop button (with a little X mark); click it to stop loading content from the current page.

- » **Sidebar:** Click this button at the left end of the Address box to hide or display the Safari sidebar.

- » **History:** Click this button, which bears a clock symbol, to display or hide the History list, which I discuss in "Using History," later in this chapter.

- » **Mail:** Click this button (bearing an envelope icon) to send an email message with a link to the current page, just as though you clicked the Share button and chose Email This Page from the drop-down menu. Safari automatically opens your default email app and creates a new message with the link already in the body.

- » **Print:** Click this button to print the contents of the Safari window.

- **Website Settings:** Click this button to change the settings you've selected for this specific website. You can use the Reader whenever possible to prevent most advertisements from appearing (more on this feature in the section titled "Working with the Reading List," later in this chapter), set the Zoom level, and enable or disable the blocking of pop-up ads.

- **Privacy Report:** Click this button to display the number of web trackers contacted by the site you're currently visiting, as well as the trackers contacted by the specific page you're viewing.

- **Profile:** Click this drop-down menu to switch among your Safari profiles. (More on profiles in the next section.)

- **iCloud Tabs:** Click this button to see a scrolling list of just the iCloud Tabs you've set on your iOS devices, PCs, and other Macs running Safari. Click an entry in the list to jump directly to that page.

- **Share:** Click the Share button to send the current page (or a link to it) to various destinations, including your Reading List, an email message, or your Notes or Messages applications. You can also add a bookmark to the current page by clicking the Share button.

Organizing with Profiles

Have you ever wished you could *really* organize your life? Like somehow separate your work life and your personal life into different neat little boxes? I've been struggling to do so for more than 50 years now — at least Safari can provide that separation for your browsing experience!

A Safari *profile* stores all the data you acquire during a browsing session (your History, Start page settings, Tab groups, and Favorites), allowing you to switch between profiles at work and at home. (For example, separate profiles are perfect if you're worried about work-related Favorites and History files showing up while you're at home.)

To create profiles, follow these steps:

1. **Choose Safari ⇨ Settings and click the Profiles tab.**

2. **Click the Add button, which bears a plus sign.**

3. **Enter the profile Name, Symbol, and Color to identify it.**

   You can also choose to use your current Favorites folder or create a new one.

4. **Click the Create Profile button.**

Choosing a home page is one of the easiest methods of speeding up your web surfing, and it's easy to do! In Safari, display the web page that you want to use for your new home page, then choose Safari ⇨ Settings. From the General tab, click the Set to Current Page button.

Visit your home page at any time by clicking the Home button on the toolbar. If it doesn't appear on your toolbar, you can add it by choosing View ⇨ Customize Toolbar.

You can also customize your default Start page with different sections! Click the Edit button at the lower-right corner of the Start page to choose what sections appear. You can add a site to your Start Page manually by dragging a bookmark from the sidebar to the Start Page icon on the Favorites bar.

From the sidebar, switch profiles using the entries at the top of the sidebar; if the sidebar is hidden, click the Profiles drop-down menu that now appears at the far left of the Safari toolbar.

Don't be surprised when your Safari profiles suddenly appear on your other Macs and iOS devices! (If you're using the same Apple ID, that is.)

TIP

Adding and Using Bookmarks

No doubt about it: Bookmarks make the web a friendly place. As you collect bookmarks in Safari, you're able to jump from one site to another with a single click of the Bookmarks menu or the buttons on the Favorites bar.

To add a bookmark, display the desired page and do any of the following:

>> **Choose Bookmarks ⇨ Add Bookmark.**

   Safari displays a sheet where you can enter a name and description for the bookmark and choose where it appears (Favorites bar, a Bookmarks folder you've created, or Bookmarks menu).

>> **Press the ⌘+D keyboard shortcut.**

>> **Drag the icon next to the web address from the Address box to the Favorites bar.**

To jump to a bookmark, do one of the following:

>> **Choose it from the Bookmarks menu.** If the bookmark is contained in a folder, which I discuss later in this section, hover your pointer over the folder name to show its contents; then click the bookmark.

>> **Click the bookmark on the Favorites bar.** If you've added a great number of items to the Favorites bar, click the More icon (which bears the >> icon) at the edge of the Favorites bar to display the rest of the buttons.

>> **Click the Show Sidebar button on the Safari toolbar,** click the Bookmarks entry in the Saved section, and then click the desired bookmark.

>> **Choose Bookmarks ⇨ Edit Bookmarks** or press ⌘+Option+B to open the Bookmarks list, which displays both the name and web address of each bookmark in your collection.

The more bookmarks you add, the more unwieldy the Bookmarks menu and the sidebar can become. To keep things organized, choose Bookmarks⇨ Add Bookmark Folder, and in the text entry box that appears, type a name for the new folder. You can drag bookmarks into the new folder to help reduce clutter.

To delete a bookmark or a folder from any of these locations, right-click the icon next to the entry and choose Delete from the shortcut menu.

Safari can share your bookmarks and Reading List selections across all Safari apps running on other Macs or iOS devices (using the same Apple ID)! You can configure what Safari shares through iCloud from the Apple ID pane in System Settings.

SAFARI THE TRANSLATOR

I'm excited about the continuing development of the Safari Translation feature in macOS, and with good reason — you can visit a foreign-language site and Safari can translate entire pages at one time! If the language is recognized and can be translated, click the Translate icon that appears at the right of the Address box — it looks like two cartoon speech bubbles — and choose Translate to English from the menu. To return the page to its original content, click the Translate icon again.

At this time, Safari recognizes English, Spanish, German, Chinese, French, Russian, Italian, Japanese, Arabic, Thai, Vietnamese, Polish, Ukranian, Korean, Dutch, and Portuguese. (Safari will identify whether it recognizes the language on a page.) The Translation feature also requires an internet connection, but that's required for surfing the web anyway. (No big deal there.)

Working with the Reading List

Now that you know all about bookmarks, I want to introduce another method of saving and retrieving specific pages in Safari. The sidebar's Reading List tab allows you to save entire pages for later perusal.

From the keyboard, press ⌘+Shift+L to display the sidebar, and click the Reading List entry in the Saved section. Click Bookmarks ➪ Add to Reading List to add the current page to the list, or hover your pointer over the left end of the Address box and click the circular icon with the plus sign. You can even click the Sharing icon on the toolbar and choose Add to Reading List to achieve the same victory. After you've saved a page to the list, just click it to return to that content!

Depending on their content, some entries in the Reading List will automatically open the Reader panel, which displays text articles free of advertisements and silly pop-ups. And if an article is continued over multiple web pages, the Reader panel automatically stitches them together to form a continuous block of text.

With the right setting, *every* compatible page on a specified website automatically displays in the Reader panel. (I always set all my news websites to use the Reader panel when possible.) When you've viewing the desired website, choose Safari ➪ Settings for This Website. Click the Use Reader When Available check box to enable it.

To delete a Reading List item, right-click the item and choose Delete.

Downloading Files

A huge chunk of the fun you'll find on the web is downloading images and files. If you're visiting a site that offers downloads, you typically click a Download button or link, and Safari takes care of the rest. While the file is transferring, you can continue browsing or even download other files; the Downloads status list tracks when everything will finish transferring. To display the Downloads status list from the keyboard, press ⌘+Option+L. By default, Safari saves all downloaded files to the Downloads folder on the Dock.

To download a specific image on a web page, move your pointer over the image, right-click, and choose Save Image As. Safari prompts you for the location where you want to store the file.

Using History

To keep track of where you've been, you can display the History list by clicking the History menu in Safari. To return to a page in the list, just choose it from the History menu.

As you might imagine, your History file leaves a clear set of footprints! To delete the contents of the menu, choose History ⇨ Clear History (at the bottom of the History menu). Safari also allows you to specify an amount of time to retain History entries. Open the Safari Settings General tab and then make a choice from the Remove History Items pop-up menu to specify the desired amount of time. You can also turn off automatic removal by selecting Manually.

Tabs Are Your Browsing Friends

Safari offers *tabbed browsing,* which many folks use to display (and organize) multiple web pages at one time. If you're comparison shopping for hardware among several online stores, for example, tabs are ideal.

When you hold down the ⌘ key and click a link or bookmark, a tab representing the new page appears at the top of the Safari window. Just click the tab to switch to that page. (Figure 7-1, shown earlier in the chapter, includes two tabs at work.)

You can also open a new tab by clicking the New Tab button in the toolbar or pressing ⌘+T. To switch tabs, click the desired tab header. You can remove a tab by hovering your pointer it and clicking the X button.

Trackpad fans will appreciate Safari's two gestures that control tabs. With multiple tabs active, you can do these things:

>> Pinch to display them all in the Tab Overview display.

>> With the Tab Overview open, swipe with two fingers to move among tabs.

To open Tab Overview without a trackpad, click the Show Tab Overview button at the right end of the Safari toolbar. From the Tab Overview display, you can click any tab thumbnail to switch to that tab. (iCloud Tabs shared from your other Apple devices appear at the bottom of the window.) To close a tab in Tab Overview, move your pointer over the thumbnail and click the X button that appears. To close the Tab Overview display, click the Hide Tab Overview button at the right end of the Safari toolbar.

To fine-tune your tabbed browsing experience, choose Safari ⇨ Settings to display the Settings dialog, and click Tabs. Here you can specify whether a new tab or window automatically becomes active in Safari and whether you can switch tabs by pressing ⌘+1 through ⌘+9.

TIP

If you open a page that plays audio — as background music or as part of a video shown on the page — you can click the speaker icon that appears on the tab header to mute that audio. (Think really, *really* irritating video advertisements.) To unmute the audio, click the speaker icon again.

Printing Web Pages

If you've encountered a page that you'd like to print, follow these steps:

1. **Display the desired page.**

2. **Choose File ⇨ Print or press ⌘+P.**

3. **In the Print dialog, select the number of copies you want to print.**

4. **Specify whether you'd like to print the entire page, only the current page, or a range of pages.**

5. **Click Print.**

A quick word about printing a page in Safari: Some combinations of background and text colors might conspire to render your printed copy worthless. In a case like that, use your printer's grayscale setting (if it has one), or click the Safari heading and deselect the Print Backgrounds and Print Header and Footers check boxes (which can save you quite a bit of ink or toner).

If you'd rather mail the contents of a web page to a friend, click the Share button and choose Email This Page from the drop-down menu (or add the Mail button to your Safari toolbar for one-click convenience).

Protecting Your Privacy

No chapter on Safari would be complete without a discussion of security, against both outside intrusion from the internet and prying eyes around your Neo. Therefore, this last section covers protecting your privacy.

A *secure site* encrypts the data that you send and receive, making it much harder for those of unscrupulous ideals to hack credit-card numbers and other personal information. Safari alerts you with the message *Not Secure* in the Address box if you visit a page that's not secure — if you don't see a message, you're connected securely and can rest easy.

Yes, there are such things as bad cookies

First, a definition of this ridiculous term. A *cookie* — a small file that a website saves on your Neo's drive — contains data that the site uses on your future visits, such as preserving your site settings for the next time or (as with Amazon.com) to customize the offerings that you see.

Unlike a virus, a cookie file isn't going to replicate itself or wreak havoc on your system, and only the original site can read the cookie that it creates. But many folks don't appreciate acting as a gracious host for a slew of snippets of personal data. You can opt to disable cookies by choosing Safari⇨ Settings, clicking the Advanced tab, and clicking the Block All Cookies check box to enable it.

If a site's cookies are blocked, you might have to take care of things manually, such as by providing a password that used to be read automatically from the cookie.

Feeling nervous about the data stored by websites? You can always delete *all* that stored information with a single click. On the Privacy pane of the Safari Settings dialog, click the Manage Website Data button; then click the Remove All button. You'll be asked to confirm your draconian decision.

Banishing pesky iCloud Keychain passwords

I'm the world's biggest critic of *keychains,* which Tahoe uses to automatically provide all sorts of login information throughout the system. In Safari, for example, the password information is automatically entered for you whenever a website you've approved requires you to log in.

To be more specific, I'm sure that many readers will adopt the *iCloud Keychain* feature, which stores password and credit-card data for Safari and pushes that information automatically to other Macs and iOS devices that use the same Apple ID. Apple even says that the passwords generated by iCloud Keychain are harder to crack, which *sounds* more secure, right?

I'd rather keep a pet piranha in a cereal bowl than use this feature! Why? Because *anyone* who's logged into your Neo with your user account gets control of your online persona (in the form of your passwords to secure websites). Safari, like an obedient puppy, automatically provides access to sites with stored keychain passwords, no matter who's at the keyboard.

If you'd like to take the far-less-convenient-but-*much*-safer, old-fashioned route of remembering your passwords yourself, follow my lead: Visit the Apple ID pane in System Settings, click the iCloud entry on the right side of the dialog, click the Passwords tile, and turn off the Sync This Mac switch.

Now that I've warned you thoroughly, I feel better about mentioning the Passwords tab of Safari's Settings dialog for those who *do* decide to use iCloud Keychain. On the Passwords tab, you can click the Open Passwords button to view the iCloud Keychain information that Safari uses and remove passwords from your iCloud Keychain.

Setting notifications

In Tahoe, Safari can allow websites you've approved to send you messages through Notification Center. The Websites tab of Safari's Settings dialog controls which sites are given this functionality. To prevent a website from sending notifications, click the Notifications entry in the list on the left side of the dialog and choose Deny from the drop-down menu next to the offending site. You can also remove a website from the list by selecting it and then clicking the Remove button.

Avoiding those @*!^%$ pop-up ads

I hate pop-up ads, and I'm sure that you do, too. To block many of those pop-up windows that advertise everything from low-rate mortgages to "sure-thing" internet casinos, open the Safari Settings dialog, click the Websites tab, and select the Pop-up Windows entry in the list on the left side. Now you can allow or block pop-up ads for each website you visit!

Chapter **8**

Expanding Your Horizons with iCloud

Readers often ask me to name my favorite reasons that they should switch platforms. In other words, why should a Windows user who thinks all is well move to the Apple universe? I believe that Apple makes superior hardware and a better operating system, but my favorite selling point is *innovation*. Apple comes up with the best ideas first, and everyone else plays catch-up.

Here's the perfect example: The folks at Apple got tired of synchronizing their iOS devices with their computers over USB cable. Remember those archaic days? When you took a photo or created a new document with your iPhone, your new additions just *sat* in their original locations until you could sync your device with your Mac. But with Apple's iCloud, your stuff gets *automatically* synchronized and backed up across the internet — something that the Windows world didn't have for years!

In this chapter, I save you the trouble of researching all the benefits of iCloud. Heck, that's one of the reasons you bought this book, right?

So How Does iCloud Work, Anyway?

All of today's iOS devices can display or play the same media: photos, music, books, TV shows, and such. Heck, iOS devices like your iPhone and iPad can even share applications. Therefore, it makes sense to share all your digital media effortlessly across these devices, and that's what iCloud is all about. Apple calls this synchronization *pushing.*

Here's how the pushing process works. Imagine that you just completed a Pages document on your Neo (an invitation for your brother's birthday party), but you're at the office and need to get the document to your family so that they can edit and print it from your iPad.

With iCloud, you simply save the document on your Neo to the Pages folder on your iCloud Drive, and macOS automatically pushes the document to the iPad (using the same Apple ID). Your document appears on the iPad, ready to be opened, edited, and printed — and it appears as well on any other devices that use the same Apple ID. Figure 8-1 gives you an idea of what's happening in the background when one of your devices pushes data with iCloud.

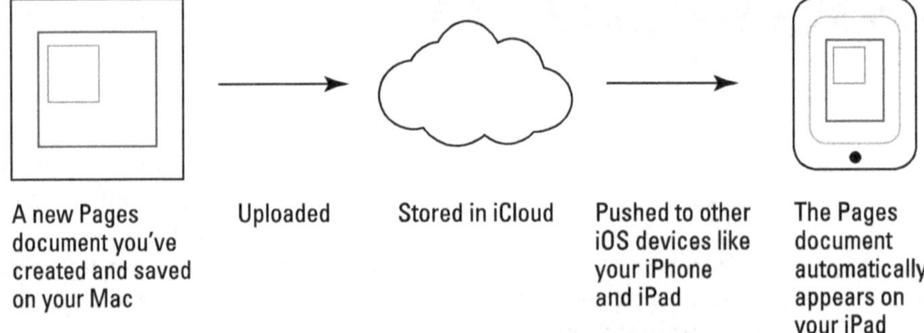

FIGURE 8-1: iCloud works by pushing data among all your iOS devices.

I'll admit that Windows *eventually* implemented a similar process with OneDrive. (That's me chuckling to myself in the background.) Yes, you can save documents within Office 365 to OneDrive and access them on other PCs and devices. Ah, but iCloud isn't limited to storing just your files and folders! Tahoe can also automatically synchronize your email, Calendar, and Contacts entries with other Apple devices across the internet (no matter where you are or which device you happen to be using).

Apple also throws in 5GB of free online storage that you can use for all sorts of things — not only digital media files, but also documents that you'd like to save online for safekeeping. Items you buy from Apple — music, podcasts, books, and apps — don't count against your 5GB limit. (More on how you can expand that 5GB limit later in the chapter.)

To join the iCloud revolution, you need an Apple ID. If you didn't create one during initial Tahoe setup — or you haven't already created one for your iPhone or iPad — you can create an Apple ID from the App Store.

You can also access your documents through the web at `https://www.icloud.com`. Log in with your Apple ID and password to send mail; access your contacts and calendar; edit your notes and reminders; locate your devices; and use online versions of Photos, Pages, Numbers, and Keynote. (Note that you may be prompted to enter a security code from an Apple device the first time you log in to iCloud on the web.)

Moving, Saving, and Opening iCloud Documents

iCloud online storage for your documents is definitely neat. Your iCloud Drive makes it easy to save documents, load documents, and move files to and from your internal drive with ease by using a Finder window. In fact, iCloud Drive keeps things tidy for you: If you move a file from your iCloud Drive to your local drive, it's also deleted automatically from iCloud Drive on your other Macs and iOS devices that use the same Apple ID. (Tahoe prompts you for permission first, of course.)

Figure 8-2 illustrates my iCloud Drive in action. You can access your iCloud Drive from the Finder window's Sidebar. Note that iCloud folders are automatically created for supported applications, such as Pages and Numbers, allowing you to click the corresponding iCloud folder from the application's Open dialog. In other words, *both* your iCloud Drive and the application-specific iCloud folder are available within the application's Open dialog. It's about as convenient as you can get.

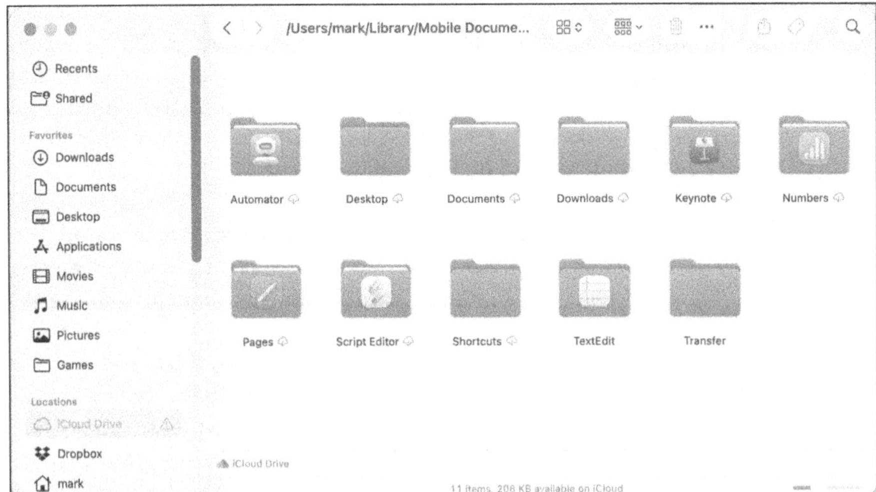

FIGURE 8-2: Each of these iCloud folders can joyously store documents.

Putting Handoff to Work

If you're like me, your favorite moment in a team track event is the all-important handoff of the baton. Handoff is the perfect name for this macOS feature, because it transfers what you're doing on your iOS devices to matching applications on your Neo!

Suppose that you're using Maps on your iPhone, and you realize that you'd rather view the location on your MacBook's larger screen (as well as print it from the USB printer connected to the Neo). If you're within Bluetooth-signal range of your MacBook, Handoff works its magic: An icon for the macOS version of Maps automatically appears on the Dock. One click of that icon, and your Neo opens Maps and displays the same location!

You're not restricted to just one app. Each time you open an app that Handoff supports (such as Safari or Mail), macOS offers you the chance to open the matching application on your Neo and displays the current data from the iOS app.

To turn Handoff on, open System Settings and click the General icon in the sidebar; then click the AirDrop & Continuity option. Click the Allow Handoff Between This Mac and Your iCloud Devices switch to enable it.

REMEMBER

Handoff must also be enabled on your iPhone or iPad to allow the connection. Open Settings on the device and display the General pane; then display the AirPlay & Continuity settings to enable the feature.

Bluetooth networking must be turned on for both the iOS device and the Neo for Handoff to work, and the iOS device must be within a 30-foot radius of your MacBook. (That's the maximum distance over which Bluetooth hardware can broadcast; walls and other obstructions reduce that range.)

Handoff works in the other direction too, allowing you to pick up where you left off on your Neo app by transferring the session to your device. Swipe the icon that appears on your iOS device to start the ball rolling.

With Handoff enabled, your old friends Copy and Paste can even be used to share text, video, or images betwixt your Neo and your iOS devices (or another Mac). This feature is called *Universal Clipboard,* and it allows you to copy items on the source device and paste them on the destination device! The process is automatic: Just copy the item as you normally would on the source device, let iCloud do all the technical stuff behind the scenes, switch to the other device, and paste the item. (Sorry, Microsoft: Only Macs and iOS devices using Bluetooth and the same Apple ID need apply.)

Expanding Your Horizons with Sidecar

Do you own a late-model iPad running iOS version 13 or later? If so, rejoice! Tahoe includes a feature called *Sidecar,* which turns your iPad into a secondary display for your Neo. As long as both devices use the same Apple ID, you can use Sidecar to extend your Tahoe Desktop (giving you more screen real estate for applications and Finder windows), or you can use the Apple Pencil input device to turn your iPad into a drawing tablet.

To turn Sidecar on, open System Settings and choose the Displays entry from the sidebar. Click the Mirror pop-up menu at the bottom of the pane (which bears a plus sign), and then choose your compatible iPad from the menu that appears. If you decide on a wired connection, you'll need a USB-C cable that can connect to your iPad. As long as your iPad is within 30 feet of your Neo, however, you can connect wirelessly by using Bluetooth.

After you've turned Sidecar on, you can click the Screen Mirroring icon that appears in the Finder menu bar to set the options for Sidecar.

Configuring iCloud

You control all the settings for iCloud from Tahoe's Apple ID pane in System Settings (shown in Figure 8-3). Click the System Settings icon on the Dock and then click the Apple ID entry at the top of the sidebar (next to your picture). Enter your Apple ID and your password, if prompted, then click the iCloud entry in the list on the right to display the iCloud pane.

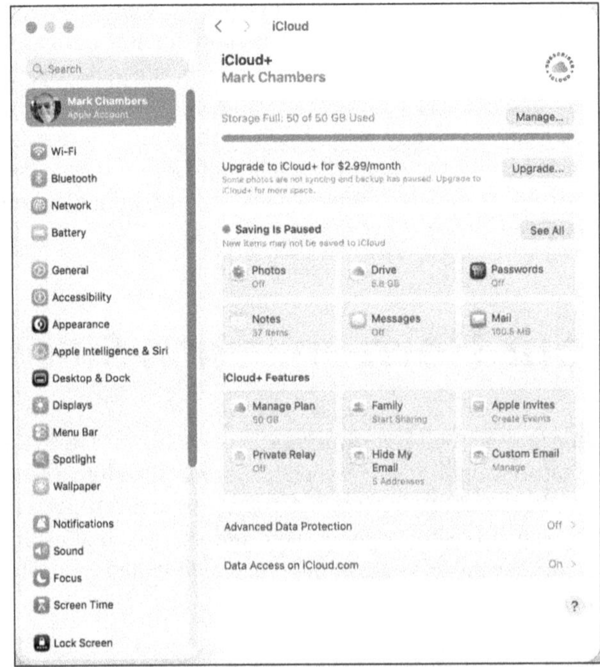

FIGURE 8-3: The iCloud pane appears in System Settings.

Most of the settings on the iCloud pane control whether a particular type of data — such as your photos, passwords, Mail message, or the contents of your iCloud Drive — is pushed to all your iOS devices. Click any of the entries to set the options for that app. (Click the See All button to display the entire list of iCloud-enabled apps.)

Note, however, that you can enable other unique features from this pane:

>> **Photos:** Click the Photos entry to enable iCloud Photos, which stores *all* your photos in iCloud. (If you have a large number of photos, you may have to buy additional iCloud storage space to use iCloud Photos.)

To turn on iCloud Photos from within Photos, choose Photos ⇨ Settings, click the iCloud tab, and select the iCloud Photos check box.

>> **Drive:** Click this entry and click Apps Syncing to iCloud Drive to specify which apps can store documents and data on your iCloud Drive. Turn off iCloud Drive access completely by disabling the Sync this Mac switch.

>> **Find My Mac:** Talk about Buck Rogers! Imagine locating your lost or stolen Neo from your iPhone or iPad. Now think about this: With Find My, you can even lock or completely wipe your Neo's internal drive *remotely,* preventing unauthorized use and erasing your private data! After you access your Neo from another iOS device, you can play a sound, remotely lock the machine, or remotely wipe the drive. To use this feature, click the See All button to display the full list, click the Find My Mac entry, and then make sure that both Find My Mac and Find My Network are turned on.

Managing Your iCloud Storage

Apple knows that you're curious about how much space you've taken up in your personal iCloud, and that information is displayed as a graph at the top of the iCloud pane.

To monitor how much space is used by individual applications, click the Manage button near the top of the iCloud pane. In the dialog that appears, you can see how much space you're using for each data type. Other items that might appear on this sheet include Mail and selected iPad and iPhone apps that support iCloud.

If you're running out of iCloud space, you can click an entry in this list and then follow any instructions that appear to delete that data type.

And if you need more elbow room than 5GB, Apple is happy to provide 50GB, 200GB, 2TB, 6TB, or even a whopping 12TB of additional iCloud storage for a monthly subscription fee of 99 cents, $2.99, $9.99, $29.99, or $59.99, respectively. Click the Upgrade button on the iCloud pane, click the desired amount of storage, and click the Upgrade to iCloud+ button to subscribe.

Chapter 9

Creating a Multiuser Neo

Everybody wants a piece. (Of your Neo, that is.)

Perhaps you live in a busy household with kids, significant others, and a wide selection of friends, all of them clamoring for a chance to spend time on the internet, take care of homework, or enjoy a good game.

On the other hand, your Neo might occupy a classroom or a break room at your office — yet everyone wants their own Private Idaho on the MacBook, complete with a folder on the drive and their own hand-picked Desktop.

Before you throw your hands up in the air in defeat, read this chapter and take heart! Here, you find all the step-by-step procedures, explanations, and tips to help you build a *safe* multiuser Neo that's accessible to all.

An Access Fairy Tale

Okay, so you don't have Cinderella, Snow White, or that porridge-loving kid with the trespassing problem. Instead, you have your brother Bob.

Every time Bob visits your place, it seems he needs to do "something" on the internet, or he needs a moment with your MacBook Neo to bang out a quick note in Word. Unfortunately, Bob's forays always end up changing stuff, such as your Desktop settings, and Safari bookmarks.

What you need, good reader, is a visit from the Account Fairy. Your problem is that you have but a single user account on your system, and macOS Tahoe thinks that Bob is *you.* By turning your mobile supercomputer into a multiuser system and giving Bob his own account, Tahoe can tell the difference between the two of you, keeping your druthers separate!

A user account keeps track of stuff such as:

>> Contacts cards

>> Safari bookmarks and settings

>> Desktop and system settings (including background images and Finder tweaks)

>> Music libraries, just in case Bob brings his own music (resigned sigh)

Also, Bob gets his own reserved Home folder on your Neo's drive, so he'll quit complaining about how he can't find his files. Oh, and did I mention how user accounts keep others from accessing *your* stuff? And how you can lock Bob out of where-he-should-not-be, such as apps like Messages and Mail? Heck, you can even lock Bob out of specific websites (hint, hint)!

The moral of my little tale? A Mark's Maxim to the rescue:

Assign others their own accounts, and let Tahoe keep track of everything. You can share your Neo with others and still live happily ever after!

MARK'S
MAXIM

Big-Shot Administrator Stuff

Get one thing straight right off the bat: *You* are the administrator of your Neo. In networkspeak, an *administrator* (*admin,* for short) is the one who has the power to Do Unto Others. (You run your multiuser show.)

I always recommend that you have only one (or perhaps two) accounts with administrator-level access on any computer. This way, you can be assured that no one can monkey with your Neo while you're away from the keyboard. (Assign a second administrator account to a *trusted* person who knows as much about your MacBook as you do. Tell 'em to buy a copy of this book.)

TIP

In the following sections, I explain the typical duties of a first-class MacBook Neo administrator. (Are you feeling important yet?)

Deciding who needs what access

The two most common user account levels are:

>> **Admin (administrator):** See the preceding section.

>> **Standard:** Perfect for most users, these accounts allow access to just about everything but don't let the user make drastic changes in Tahoe or create new accounts.

Another Mark's Maxim is in order:

Assign other folks standard-level accounts and then decide whether each new account needs to be modified to restrict access. *Never* **assign an account admin-level access unless you deem that access to be truly necessary.**

MARK'S
MAXIM

Standard accounts are quick and easy to set up, and they're highly configurable, so you can make sure that your kids don't end up trashing your Neo's drive or sending junk mail. (Attention, parents, teachers, and those designing a single public-access account: This means *you.*)

Adding users

All right, Mark. Enough pregame jabbering. Show this good reader how to set up new accounts! Your Neo already has one admin-level account (created for *you* during the initial Tahoe setup process). You need to be logged in to that account to add a user. Follow these steps:

1. **In the Users & Groups pane of System Settings, click the Add User button.**

    The empty user record sheet shown in Figure 9-1 appears.

    If Settings prompts you for permission to add a user, enter your login password to proceed.

    TIP

2. **Choose the level for this user from the New User pop-up menu.**

    By default, the user receives a standard-level account. You can also choose an administrator account or a sharing-only account.

    The sharing-only account allows the user to copy or open shared files from your Neo from another computer, but that user can't directly log in.

TECHNICAL
STUFF

3. **In the Full Name text box, type the name you want to display for this account in the Current User list and on the Login screen; then press Tab to move to the next field.**

TIP

macOS automatically generates an *account name* in the Account Name field for use in Messages and various network applications. The account name is also the name of the folder that macOS creates on the Neo's drive for this user. You can keep the default account name or type a new one, but this name can't contain any spaces.

4. **Type the password for the new account; then press Tab.**

As always, when you enter or verify a password, macOS displays bullet characters for security.

5. **Type the password again in the Verify text box and press Tab.**

6. **(Optional) If you decide to use the password-hint feature, you can enter a short sentence or question in the Password Hint text box.**

The hint is displayed after three unsuccessful attempts to enter the account's password.

WARNING

From a security standpoint, password hints are taboo. (I *never* use 'em. If someone is having trouble logging in to a computer I administer, you'd better believe I want to know *why*.) I recommend that you skip this field!

7. **Click the Create User button to finish and create the account.**

The new account shows up in the Current User list and the Login screen.

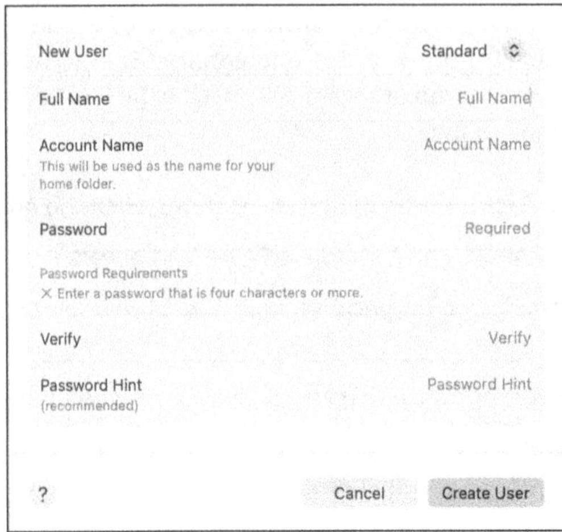

FIGURE 9-1:
Fill out these fields, and you have a new user.

Each user's Home folder has the same default subfolders, including Desktop, Documents, Movies, Music, Pictures, Public, and Downloads. A user can create new subfolders within their Home folder at any time.

No matter what the account level, most of the contents of a Home folder can't be viewed by other users. (Yes, that includes admin-level users. This way, everyone who uses your Neo gets their own little area of privacy.) In the Home folder, only the Public folder can be accessed by other users — and only in a limited fashion. (Read all about Home folders in Chapter 3.)

Modifying user accounts

Next, consider the basic modifications you can make to a user account, such as changing existing information or selecting a new user picture.

To edit an existing account, log in with your admin account, open System Settings, and click Users & Groups. Then follow these steps:

1. **In the list on the right side of the window, click the Info icon (a circle with a letter *I*) next to the account you want to change.**

2. **Edit the settings you need to change.**

   Examples include temporarily enabling administrator rights for an account (by selecting the Allow This User to Administer This Computer switch) and resetting the account password (by clicking the Reset button).

3. **Click the round *picture well* (the circle that displays the image) to select the image shown in the Login list next to the account name.**

   Apple provides several good images (including emojis) in the preview collection. Just click a thumbnail to select it. You can also drag an image from a Finder window or the Photos app and drop it into the picture well.

   Alternatively, you can click the picture well and then click the Camera entry to grab a picture from your Neo's built-in FaceTime HD camera.

4. **After you make your changes, press ⌘+Q to save them.**

Standard-level users have some control of their accounts; they're not helpless, after all. Standard users can log in, open Settings, and click Users & Groups to change the account password or picture as well as the Contacts Card assigned to them in the Contacts app.

Note, however, that users with limits set may not have access to Account Settings, so they can't make changes. (Read about this topic in the upcoming section "Managing an account's access settings.")

I banish thee, mischievous user!

Not all user accounts last forever. Students graduate, coworkers quit, kids move out (at last!), and Bob might find someone with a faster broadband connection. (Or he might finally invest in an iPhone.) We can only hope.

Anyway, no matter what the reason, you can delete a user account at any time. Log in with your admin account, display the Users & Groups pane in System Settings, and then follow these steps to eradicate an account:

1. **In the user list on the right side of the window, click the Info button next to the account you want to delete.**

2. **Click the Delete User button.**

TIP

   Note that the contents of the user's Home folder can be saved as a disk image in the Deleted Users folder (just in case you need to retrieve something). You can also choose to leave the deleted user's Home folder as is, without removing it, but naturally you won't regain any space.

   If you're absolutely sure that you won't be dating that person again, select the Delete the Home Folder radio button (which doesn't save anything in the Deleted Users folder). You regain *all* the drive space that was being occupied by the contents of the deleted user's Home folder.

3. **To delete the account, click the Delete User button.**

MARK'S MAXIM

Always delete unnecessary user accounts. Otherwise, you're leaving holes in your security.

WORKING WITH THE GUEST ACCOUNT

The *Guest* account is a convenient method of granting someone temporary access to your Neo. Your guest doesn't even need a password to log in! Your Guest account has all the attributes of a standard account, so the visitor has little chance of accidentally (or purposely) damaging your system. Nevertheless, after the guest user logs out, the Guest account is "flushed," and all the data that person created in the account are deleted automatically, allowing the next guest to start with a clean slate.

By default, the Guest account is disabled. To turn this feature on, open System Settings, click Users & Groups, and then click the Info button next to the Guest User entry in the list. Click the switch titled Allow Guests to Log In to This Computer to enable the Guest account. (You can limit access to adult websites and allow access to shared folders as well.) Click OK to save the change. You can limit the Guest account using the Screen Time pane in System Settings, like any other standard-level account.

Setting up login items and managing access

Every account on your Neo can be customized. Understandably, some settings are accessible only to admin-level accounts, and others can be adjusted by standard-level accounts. In the following sections, I introduce you to the things that can be enabled (or disabled) in a user account.

Automating with login items

Login items are apps, such as Apple Mail, or documents that can be set to launch or load automatically as soon as a specific user logs in. In fact, a user *must* be logged in to add or remove login items. Even an admin-level account can't change login items for another user.

REMEMBER

A user must have access to the Users & Groups pane to use login items. As you see in the following section, a user can be locked out of System Settings, which makes it impossible for login items to be changed for that account. In this case, an administrator must temporarily enable access to System Settings so the restricted user can add or delete login items.

To set login items for your account, follow these steps:

1. **Click the System Settings Dock icon and then click the General entry.**

2. **Click the Login Items & Extensions entry.**

   It bears repeating: You can change the Login Items for only the account that's *currently* logged in, so be sure that the desired account appears at the top of the Settings sidebar.

3. **Click the Add button (with the plus sign).**

4. **Navigate to the app or document you want to launch each time you log in, click it to select it, and then click Open.**

5. **Press ⌘+Q to quit Settings and save your changes.**

Login items are launched in the order in which they appear in the list, so feel free to drag the items into any order you like.

It's a good idea to limit the amount of login items — they may be automatic and convenient, but too many of them can dramatically slow the boot process. No one wants to wait two minutes each time you start your Neo!

Managing an account's access settings

Any account on your Neo can be limited or restricted as necessary. You can restrict access to many places in Tahoe and your MacBook's apps. Note that you can use Screen Time with your administrator account as well.

In short, limits come in handy for preventing users — family members, students, coworkers, friends, or the public — from damaging your system.

To display the access controls for a standard account, start here:

1. **Log in by using your Administrator account.**

2. **Open Settings and click the Screen Time entry in the Settings sidebar.**

3. **Click the Lock Screen Time switch to enable it and specify a passcode.**

   If prompted to convert this account to a Standard account, click Allow This User to Administer This Computer and click Continue. (You're setting just the passcode at this point.)

4. **Click the red Close button in the top-left corner of Settings to close the Settings window and save your changes.**

5. **Log out of your administrator account and login using the Standard-level account you want to manage; then return to the Screen Time pane in Settings.**

6. **Select App & Website Activity and click Turn On App & Website Activity; then click Downtime on the right side of the pane.**

   To set a downtime schedule, click the switch in the top-right section of the pane to turn on Downtime, and then click the Schedule pop-up menu to specify whether the schedule applies every day or on a specified custom range of days. Click the Back button to return to the Screen Time settings.

7. **Select App Limits on the right side of the pane.**

   When you click the App Limits switch in the top-right section of the pane, you can click the Add Limit button to specify a category of applications to add to the list. Click the check box next to the category to limit, and then use the Time controls to set the schedule. To disable the limits on an application category, disable the check box next to the category. Click the Back button to return to the Screen Time settings.

8. **Select Always Allowed on the right side of the pane to specify applications that can be used at any time.**

   The selected apps will *always* be available, even during downtime (and after app limits have been reached). Click the Back button.

9. **Select Content & Privacy to set restrictions on purchases through Apple Stores as well as age-appropriate content.**

   Click the switch next to the Content & Privacy heading to enable restrictions.

10. **Click the Store Restrictions entry and make the desired changes.**

    Ratings limits are available for purchasing applications, movies, TV shows, books, and music across all the content available in the iTunes Store. (Powerful stuff, parents!) Besides restricting the user's ability to shop for explicit books, music, and video, you can prevent the user from installing or deleting apps on iOS devices. Click Done when you're finished.

11. **Click the App Store, Media, Web & Games entry to choose limits on websites, apps, and games.**

    Tahoe offers three levels of control for websites from this screen. Click the Access to Web Content pop-up menu and choose the desired setting:

    - **Unrestricted Access:** Select this to allow unfettered access.

    - **Limit Adult Websites:** You can allow Safari to automatically block websites that it deems to be adult. To specify sites that the automatic "adult filter" should allow or deny, click Customize.

    - **Allowed Websites Only:** Choose this menu item to specify which websites the user can view. To add an approved website, click Customize, click the Add (plus sign) button, and respond to the prompt for a title and the website address.

    Click the Done button to return to the Content & Privacy settings.

12. **Click the Preference Restrictions button to set restrictions on a range of Tahoe features.**

    Click the Done button to return to the Content & Privacy settings.

    If you want to prevent the user from removing the restrictions you've set within Screen Time, disable the Allow Account Changes switch on the Preference Restrictions dialog! (This locks the settings throughout Screen Time, requiring the passcode you set up in Step 3 to unlock them.)

13. **Click the red Close button in the System Settings window.**

Tackling Mundane Chores

Now that you're hip to user accounts, you can turn to topics that affect all users of your Neo: how users log in, how they can share data with others on the MacBook, and how each account can be protected with state-of-the-art encryption. (I told you that Tahoe would open new doors for you!)

Logging in and out of Tahoe For Dummies

Hey, how about the login screen itself? How do your users identify themselves? This section covers the login process like a blanket.

Exploring your login options

Tahoe offers four methods of logging folks in to your multiuser Neo, all of which you can access by clicking the Lock Screen entry in System Settings:

>> **Name and Password login:** This is the most secure type of login available, requiring your account username and password. (A typical hacker won't know any usernames.) Press Return to complete the process.

When you enter your password, Tahoe displays bullet characters to ensure security.

Keep your Neo secure: Use the Name and Password login method, and always choose a password that's tough to guess.

>> **List of Users login:** This login screen offers a good middle of the road between security and convenience. Hover your pointer over the account image on the login screen and click your username; then type your password. Press Return to continue.

>> **Fast User Switching:** This feature allows another user to log in while the previous user's apps are still running in the background (perfect for a fast email check or a scan of your eBay bids without forcing someone else off the Neo). To turn on Fast User Switching, follow these steps:

1. **Open System Settings.**

2. **Click the Menu Bar entry in the sidebar.**

3. **Click the Fast User Switching check box to enable it.**

4. **Click the Show In Menu Bar menu and choose Account Name.**

5. **Click the Back arrow.**

Tahoe now displays the active user's name on the Finder menu bar.

To switch to another account:

1. **Click the current user's name in the Finder menu.**

2. **Choose the name of the user who wants to log in.**

Tahoe displays the login window, as though your Neo had been rebooted.

The previous user's stuff is still running, so **do not** reboot or shut down!

To switch back to the previous user:

1. **Click the username on the Finder menu again.**

2. **Choose the previous user's name.**

For security, Tahoe prompts you for that account's login password.

>> **Auto Login:** This option (set from the Users & Groups pane) is the most convenient method of logging in but offers **no security whatsoever.** Tahoe automatically logs in to the specified account when you start or reboot your Neo.

I *strongly recommend* that you use Auto Login *only* if:

- Your Neo is in a secure location, such as your home. Otherwise, you need the protection of a name and password login!

- You can guarantee that you're the only one using your Neo. *Period.*

- You're setting up a public-access Mac kiosk, in which case you want your Neo to automatically log in with the public account.

Logging out

Logging out of Tahoe is a cinch. Just choose Log Out or press ⌘+Shift+Q. A confirmation dialog appears that automatically logs you off in one minute. And that one minute is important, because if someone walks up and clicks Cancel, they'll be using your account! I recommend bypassing the confirmation dialog by pressing Option while choosing Log Out from the menu (or by adding the Option key to the keyboard shortcut). Heed this Mark's Maxim:

Always **click the Log Out button in the confirmation dialog before you leave your Neo (or use the Option key to bypass the confirmation dialog), and double-check to make sure that the logout completes successfully.**

Interesting stuff about sharing stuff

You may wonder where shared documents and files reside on your Neo. That's a good question. The answer is simple: The Users folder on your MacBook has a Shared folder within it. To share a file or folder, place it in the Shared folder.

You don't have to turn on file sharing in the Sharing pane of Settings to use Shared folders on your Neo. File sharing affects only network access to your machine by users of other computers.

Each user account on your Neo also has a Public folder in that user's Home folder. The Public folder is a read-only folder that other users on your system (and across the network) can access. They can only open and copy the files it contains. (Sorry, they can't create new documents or change existing documents created by other users.)

Encrypting your Home folder can be fun

Allowing others to use your Neo always incurs a risk — especially if you store sensitive information and documents on your MacBook. Although your login password will ensure that your Home folder is off limits to everyone else, consider adding an extra level of security to stymie even dedicated hackers. Superlative security is a Supremely Good Thing!

To this end, Tahoe includes *FileVault,* which automatically encrypts the contents of your Neo's drive. Without the proper key (in this case, your login password, your Apple ID, or the FileVault recovery key), the data stored on your drive is impossible for just about anyone to read.

The nice thing about FileVault is that it's transparent to you and your users. In other words, when you log in, Tahoe automatically decrypts your encrypted files and folders. You won't even know that FileVault is on the job (which is how computers are *supposed* to work).

To turn on FileVault protection for a specific account, follow these steps:

1. **Click the System Settings icon on the Dock and then click the Privacy & Security entry in the sidebar.**

2. **On the Privacy & Security pane, click the FileVault entry.**

3. **Click the Turn On button.**

4. **Specify whether your iCloud (Apple ID) account can be used to reset your password and unlock your disk; then click Continue.**

   For most Neo owners, the iCloud Account option is fine. If you're security-conscious, or if you've shared your iCloud account information with others, select Create a Recovery Key and Do Not Use My iCloud Account.

5. **If you decide to create a separate recovery key, *write down the FileVault recovery key displayed by Tahoe and store it in a safe place.***

   I love the FileVault feature and use it on all my Macs. Yet risk is involved (insert ominous chord here). *Do not forget your login and iCloud account passwords (or make DOGGONE sure that you have access to a copy of that all-important FileVault recovery key)!* If you forget these passwords and the key, you can't retrieve any data from your Neo's drive. An Apple support technician will tell you that nothing can be done. As Jerry Reed used to say, "It's a gone pecan" (pronounced Southern style, as "puh-*kahn*").

6. **If necessary, click Enable User, provide the login password for each user on your account, and then click Continue.**

   Each user on your Neo must be enabled after FileVault has been turned on. If you don't know the login passwords for the other user accounts on your system, you have to ask each person to provide their password to continue.

   Your MacBook automatically begins the encryption process. You can continue to use your laptop normally during encryption. Click the Back button to return to System Settings.

IN THIS CHAPTER

» **Considering the benefits of a network**

» **Choosing between wired and wireless networks**

» **Gathering the stuff you need to network**

» **Making the network connection**

» **Using and sharing your network**

» **Protecting your Neo with a firewall**

Chapter **10**

Working Well with Networks

In my opinion, network access ranks right up there with air conditioning and the microwave oven. Like other "I can't imagine life without them" kinds of technologies, it's hard to imagine sharing data from your Neo with others around you without a network. I guess you could still use a *sneakernet* (the old-fashioned term for running back and forth between computers with a floppy disk), but these days, Apple computers don't even *have* floppy drives.

Nope, networking is here to stay. Whether you network for an internet connection, to challenge your friends to a game of battlefield action, or to stream your MP3 collection to others, you'll wonder how you ever got along without one. In this chapter, I provide all the details you need to know to get your svelte Neo hooked up to a new (or existing) network.

What Exactly Is the Network Advantage?

If other members of your family have computers, or if your Neo is in an office with other computers (*including* those rascally PCs), here's just a sample of what you can do with a network connection:

>> **Share an internet connection.** This is *the* major reason why many families and most small businesses install a network — everyone simultaneously using the same broadband connection on every computer on the network. You'll either need to buy a standalone router as a sharing device or rent one as part of your internet service.

>> **Share a printer.** You say your fellow employee — or, even worse, your big sister — has a great printer connected to her computer? Luckily, that printer can be shared with anyone across your network.

>> **Copy and move files of all sizes.** Need to get a Keynote presentation from one Mac to another? With a network connection, you can accomplish this task in literally seconds. Otherwise, you'd have to copy that file to a USB flash drive, use AirDrop, or use an external hard drive. A network connection makes copying as simple as dragging a file from one Finder window to another. (Or you could use your iCloud Drive. Your choice!)

>> **Share documents across your network.** Talk about a wonderful collaboration tool! You can drop a Microsoft Word document or Keynote presentation file in your Public folder (or save it in your iCloud Drive) and ask for comments from others in your office (or around the planet).

>> **Communicate with friends and family.** Use the Messages app to send and receive instant messages, or enjoy a video chat using FaceTime. Chapter 11 covers the joys of messaging.

>> **Stream music and video.** With macOS Tahoe, you can share your audio and video media collection on your Neo with other Macs and PCs (and even devices such as an Apple TV or an AirPlay speaker system) on your network. Using a network connection, you can also watch streaming TV and movies from services such as Netflix and Hulu.

>> **Play multiplayer games.** You can play virtually all of today's games remotely, challenging other players across the internet — a great feature if you're stuck in a hotel room for the evening. (Or, as many MacBook owners discovered, if you're quarantined at home during a pandemic.)

If your Neo isn't within shouting distance of an existing network, or if you don't plan on buying any additional devices or computers, you may not need to create a network. A lone MacBook hanging out in your home with no other computers around should need a network only for internet access.

Should You Go Wired or Wireless?

After you decide that you indeed need a network for your home or office, you have another decision to make: Should you install a *wired* network (running cables between your computers) or a *wireless* network? Heck, should you throw caution to the wind and build a combination network with both wireless and wired hardware?

Your first instinct is probably to choose a wireless network for convenience. After all, this option allows you to eliminate running cables behind furniture or in your office ceiling. Ah, but I must show you the advantages of a wired network as well. Table 10-1 gives you the lowdown to help you make up your mind.

TABLE 10-1 ## Wireless versus Wired Networks

Factor	Wireless Networks	Wired Networks
Speed	Moderate	Much faster
Security	Moderate	Better
Convenience	Much better	Worse
Cables	Few (or none)	Required

As I see it, here are the advantages of choosing a wired versus a wireless network setup:

>> **Wired:** Using a wired network offers two perks over a wireless network:

- **Faster speeds:** In general, wired networks are *many* times faster than an 802.11ax wireless connection.

  The performance of a wireless connection can be compromised by interference (from impeding structures, such as concrete walls, and from household devices) as well as by distance. A wireless network can also slow down because of proximity to other wireless networks, especially in densely populated areas. Wired networks have no such problems as long as cables are lengths of 25 feet or less.

- **Better security:** A wired network doesn't broadcast a signal that can be picked up outside your home or office, so it's more secure.

  Hackers can attack through your internet connection, even if you're using a wired network. Hence the final section of this chapter, "Use Your Firewall!"

Maybe you're caught in the middle when trying to choose between wired and wireless networking. Or perhaps you're already using a wired network with your other computers but are thrilled by the idea of sitting on your deck in the sunshine, checking your email on your Neo, untethered. By combining *both* technologies, you can get the faster transfers of a wired network among all the computers in your home or office and the freedom you crave. In fact, your cable, fiber, or DSL internet provider may offer a combo router that provides both wired and wireless connections.

In my home office, I use a wireless base station that includes a built-in wired switch. My family gets all the convenience of a wireless network, and everyone can connect to the internet from anywhere in our house. On the other hand, my office computers have the faster performance and tighter security of a wired network. *Sassy* indeed!

>> **Wireless:** A wireless connection really has only one advantage, but it's a big one: *convenience* (which in this case is another word for *mobility* for all your networked devices). Accessing your network anywhere within your home or office — without cables — is easy. Connecting a wireless printer is a breeze.

Be a Pal: Share Your Internet!

It's time to see what's necessary to share an internet connection betwixt all your devices and computers. (Don't worry, it's less daunting than doing your taxes.) Note that if you already have a wired or wireless network set up in your home or office and it's running to your satisfaction, you can blissfully skip this section.

Naturally, sharing an internet connection should be done only with those devices and computers that you trust and consider to be secure (typically, only the hardware within your home or office network).

I recommend a dedicated internet-sharing device (often called an *internet router*) to connect to your broadband modem. You do have to buy or rent this additional hardware. Such is the computing life. As I mention earlier, internet routers usually include wired or wireless network connections, and many include both.

Setting up an internet router is usually a simple matter, but the configuration depends on the device manufacturer and usually involves changes in System Settings that vary according to the router model. Grab a diet cola, sit down with the router's manual, and follow the installation instructions you find there.

What Do I Need to Connect?

Most *normal* folks (whom I define as "those who have never met a network system administrator and couldn't care less") think that connecting to a network probably involves all sorts of arcane chants and a mystical symbol or two. In the following sections, I provide you the shopping list you need to set up your own network or connect to a network that's already running.

Wireless connections

You Neo arrives with built-in wireless hardware, so if you already have a network base station, you're all set. Otherwise, hold on tight while I lead you through the hardware requirements for wireless networking.

The maximum signal range of any wireless network can be impeded by walls or electrical devices, all of which can generate interference.

Connecting a Neo to an existing wireless network

Connecting your awesome Neo to an existing wireless network requires no extra hardware, because your hardware is built in. (Whew. That was easy!)

Using a base station to go wireless

If you decide that you want to build your own wireless network, you eschew cables, or you want to add wireless support to your existing wired network, you need a *base station.* (If you do have an existing wired network, the base station can act as a bridge between computers using wireless hardware and your wired network, allowing both types of computers to talk to each other.) Such a wireless base station will have either:

>> A port that can connect to your existing wired network's switch

>> A full built-in switch for wired connectivity (which means that you can sell your old wired Ethernet switch to your sister in Tucson)

And, of course, a base station can simply act as a central switch for your wireless network (with no support for a wired network).

It's important to note that most Internet service providers (ISPs) can supply you with a modem for your broadband connection that has a built-in wireless base station — so your existing internet connection hardware may already *have* wireless capability! Contact your ISP and ask them whether you have wireless support (and, if you do, ask for a tech visit to help you set up a wireless network).

"Can I use an older wireless base station?" Technically, the answer is yes, because the 802.11ax hardware that comes with the Neo is compatible with *all* the older wireless standards — 802.11b/a/g/n/ac — but I highly recommend that you stick with 802.11ax in the future, which both plays well with others and provides much better performance to boot!

You'll find a plethora of third-party base stations that will do the job just fine. Naturally, you should take a gander at the manufacturer's installation guide just to make sure, but I've added many brands of these devices, and I used the same general steps for each one.

It's always a good idea to invest in non-Apple hardware that explicitly supports macOS Tahoe. That way, you're guaranteed both documentation and support for the Mac, and possibly even installation software! Moral of the story? Check the supported hardware and software before you buy!

Follow these steps to add a base station to your broadband connection:

1. **If you have a broadband modem, connect it to the WAN (wide-area network) port on the base station with an Ethernet cable.**

2. **If you have an existing wired Ethernet computer network with a switch or router, connect it to the Ethernet LAN (local-area network) port on the base station with an Ethernet cable.**

3. **If you have a USB printer, connect it to the USB port on the base station.**

   I cover the steps for sharing a printer in the later section "Sharing a network printer."

4. **Connect the power cable.**

5. **Switch on your base station.**

6. **If your base station has macOS installation software, launch the installer on your Neo.**

Joining a wireless network

To join a wireless network, follow these steps:

1. **Click the Wi-Fi status icon (which looks like a fan) on the Finder's menu bar. If the Wi-Fi switch at the top of the menu is turned off — the switch is toggled to the left — click the Wi-Fi switch to turn it on.**

2. **Next choose an existing network connection that you'd like to join.**

    The network name is the same as the network name you chose when you set up your base station.

3. **If you set up a secure network, enter the password you assigned to the network during setup.**

    By the way, security is always A Good Thing. I strongly recommend that you enable the password-encryption features of your base station while installing it. In the words of an important Mark's Maxim:

    Keep uninvited guests out of your network! Use your base station's security features and encrypt your data by using WPA2 encryption!

Some wireless networks may not appear in your Wi-Fi menu list. These are *closed networks*, which can be specified when you set up your base station. You can't join a closed network unless you know the exact network name (which is far more secure than the base station simply broadcasting the network name). To join a closed network, follow these steps:

1. **Click the Wi-Fi status icon on the Finder's menu bar, choose Other Networks, and then click Other . . . at the bottom of the menu.**

2. **Type the network's name.**

3. **If the network is secured with WPA/WPA2, WPA2/WPA3, WEP, or Dynamic WEP encryption (the security standards for protecting your data through encryption), click the Security pop-up menu, and choose which type of encryption is being used.**

    I recommend avoiding WEP and Dynamic WEP encryption whenever possible. Your best bet is WPA2 or WPA3 encryption. These types are the current standards for home wireless networks, so always choose one of them when available. Most home base stations will use the WPA2/WPA3 Personal setting.

4. **Enter the network password, if required.**

5. **Click Join.**

AirDrop is the local Mac-to-Mac file transfer feature built into macOS Tahoe, and it couldn't be easier to use. No setup and no passwords are involved! But it comes with two caveats:

- AirDrop uses the Bluetooth and Wi-Fi hardware built into today's Macs, so don't forget to turn on both Bluetooth and Wi-Fi first. (AirDrop will prompt you to turn on either wireless system when necessary.)

- You have to be within Wi-Fi signal range of another Mac to use AirDrop. Note, however, that the two computers *don't* have to be using the same Wi-Fi network. (My iMac uses a wired connection to my network, but because it has internal Wi-Fi hardware, I can use AirDrop to send files to my Neo.) Because AirDrop uses a Wi-Fi connection, file transfers are significantly slower (and far less secure) than they'd be over a wired Ethernet network. (It's a good idea to AirDrop only with folks you know.)

To use AirDrop to transfer files to another Mac, both users should click the AirDrop icon in any Finder window's Sidebar to join the AirDrop group. After a short delay, you see the account pictures for all Macs within signal range and with AirDrop open. Just drag the files you want to transfer to the person's picture. Both you and the recipient are prompted for confirmation before the transfer begins. When the transfer is complete, the files you sent are saved in the recipient's Downloads folder.

When you're done using AirDrop, just close the Finder window displaying the account pictures (or click another location on the Finder window's Sidebar) to exit the AirDrop group. (Don't forget that you have to reopen AirDrop if someone wants to send you files. I leave my AirDrop Finder window open and minimized to the Dock.)

To disconnect from a Wi-Fi network, click the Wi-Fi menu and then click the Wi-Fi switch to turn it off (or connect to another wireless network). In other words, if you choose another available wireless network from the Wi-Fi menu, your Neo automatically drops the previous connection. (You can be connected to only one wireless network at a time.)

Wired connections

Unfortunately, your Neo didn't come from Apple with a wired Ethernet port onboard, but you can add a USB-C-to-Ethernet connector that allows you to use a wired network. After you add the connector to your system, you can follow along without any problem. Don't forget that you also need cables and an inexpensive

Ethernet switch. (If you're using an internet router or other hardware-sharing device, it almost certainly has a built-in four- or eight-port switch.)

If you've (wisely) invested in a docking station for your Neo, it very likely has a wired Ethernet port as one of its array of connections — no need for a separate adapter! Check your docking station's user manual to see whether it includes an Ethernet port.

Making a connection to a wired network

If you're connecting to an existing wired network, you need a standard Cat5/Cat5E/Cat6 Ethernet cable of the necessary length. I recommend a length of no more than 25 feet, because longer cables are often subject to line interference (which can slow or even cripple your connection). You also need a live Ethernet port from the network near your Neo. Plug the cable into your USB-C Ethernet adapter (or your dock) and then plug the other end into the network port.

Wired network hardware

If you don't know your switch from your NIC, don't worry. Here, I describe the hardware you need for your wired network.

WIRED NETWORK COMPONENTS

If you're building your own wired network, you need:

>> **A switch:** This gizmo's job is to provide more network ports for the other computers in your network. Switches typically come in four- and eight-port configurations.

   As I mention earlier in this chapter, most internet routers (sometimes called *internet-sharing devices*) and wireless base stations include a built-in switch. So if you've already invested in an internet router or base station, make doggone sure that it doesn't come equipped with the ports you need before you go shopping for a switch.

>> **Ethernet cables:** Exactly how many cables you need is determined by how many computers and other devices (such as a network printer) you're connecting. If you're working with a Gigabit Ethernet system, you need Cat5E or Cat6 cables. Cat6 cables provide better performance but are more expensive.

Naturally, if you're using a broadband internet connection, you also have a DSL, fiber, or cable modem. These boxes always include a port for connecting to your wired Ethernet network. If you have a *wireless* modem, which act as wireless base stations, don't panic. A wireless modem should also have a wired port for connecting to your existing switch.

WIRED NETWORK CONNECTIONS

After you assemble your cables and your router or switch, connect the Ethernet cables from each of your computers to the router or switch, and then turn on the device. (Most need AC power to work.) Check the device manual to make sure that the lights on the front indicate normal operation. (Green is usually A Good Color.)

Next, connect your broadband modem's Ethernet port to the WAN port on your switch with an Ethernet cable. If your modem isn't already on, turn it on now, and check for normal operation.

When your router or switch is powered on and operating normally, you're ready to configure macOS. Hop to the upcoming section "Connecting to the Network." (Now add *network technician* to your growing computer résumé!)

Joining a wired Ethernet network

After all the cables are connected, and your central connection gizmo is plugged in and turned on, you've essentially created the hardware portion of your network. Congratulations!

With the hardware in place, it's time to configure Tahoe. In this section, I assume that you're connecting to a network with an internet router or switch that includes a DHCP server. (Jump to the sidebar "The little abbreviation that definitely could" for more on DHCP.)

Follow these steps on each Mac running macOS that you want to connect to the network:

1. **Click the System Settings icon on the Dock.**

2. **Click the Network entry in the sidebar.**

3. **In the Connection list on the right, select Ethernet (or Thunderbolt Bridge).**

   The entry may also be named Ethernet 1. Make sure that you select the Ethernet entry that does *not* carry the Wi-Fi fan symbol.

4. **Click the Details button and click the TCP/IP entry in the list at the left.**

5. **Click the Configure IPv4 pop-up menu and choose Using DHCP.**

6. **Click the OK button.**

   Enjoy the automatic goodness as macOS connects to the DHCP server to obtain an IP address, a subnet mask, a gateway router IP address, and a Domain Name System (DNS) address. (Without a DHCP server, you'd have to add all this stuff manually. Ugh.)

A few seconds after clicking the OK button, you should see the information on your connection appear.

7. Press ⌘+Q to quit System Settings and save your work.

You're on!

Connecting to the Network

All right! The hardware is powered up, the cables (if any) are installed and connected, and you've configured macOS Tahoe. You're ready to start (or join) the party. It's time I show you how to verify that you're connected, as well as how to share data and devices with others on your network.

You can use the macOS Wireless Diagnostics app at any time to check on the condition of your network. Click the Spotlight search icon on the Finder menu bar and type **Wireless Diagnostics** in the Spotlight search box; then double-click the app in the results list to launch it. The onscreen instructions will guide you through the diagnostic process.

THE LITTLE ABBREVIATION THAT *DEFINITELY* COULD

You know, some technologies are *peachy*. (So much for my über-tech image.) Anyway, these well-designed technologies work instantly; you don't have to guess any network settings, and every computer can use them.

Dynamic Host Configuration Protocol (*DHCP* for short) is about as peachy as it gets. This protocol enables a computer to automatically get all the technical information necessary to join a network. Virtually all network devices can use DHCP these days, as well as macOS. Basically, the DHCP server simply flings the proper settings at every computer on the network all by itself. Your Neo accepts the settings and relaxes in a placid networking nirvana.

If you're connecting to an existing network, tell the network administrator that you're taking the easy route and using DHCP. A warning, however: Adding more than one DHCP server on a single network will cause a civil war, and your system will lock up tight. Therefore, before adding hardware with a DHCP server to an existing network, ask your network administrator to ensure that you aren't making a mistake.

Sharing stuff nicely with others

By golly, it works! Okay, now what do you *do* with your all-new chrome-plated network connection? Ah, my friend, let me be the first to show you around! In the following sections, I cover the most popular network perks. (These perks work with both wired and wireless connections.)

Network internet connections

If your broadband modem plugs directly into your Neo (rather than into a dedicated internet-sharing device or internet router), you might ponder just how the other computers (or iPhones or iPads) on your network can share that spiffy high-speed connection. If you're running a wireless network, it comes to the rescue!

Follow these steps to share your connection wirelessly:

1. **Click the System Settings icon on the Dock.**

2. **Click the General entry in the sidebar, and then click the Sharing entry in the list on the right.**

3. **Click the Internet Sharing switch in the list on the right to turn it on.**

    Tahoe displays a warning dialog stating that connection sharing could affect your network. If you intend to share the internet connection provided on an existing network that you *didn't* set up, contact your network administrator first! (It's best to avoid sowing chaos and disorder.)

4. **Click Configure.**

5. **From the Share Your Connection From pop-up menu, choose Ethernet.**

6. **Click the Wi-Fi switch in the To Devices Using list to turn it on.**

7. **Click the Internet Sharing switch at the top of the dialog to turn it on.**

    Again, Tahoe requests confirmation.

8. **Click Turn On to continue.**

9. **Click the Close button to exit System Settings.**

Sharing an internet connection (without an internet router or dedicated hardware device) through macOS *requires* your Neo to remain on continuously. Remind others in your office or home that your svelte MacBook *must* remain on; otherwise, they'll lose their internet connection!

Don't forget — you don't need to configure Internet Sharing if your broadband modem connects to a dedicated sharing device or router. That snazzy equipment automatically connects your network to the internet.

Network file sharing

You can swap all sorts of interesting files with other Macs on your network. When you turn on File Sharing, Tahoe allows all Macs on the network to connect to your Neo and share the files in your Public folder. (Note that sharing across a network is different from sharing a single computer among several people. I cover that environment in Chapter 9.)

Follow these steps to start sharing files and folders with others across your network:

1. **Click the System Settings icon on the Dock.**

2. **Click the General icon in the sidebar, and then click the Sharing entry in the list on the right.**

3. **Click the switch next to the File Sharing service entry to toggle it on, enabling the connections for Mac and Windows sharing.**

   Other Mac users can connect to your laptop by choosing Go from the Finder's menu bar and choosing the Network menu item. The Network window appears, and your Neo is among the choices. For other Macs on your network, your MacBook's shared files and folders appear in a Finder window, listed below the Shared heading on the Sidebar.

   Windows 11 users should head to the Network panel. Those lucky Windows folks also get to print to any shared printers you've set up. (The following section covers shared printers.)

4. **Click the Close button to exit System Settings.**

   Tahoe conveniently reminds you of the network name for your Neo at the bottom of the Sharing list, and you can change it if you like.

Sharing a network printer

I love describing easy procedures, and sharing a printer on a Mac network ranks high on the list! You can share a printer that's connected to your Neo by following these simple steps:

1. **Click the System Settings icon on the Dock.**

2. **Click the General icon in the sidebar; then click the Sharing entry in the list on the right.**

3. **Click the Printer Sharing switch to toggle it on.**

   To specify the printer you want to share, click the Info button next to the Printer Sharing switch. From here, you can toggle a printer as shared or private, and you can allow everyone (or just specific people) to share your printer. Click Done to return to the Sharing list.

4. **Click the Close button to exit System Settings.**

   A printer you share automatically appears in the Print dialog on other computers connected to your network.

Use Your Firewall!

Yep. That's an exclamation point at the end of that title. It's that important. The following Mark's Maxim, good reader, isn't a request, a strong recommendation, or even a regular Maxim. Consider it to be an *absolute command* (right up there with "Pay your taxes!").

Turn on your firewall *now.*

When you connect a network to the internet, you open a door to the outside world. As a consultant to organizations in my hometown, I attest that the outside world is chock-full of malicious turkeys who *dearly love* to inflict damage on data and would like to take control of your Neo. Call 'em hackers (or call 'em something I can't repeat), but *don't let 'em in!*

Tahoe comes to the rescue again with a built-in firewall. When you use the firewall, you build a virtual barrier between yourself and the hackers (both on the internet and within your local network). Follow these steps:

1. **Click the System Settings icon on the Dock.**

2. **Click the Network entry in the sidebar.**

3. **Click the Firewall entry in the list at the right.**

4. **Click the Firewall switch to toggle it on.**

5. **Click the Options button.**

6. **Click the switch titled Automatically Allow Built-In Software to Receive Incoming Connections to toggle it on.**

7. **Click the switch titled Automatically Allow Downloaded Signed Software to Receive Incoming Connections to toggle it on.**

8. **Click the Enable Stealth Mode switch to toggle it on.**

   This important feature prevents hackers from *trolling* for your Neo on the internet — in other words, searching for an unprotected computer.

9. **Click OK.**

10. **Click the Close button to exit System Settings.**

Tahoe even keeps track of the internet traffic that you *do* want to reach your Neo, such as printer and file sharing. When you activate one of the network features described in the earlier section "Sharing stuff nicely with others," Tahoe automatically opens a tiny hole (called a *port* by net types) in your firewall to allow just that type of communication with your Mac.

If you decide to turn on printer sharing (as described in the preceding section), for example, Tahoe automatically allows incoming print jobs over the network from other computers.

You can also add ports for applications that aren't on the firewall's Allow list, such as third-party instant-messaging clients and multiplayer-game servers. Depending on the type of connection, Tahoe often displays a dialog prompting you for confirmation before allowing certain traffic, so you probably won't need to do anything manually.

You *can* manually add a program to your list of allowed (or blocked) firewall ports, however. Follow these steps:

1. **Click the System Settings icon on the Dock.**

2. **Click the Network entry in the sidebar.**

3. **Click the Firewall entry in the list on the right and then click the Firewall Options button.**

4. **Click the Add button (which carries a plus sign).**

5. **Browse to the application that requires access to the outside world — or the application that you want to block from outside communication — and click it to select it.**

6. **Click the Open button on the File sheet.**

   The application appears in the Firewall list. By default, it's set to Allow Incoming Connections.

7. **If you want to block any communications coming into the application, click the Allow Incoming Connections pop-up menu, and choose Block Incoming Connections instead.**

8. **Click OK and then click the Close button to exit System Settings.**

IN THIS CHAPTER

» **Using Photo Booth**

» **Chatting with Messages**

» **Using Continuity Camera**

» **Sharing screens with others**

» **Connecting with FaceTime**

Chapter **11**

Hooking Up with Your World

This chapter is all about getting interesting things into — and out of — your MacBook Neo. I might surprise you with something new to you, such as your laptop's built-in FaceTime HD video camera, which gives you the ability to place and receive video and audio calls to friends and family on their Macs, iPhones, and iPads. You can send and receive instant messages from your friends as well, whether they have Macs, iOS devices, or smartphones from another manufacturer. Your Neo can share its display with others, too.

Heck, I also show you how to turn your MacBook into an old-fashioned photo booth, just like the expensive models at your local mall or amusement park. Think "Neo selfies" at your next party — complete with outrageous effects!

Using Photo Booth

Although the lens of your Neo's built-in FaceTime HD camera is difficult to see at the top of your laptop's display, it's a first-rate performer! It allows you to capture video in iMovie, video chat with FaceTime, or snap a quick, fun series of photos or video clips via the Photo Booth application that comes with macOS Tahoe.

The FaceTime HD camera's indicator light appears as a green dot in the upper right corner of your display (or at the far right side of the Finder menu) whenever you're taking a snapshot or recording video . . . which, when you think about it, is A Good Thing (especially if you prefer chatting at home in Leisure Mode). If you're security conscious, a number of manufacturers produce clips with sliding lens covers that can block the camera when not in use. Or, in a pinch, you can cover the camera lens with a sticky note!

TIP

If you need a quick picture of yourself for use on your web page, or perhaps your user account icon needs an update to show off your new haircut, use Photo Booth to capture images. Although today's digital cameras can produce a much higher-quality photo, you can't beat the built-in convenience of Photo Booth for that quick snapshot!

To snap an image in Photo Booth, follow these steps:

1. **Launch Photo Booth from the Spotlight box.**

   To try things out in full-screen mode, choose View ⇨ Enter Full Screen.

2. **Choose to take one image, four quick photos as a group, or digital video.**

   The three buttons in the bottom-left corner of the window allow you to switch among four photos in a row (arranged as a square group), taking one photo or a movie clip.

3. **(Optional) Click the Effects button to choose an effect you'd like to apply to your image.**

   Photo Booth displays a screen of thumbnail preview images so that you can see how each effect changes the photo. To move through the thumbnail screens, click the Previous and Next arrow buttons that appear at the bottom of the window.

   You can always launch your favorite image editor afterward to use a filter or effect on a photo (such as the effects available in the Photos application), but Photo Booth can apply these effects automatically as soon as you take the picture.

4. **(Optional) Click a thumbnail to apply the desired effect.**

   When you choose an effect, Photo Booth automatically closes the Effects display.

TIP

   To return the display to normal, click the Normal thumbnail, which appears in the center. (That would be Paul Lynde's spot, for those old enough to remember *Hollywood Squares.*)

5. **Click the red Camera button.**

   The image (or video clip) appears in the filmstrip at the bottom of the window.

Photo Booth keeps a copy of all the images and clips you take in the filmstrip so that you can use them later. After you click a photo or film clip in the filmstrip, the Share button appears in the bottom-right corner of the window, inviting you to take any of a series of actions, including:

>> Sending the photo in an email or as a Messages attachment

>> Saving the photo directly to Photos

>> Using the photo to create a new Notes entry or Reminder

>> Sending the photo to another device via AirDrop

>> Creating a Journal entry with the photo

>> Using the image as your macOS user account icon

To delete an image from the Photo Booth filmstrip, click the offending photo and then click the *X* button that appears in the top-left corner of the thumbnail.

TIP

Conversing with FaceTime

With Apple's FaceTime technology, you can video-chat with owners of iOS devices and Macs, and if they can run the FaceTime app, they're guaranteed to have the right video hardware!

Most iOS devices can use either a Wi-Fi or cellular connection for FaceTime, and your Neo requires a connection to the internet.

REMEMBER

To launch FaceTime, display the Spotlight search box, type **Facetime** and click on the first result in the search list. The first time you use the application, you have to enter your Apple ID and your email address. The folks you chat with on the other end use that same email address to call you via FaceTime. (You can call iPhone owners by using their telephone numbers.)

After you sign in, initiate a call with any contact by clicking the New FaceTime button near the top of the FaceTime window and typing the desired name, email address, or phone number. Click the desired email or telephone number, and the connection process begins.

Apple isn't satisfied with providing access to your Contacts list, however. You can use the Recent Calls list (which appears as a sidebar along the left side of the window) to choose a contact whom you've called or attempted to call, or who has called you within the recent past. Hover your pointer over the contact and click the video camera icon to initiate the call.

When the call is accepted, you see a large video window with a smaller picture-in-picture display. The video of the other person fills the large window, and the video that you're sending appears in the small display. Click the End icon (the red button with the X) to end the call.

To take advantage of your Neo's widescreen display, choose Video ⇨ Use Landscape or press ⌘+R. (Why let iPhone and iPad owners have all the landscape fun?)

Sending and Receiving Instant Messages

"If I can FaceTime or send an email, why use Messages?" you may ask. When family and friends want to communicate with you by using their computers, they could certainly use Mail or FaceTime — but video and email may not be convenient (or as fast), and you'd miss that communication. Messages allows you to plug into the popular world of internet instant messaging made familiar between smartphones and devices.

Sending a text message to another person is practically instantaneous — hence the name — and you can switch to an audio chat (sound only) or a video chat (using FaceTime) if the other person has a compatible device.

When you first run Messages, you'll be prompted to use the Messages account that you've created on your iPhone or iPad. If you don't have either of those devices, you can create a Messages account using your Apple ID. If you've already set up SMS and MMS text messaging on your iPhone, those texts are also shown, and you can reply to them within the app as well!

Your Neo must be signed in to the same iCloud account as your iPhone to send and receive SMS or MMS messages.

To send a new message, click the Create New Message icon in the Messages toolbar, or press ⌘+N. Messages prompts you to type a name from your Contacts list that contains an instant message address, or enter an email address or telephone number if the recipient isn't in your Contacts list. If you have already sent and received messages with the recipient, they'll be displayed in the list. Now type your text in the entry box at the bottom of the window.

If you prefer using the Siri voice assistant, you can click the Siri icon in the Finder toolbar and say "Send a message to" followed by the person's name and the message text.

If you want to use bold or italic text, highlight the text and then press ⌘+B for Bold **(B)** or ⌘+I for Italic *(I)*. You can also add an *emoji* (a symbol, also called a *smiley*) to your text: Click the text where you want the emoji to appear, click the Smiley button to the right of the text entry field, and then choose the proper smiley from the list.

To send a file (such as a photo) during a chat, simply drag the file into the entry box.

When your message is perfect, press Return to send it. You'll note that Messages creates an entry (called a *conversation*) in the sidebar at the left. You can click another conversation at any time to switch to that message exchange, allowing you to communicate with several people (or groups) at one time.

Sharing Your Screen

There are a slew of reasons why you'd want to share your Neo's display over a network connection. They include:

>> Allowing someone with Mac technical skills to troubleshoot a problem with your Neo

>> Allowing your family member, friend, or coworker to demonstrate how to use an app

>> Allowing another person to flip through your Photos library to find just the right image (without having to export and send them separately)

Before going any further, though, I'd like to stress the common verb in all three scenarios — the word *allowing!* **Under no circumstances should you allow a stranger to share your Neo's screen, unless they're an authorized Apple technician or a legitimate member of a tech support organization.** A person sharing your MacBook has all the permissions that you do, so deleting files and folders (and even formatting your drive) would be a simple task.

Now that you've weighed the gravity of screen sharing, follow these steps to share your Neo's screen with another Mac:

1. **Open System Settings and click the General entry in the sidebar.**

2. **Click Sharing, and then click the Screen Sharing switch to enable it.**

   Note that screen sharing is disabled if you've already turned on the Remote Management switch at the bottom of the pane.

3. **Click the Info icon next to the Screen Sharing switch.**

   You can elect to allow anyone to request a connection, or you can click the Add button (which bears a plus sign) to select a user account on your Neo that will have access.

4. **Close the System Settings window.**

5. **The person sharing your screen should launch the Screen Sharing app using the Spotlight search box.**

6. **If the other Mac is on the same local network, the other person should click the Network entry in the Screen Sharing sidebar, select your Neo, and click Connect.**

7. **If the person is connecting with you over the internet, they should click the Connection button (which bears a plus sign) in the toolbar at the top of the window. The person should enter your Apple ID.**

   Do not provide both your Apple ID and your password. Only the Apple ID is required for the other person to connect.

   Your visitor can now see the contents of your screen and shares control of your pointer and keyboard, allowing them to run apps and change settings on your Neo. (You can still control your pointer and use your keyboard as well.) You can monitor everything that they see, making Screen Sharing an excellent tool for remote technical support.

   Note that you can disconnect your visitor at *any time* by clicking the Screen Sharing icon in the Finder menu (it resembles a laptop screen with a human figure next to it) and choosing End Screen Sharing from the menu that appears.

For security, it's always a good idea to return to the Sharing pane in System Settings and turn off the Screen Sharing switch when you're not using it.

Using Continuity Camera

Here's a macOS feature that every Neo owner with an iPhone should love! With Continuity Camera, the rear-facing camera on your iPhone is transformed into a high-resolution video camera for your Neo, surpassing even the FaceTime HD camera that's built-in to the MacBook.

First, the requirements: Your iPhone must be an iPhone XR model (or later) running iOS 17 or above to use all the bells and whistles offered by Continuity Camera, and you must use the same Apple ID on both devices. Make sure that Bluetooth and Wi-Fi are enabled on both devices. If you're capturing high-quality video for use in other projects, you may want to invest in a display clip or iPhone stand that can keep your iPhone steady.

Looking forward to a long FaceTime call? Consider connecting your iPhone to your Neo with a USB-C cable, allowing it to charge during the conversation.

Now the fun begins, as you open any app that uses your FaceTime HD camera (including FaceTime, Photo Booth, and iMovie). Choose your iPhone as the camera from within that application, which usually involves a selection from the app's menu bar, or displaying the settings for that application. (For example, in Photo Booth, you can click Camera ⇨ iPhone Camera.) Your iPhone automatically begins streaming video from the rear camera. You can pause and resume the video stream from your iPhone's screen. The streaming ends when you close the app on your Neo, or when you click Disconnect on your iPhone.

Wondering what happens if you get a call while using Continuity Camera? Your iPhone will display a notification and give you the option of answering the call, which pauses the video streaming.

4

Living the iLife

Chapter **12**

The Multimedia Joys of Music and TV

Sometimes, words just aren't enough. Apple's Music application is that kind of perfection.

To envision how Music changes your Neo, you have to paint the picture with *music* — music that's easy to play, search for, and transfer from device to device. Whether it be classical, alternative, jazz, rock, hip-hop, blues, or folk, I guarantee you won't find a better application than Music to fill your life with . . . well . . . *music!*

But wait, there's more: Apple also supplies an app called TV for watching video — both TV shows and movies that you purchase or rent from the iTunes Store. I provide all the details you need to start watching video on your Neo's spectacular screen.

In this chapter, I lead you through all the features of my two absolute favorite Apple applications: Music and TV.

What Can I Play in Music?

Simply put, Music is a media player that plays audio files (and music videos). These files can be in any of many different formats. Music supports these common audio formats:

- **MP3:** The small size of MP3 files has made them popular for file trading on the internet. You can reduce MP3 files to a ridiculously small size (albeit at the expense of audio fidelity), but a typical CD-quality, three-minute pop song in MP3 format has a size of 3–5MB.

- **AAC:** Advanced Audio Coding is an audio format that's similar to MP3 but offers better recording quality at the same file sizes. However, this format is somewhat less compatible with non-Apple music players and software. (Luckily, you can still burn AAC tracks to an audio CD, just as you can MP3 tracks. They can also be exported from Music in MP3 format.) The tracks that you download from the Music Store are in AAC format, and AAC music files are becoming more popular for downloading on the internet.

- **Apple Lossless:** Another format direct from Apple, *Apple Lossless* format (also known as ALAC) provides the best compromise between file size and sound quality. These tracks are encoded without loss of quality, although Apple Lossless tracks are somewhat larger than AAC. This format is generally the favorite of discerning audiophiles.

- **CD audio:** If you have an external optical drive connected to your Neo, Music can play audio CDs.

- **Audiobooks:** You no longer need cassettes or audio CDs to enjoy your spoken books. Music can play them for you, or you can send them to your iOS device for listening on the go.

- **Streaming internet radio:** You can listen to a continuous broadcast of songs from your favorite internet radio stations, with quality levels ranging from what you'd expect from FM radio to the full quality of an audio CD. You can't save the songs within Music, but streaming radio is still great fun. Unlike services like Spotify, Pandora, and Apple Music, these streaming radio stations are free and don't require a subscription!

Playing Digital Audio Files

Music can play the digital audio files that you download from the internet or obtain from other sources (typically in the MP3 file format). After saving your audio files to your Neo, open a Finder window and navigate to wherever you stored the files. Launch Music and click the Songs entry in the sidebar. Now you can simply drag the music files (or an entire folder of music) from the Finder window to the list of your songs on the right side of the Music window. The new files appear in your Music library. You can also drag a song file from a Finder window and drop it on the Music icon on the Dock, which adds it to your Music library as well.

To play a song, just double-click it in the Music list and use the Music interface, which resembles that of a traditional CD player. The main playback controls of Music are Play, Previous, Next, the Progress bar, and the Volume slider, as shown in Figure 12-1.

Click the Play button to begin listening to a song. While a song is playing, the Play button toggles to a Pause button. As you might imagine, clicking that button again pauses the music. From the keyboard, the spacebar acts as the Play and Pause buttons.

Click the Next button to advance to the next song. The Previous button works like the Next button but with a slight twist: If a song is currently playing and you click the Previous button, Music first returns to the beginning of the current song (just like an audio CD player). To return to the previous song, double-click the Previous button. To change the volume of your music, click and drag the volume slider.

To move forward or rewind while playing a song, click and hold the Progress bar while you drag it in either direction.

TIP

As with other Mac apps, you can control much of Music with the keyboard. Table 12-1 lists some of the more common Music keyboard shortcuts.

The Music sidebar is a convenient beast indeed. You can drop music file(s) on top of a playlist's name in the list, and Music adds it to that particular playlist as well as to the main library. (More about playlists in a bit.) If you drop a folder of songs on top of the Playlists header in the sidebar, Music creates a new playlist using the folder name and adds all the songs in the folder to the new playlist. *Bam!*

TIP

If you have an external DVD drive, playing an audio CD in Music is similar to playing digital audio files. Just insert the CD in the drive, start Music by clicking its icon on the Dock, and click the Play button. The controls I describe in the previous section work with the tracks on an audio CD.

Common Music Keyboard Shortcuts

Press This Key or Key Combination	To Do This
Spacebar	Play the currently selected song if Music is idle.
Spacebar	Pause a playing song.
→	Advance to the next song.
←	Go back to the beginning of a song. Press a second time to return to the previous song.
⌘+↑	Increase the volume of the music.
⌘+↓	Decrease the volume of the music.

TIP

You can customize the Music sidebar to display only those media types and criteria that you prefer. (I like the Composers and Music Videos entries to be visible, for example.) To edit the entries in the sidebar, hover your pointer over the Library heading and click the Edit link that appears; then enable or disable the check boxes next to each heading as desired.

Think of the library as a master list of your audio media. To view the Music library, click the Songs entry in the sidebar, as shown in Figure 12-2.

FIGURE 12-2: The Music library keeps track of all your audio files.

The Music window can play media from a surprising number of sources:

>> **Library:** The sidebar can display Music, Music Videos, and Audiobooks.

>> **iTunes Store:** I discuss this music source in the final section, "Buying Digital Media the Apple Way."

>> **Radio and Home:** I discuss Apple Music Radio and Home in the section titled "A New Kind of Radio Station," later in this chapter.

>> **Shared:** If another Mac or PC on your local network is running Music and is set to sync its library, the songs in that Music library appear on all devices that use the same Apple ID.

>> **Devices:** If you connect an iPhone or iPad to your Neo, they appear in the sidebar. (And yes, Virginia, smartphones and MP3 players from other companies also appear in the list if they're supported in Music.)

>> **Genius:** Choose File ➪ New ➪ Genius Playlist to allow Music to automatically create playlists from selected songs in your Music library. (More on this feature in "Separating Slim Whitman and Slim Shady: Organizing with Playlists," later in this chapter.)

>> **Audio CD:** An audio CD entry appears in the sidebar once the disc is loaded in your external DVD drive.

>> **Playlists:** Think of playlists as folders that you use to organize your music. (More on playlists later in the section titled "Separating Slim Whitman and Slim Shady: Organizing with Playlists.")

If you've invested in an Apple TV device, it appears when you click the AirPlay icon in the Music toolbar (which looks like a triangle topped with circular waves at the right side of the Music controls). Choose the Apple TV entry from the list that appears to allow Music to share media with your Apple TV, which sends it to your HDTV.

You can browse your Music library in several ways. By default, the application sorts by *Songs*, but you can choose View➪ Sort By to sort by different criteria (including Album, Artist [active in Figure 12-2], Genre, Plays, Title, and Time).

If you're using Songs view, the Music library may display information for each song that you add to it. If any song you're adding doesn't display anything for the title, album, or artist information, don't panic; most MP3 files have embedded data that Music can read. If a song *doesn't* include any data, you can always add the information to these fields manually. I show you how later, in "Setting or changing the song information manually."

You can also change your sort order by clicking any column heading in the Music library list; Music reorders the list according to that category. Clicking the Artist column heading, for example, alphabetizes your library by artist name. Drag the column titles to reorder them as you like (except for the check-box column displayed when you're selecting songs).

While listening to your music, you can always display the tracks that Music will play next — and even change their order. (Great fun for us amateur party DJs!) Choose View ⇨ Show Playing Next to display the list at the right side of the window, and drag songs into the perfect order!

Finding songs in your Music library

After your collection of audio files grows large, you may have trouble locating that Swedish remix version of "I'm Your Boogie Man." To help you out, Music has a built-in Search function. To find a song, click the magnifying glass icon to open the search box and type some text. While you type, Music tries to find a selection that matches your search text. The search displays any matching text from your library, as well as the Apple Music service and the iTunes Store. If you type **Electronic** in the field, Music might return results for a band named Electronic or other tunes that you classified as *electronic* in the Genre field. (The section "Knowing Your Songs," later in this chapter, describes how to classify songs by genre.)

To close the search results, click the circle with the *x* icon at the right side of the search box.

Removing old music from the library

After you spend some time playing songs with Music, you might decide that you didn't *really* need 10 versions of "Louie Louie" in your library. To remove a song from the library, click the song to select it and press the Delete key, or right-click the song entry and choose Delete from Library.

You can also remove a song from the library by dragging it to the Trash on the Dock.

Separating Slim Whitman and Slim Shady: Organizing with Playlists

As I mention earlier, the Music library can quickly become a fearsomely huge beastie, containing thousands upon thousands of songs. If your library grows anywhere near that large, finding all the songs in your collection of Paul Simon albums is *not* a fun task. Furthermore, with the library, you're stuck playing songs in the order in which Music lists them.

To help you organize your music in groups, use the Music playlist feature. Typically, a *playlist* is a collection of songs from the library, but playlists can also include media such as music videos and audiobooks. You can create as many playlists as you want, and each playlist can contain any number of items. Whereas the Music library lists all available songs, a playlist displays only the items that you add to it. Further, any changes you make in a playlist affect only that playlist, leaving the library untouched.

To create a playlist, you can do any of the following:

- **Choose File ⇨ New ⇨ Playlist.**

- **Press ⌘+N.**

- **Choose File ⇨ New ⇨ Playlist from Selection.** This command creates a playlist and automatically adds the selected tracks.

- **Choose File ⇨ New ⇨ Genius Playlist.** Music builds a playlist of songs that are similar in some way (typically by matching the genre of the selection or the beats per minute). Note that your Neo needs an internet connection to create a Genius playlist. You also need to turn on the Genius feature by choosing File ⇨ Library ⇨ Turn on Genius.

- **Drag a folder containing audio files from a Finder window to the Playlists heading in the sidebar.**

To help organize your playlists, it's a good idea to . . . well, *name* them. (Aren't you glad now that you have this book?) Suppose that you want to plan a party for your polka-loving friends. Instead of running to your Neo after each song to change the music, you could create a polka-only playlist. Start the playlist at the beginning of the party, and you won't have to worry about changing the music the whole night! To load a playlist, select it in the sidebar; Music displays the songs in the playlist.

The same items can appear in any number of playlists because the items in a play-list are simply pointers to the media in your Music library — *not* the actual songs themselves. Add and remove them at will to or from any playlist, secure in the knowledge that the items remain safe in your library. You can remove a selected playlist by pressing Delete.

Removing a playlist doesn't delete any songs from your library.

SOME PLAYLISTS ARE SMARTER THAN OTHERS

You can create a Smart Playlist in the Music sidebar by choosing File ⇨ New Smart Playlist.

The contents of a Smart Playlist are automatically created from a specific set of conditions that you set via the Smart Playlist dialog. You can limit the track selection by mundane things such as album, genre, or artist; or you can get funky and specify songs that were played last, or by the dates when you added tracks, or even by the total length of the song. If you want to add another criterion, click the plus sign on the right side of the dialog to display another condition field.

Select the Live Updating check box for the ultimate in convenience. Music automatically maintains the contents of the Smart Playlist to keep it current with your criteria at all times in the future. (If you remove tracks from a Smart Playlist manually, Music adds other tracks that match your criteria.)

Now think about what all these settings mean when combined. I created a Smart Playlist that selects only songs in the Rock genre. It's limited to 25 songs, selected by least often played, and live updating is turned on. The playlist is named Tracks I've Gotta Hear because it finds the 25 rock songs that I've heard least often! After I listen to a song from this Smart Playlist, Music automatically freshens it with another song, allowing me to catch up on the tracks I've been ignoring.

Knowing Your Songs

Besides organizing your music into Elvis and non-Elvis playlists, Music gives you the option to track your music at song level. Each song you add to the Music library has a set of data associated with it. Music displays this data (see Figure 12-3) on the Details tab of the Info dialog, including:

>> **Title:** The name of the song

>> **Artist:** The name of the artist who performed the song

>> **Album:** The album where the song appears

>> **Album Artist:** The name of the artist responsible for a compilation or tribute album

>> **Composer:** The name of the astute individual who *wrote* the song

>> **Genre:** The classification of the song (such as rock, jazz, or pop)

>> **Year:** The year the artist recorded the song

>> **Track:** The position of the song on the original album

>> **Disc Number:** The original disc number in a multi-CD set

>> **Comments:** A text field that can contain any comments on the song

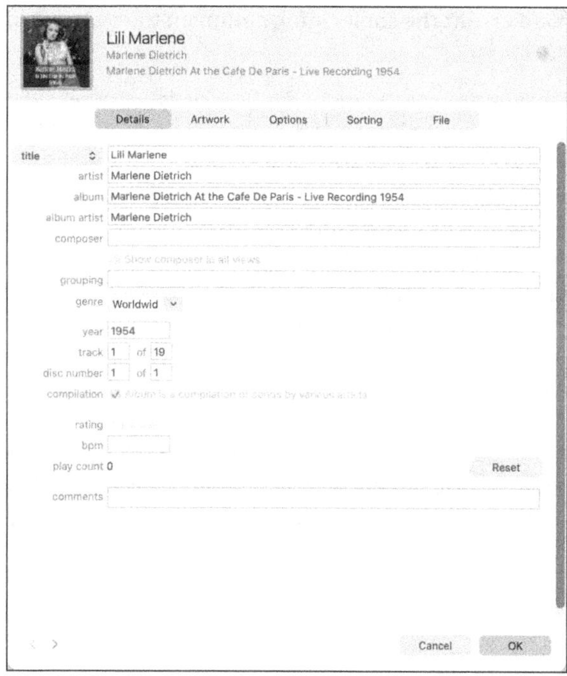

FIGURE 12-3: View and edit song information here.

You can display this information by clicking a song name and pressing ⌘+I. The fields appear on the Details tab.

Adding song information automatically

Each song you add to the Music library may have song data included with it. If you add music from an audio CD, Music connects to the internet and attempts to find the information for each song. If you download a song from the internet, it often comes with some information embedded in the file already; the amount of included data depends on what the creator supplied. (And it's often misspelled as well; think *Leenard Skeenard*.) If you don't have an internet connection, Music displays generic titles instead.

Setting the song information manually

If Music can't find your CD in the online database, or someone gives you an MP3 with incomplete or inaccurate information, you can change the information yourself. Believe me, you want *at least* the artist and song name! To view and change the information for a song, follow these steps:

1. **Select the song in the Song list or a playlist.**

2. **Press ⌘+I, or choose Song ⇨ Info.**

3. **Click a field to edit the song's information on the Details tab (refer to Figure 12-3).**

Move to the next or previous track in the library list or playlist by clicking the Next or Previous button in the bottom-left corner of the Info dialog.

The more work you put into setting the information of the songs in your Music library, the easier it is to browse and use Music. Incomplete song information can make it more difficult to find your songs in a hurry. You don't have to change *all* the information about a song — normally, you can get away with setting only a song's title, artist, and genre — but the more data you add, the faster you can locate songs. Music tries to help by automatically retrieving known song information, but sometimes you have to roll up your sleeves and do a little work.

"What about cover art, Mark?" Well, I'm overjoyed that you asked! If you have an internet connection, Music can try to locate artwork automatically for the tracks you select. (Note that embedding large images can significantly increase the size of the song file.) Follow these steps:

1. **Select the desired songs from the track list.**

2. **Choose File ⇨ Library ⇨ Get Album Artwork.**

Want to add album covers to your song info manually? Select one or more songs in the track list, display the Info dialog, and click the Artwork tab. Now launch Safari, visit Amazon.com and do a search for the same album. Drag the cover image from the web page right into the Info dialog, drop it in the center of the Artwork square, and click OK.

If you've subscribed to Apple Music, you can view the lyrics to many songs while you listen! When the music is playing, click the Lyrics button at the right side of the Music controls (it looks like a speech bubble with two periods inside it). To close the Lyrics window, click the Lyrics button again.

Ripping Audio Files

You don't have to rely on internet downloads or the iTunes Store to get audio files: If you have an external optical drive, you can create your own MP3, AAC, or Apple Lossless files from your audio CDs with Music. The process of converting CD tracks to audio files is called *ripping.* (Audiophiles with technical teeth also call this process *digital extraction,* but they're usually ignored at parties by the popular crowd.)

To rip MP3s from an audio CD using an external DVD drive, follow these steps:

1. **Launch Music by clicking its icon on the Dock.**

   Alternatively, you can locate Music in your Applications folder.

2. **Choose Music ⇨ Settings.**

3. **In the Settings dialog that appears, click the Files tab.**

4. **Click the Import Settings button.**

5. **Choose MP3 Encoder from the Import Using pop-up menu.**

6. **Choose High Quality (160 Kbps) from the Setting pop-up menu, and click OK to return to the Settings dialog; click OK again to return to Music.**

7. **Load an audio CD into your Neo's external optical drive.**

   The CD title shows up in the Source list in the sidebar on the left side of the window. The CD track listing appears on the right side of the window.

If Music asks whether you want to import the contents of the CD into your Music library, you can click Yes and skip the rest of the steps. If you've disabled this prompt or want to import only certain songs, continue with the remaining two steps.

8. **Deselect the check box next to any song you don't want to import.**

   All songs on the CD have a check box next to their title by default. Unmarked songs aren't imported.

9. **Click the Import CD button.**

Tweaking the Audio for Your Ears

Besides the volume controls that I mention earlier in this chapter, Music offers an equalizer. An *equalizer* allows you to alter the volume of various frequencies in your music, allowing you to fine-tune your tunes.

To open the Equalizer, choose Window ⇨ Equalizer or press ⌘+Option+E. Use the leftmost slider (Preamp) to set the overall level of the Equalizer. The remaining sliders represent various frequencies that the human ear can perceive. Setting a slider to a middle position causes that frequency to play back with no change.

Adjust each slider until your music sounds the way you like it. The Music Equalizer also has several predefined settings to match most musical styles. Open the pop-up menu at the top of the Equalizer window to choose a genre. Music saves your settings when you close the Equalizer window.

A New Kind of Radio Station

Besides playing back your favorite audio files, Music can tune in internet radio stations around the globe. You can add your favorite stations to your playlists. You can also subscribe to the Apple Music Radio feature to create a custom station dedicated to the genres and artists you prefer. This section shows you how to do it all.

When choosing an internet radio station, keep your internet connection speed in mind. If you're using a broadband connection — or if you're at work using your company's high-speed network — you can listen to stations broadcasting at 128 Kbps or even higher. The higher the bit rate, the better the music sounds.

DISCOVERING NEW MUSIC WITH HOME

Have you ever wondered what great music lies "just out of reach"? Perhaps a buddy hasn't yet recommended that new band, or there's an album from one of your favorite artists that you don't even know exists! If you're an Apple Music subscriber, just click the Home entry in the sidebar and start exploring. (And no wasting time trying to guess which new artists may appeal to you.)

Let me explain: Home starts with the music and playlists that you've enjoyed in the past, but it actually "learns" your taste in music and mixes! Literally, the more you listen, the better it gets at predicting your musical tastes. (I've been pleasantly surprised by the jazz and techno suggestions that Home has recommended, based on my love of anything from Charlie Parker and Propellerheads.)

Tuning in your own stations

To listen to an internet radio station, you need the station's internet address, or *URL*.

In Music, choose File ⇨ Open Stream URL or press ⌘+U. In the Open Stream dialog that appears, enter the URL of your desired radio station, and click OK. In seconds, Music tunes in your station and adds the station as an item in your Songs list so that you can listen again in the future with a single click.

Radio stations in your playlists

If you find yourself visiting a particular online radio station often, you'll be glad to know that Music supports radio stations in its playlists. To add a radio station to a playlist from your library, follow these steps:

1. **Click the Songs entry in the sidebar and locate the radio station.**

2. **Drag the station entry from the Song list to the desired playlist in the sidebar.**

If you haven't created any playlists yet, see the section "Separating Slim Whitman and Slim Shady: Organizing with Playlists," earlier in this chapter, to find out how.

Creating a custom Music Radio station

Apple Music Radio makes it possible for you to listen to the artists, songs, and genres that you prefer in Music without selecting a specific internet radio station.

To use Apple Music Radio, click the Radio entry below the Apple Music heading in the sidebar. After you've set up your subscription, type the artist name, song name, or genre in the Search field.

Like internet radio, the Apple Music subscription service requires an internet connection — but unlike typical streaming stations, Apple Music also requires an Apple ID.

Your Music Radio station is automatically shared among all your Macs running macOS (as well as any iOS devices you own). In fact, Music is connected closely with the Apple iCloud service. To download a local copy of any iCloud item, simply click the iCloud icon next to the item. After the local copy has been saved to your Mac's drive, the iCloud icon disappears, and you're ready to listen (even without an internet connection).

iSending iStuff to iPhone and iPad

If you own an iPhone or iPad, you probably already know that these devices can act as your personal music player. You can buy all sorts of music and video through the iTunes Store app.

To sync, both your Neo and the device *must* use the same Apple ID.

You connect your iOS device to any Mac or Windows PC that has USB ports by using the included cable. After the device is connected, you can synchronize it with Music. By default, this process is automatic: Your iPhone or iPad and the Music software communicate and figure out what items are in your Music library (as compared with the device's library). If they discover songs, podcasts, and video in your Music library that are missing from your device, the items automatically transfer to the device. Conversely, if the iPhone or iPad contains stuff that's no longer in Music, the device automatically removes those files from its drive.

You can change your settings in the device's Summary pane so that Music auto-syncs only selected playlists. (Click the device icon in the Music sidebar to display the Summary pane; then click the Sync Settings button.) Or, if you're really nervous, you can choose to manage the contents of your device manually, from the Summary pane.

If you'd rather lose the cable connection and sync your device wirelessly, you can first connect with a USB cable and then click the device in any Finder window sidebar. Select the General tab and then enable the Show this Device when on Wi-Fi.

To see your music onscreen, try Music's visuals! Choose Window⇨Visualizer or press ⌘+T. Most of your Music interface disappears, replaced by groovy lava-lamp–style animations. To stop the visuals, press Esc (or press ⌘+T again). The familiar face of Music returns.

You can still control Music with the keyboard while the visuals are zooming around your screen. See Table 12-1, earlier in this chapter, for a rundown on common keyboard shortcuts.

Exercising Parental Authority

Do young children use your Mac? I'll be honest here: A large amount of content in the iTunes Store (including audio, movies and music videos) is stuff I don't consider to be suitable for kids. And what about the media that others in the family may decide to share? Such is the world we live in today, and the good folks at Apple recognize that you may not want to inadvertently allow your kids to have access to explicit content.

Luckily, you can use the Restrictions settings in System Settings to build a secure fence around adult content. Open System Settings and click the Screen Time pane to see the Content & Privacy settings.

To restrict an account, you must log in with the child's username and password. (If you use your administrator account to make changes, you're actually placing Music restrictions on *yourself!*)

After you're logged in to your child's account, follow these steps:

1. **Click the Settings icon on the Dock.**

2. **Click the Screen Time pane in the Settings sidebar.**

3. **Click the Content & Privacy entry.**

4. **Click the Content Restrictions entry, choose App Store, Media, Web, & Games and click the Allow Music & TV Shared Libraries switch to turn it off.**

5. **Click Done.**

   Because Apple maintains separate iTunes Stores for different nations, you can choose which country's iTunes Store to monitor.

6. **To restrict specific content in the iTunes Store, click the Store Restrictions entry.**

   Click the Movies or TV Shows pop-up menu to choose a restriction level.

   Note that these restrictions apply only to content in the iTunes Store, content that can be downloaded through iCloud, and media shared with your Neo.

7. **Click the Allow Explicit Music, Podcasts, and News switch to turn it off.**

8. **Click Done, and then close the Settings dialog to save your changes.**

You can now log out of your child's account.

Watching Video with TV

"But Mark, what about the TV shows and movies you mentioned earlier?" Fear not, good reader. Apple organizes all the video you've bought from the iTunes Store into the separate TV application; full-length movies and TV shows are easy to browse and enjoy on your Neo.

Figure 12-4 illustrates the TV window, which is quite similar to the Music window. (Why mess with perfection?) You'll note the sidebar, which makes it easy to display all your films and TV shows, as well as top movies or TV shows that you can rent or purchase. Some selections are free, but most are pay-to-view. The Library categories, however, display only the video content that you've already purchased, so it's always available.

Wondering what app to launch when you've downloaded a new movie? It's important to consider all your TV shows and movies as content that you'll watch within the TV app. (Apple has decided to retain your music videos within the Music app — somewhat confusing, I know.)

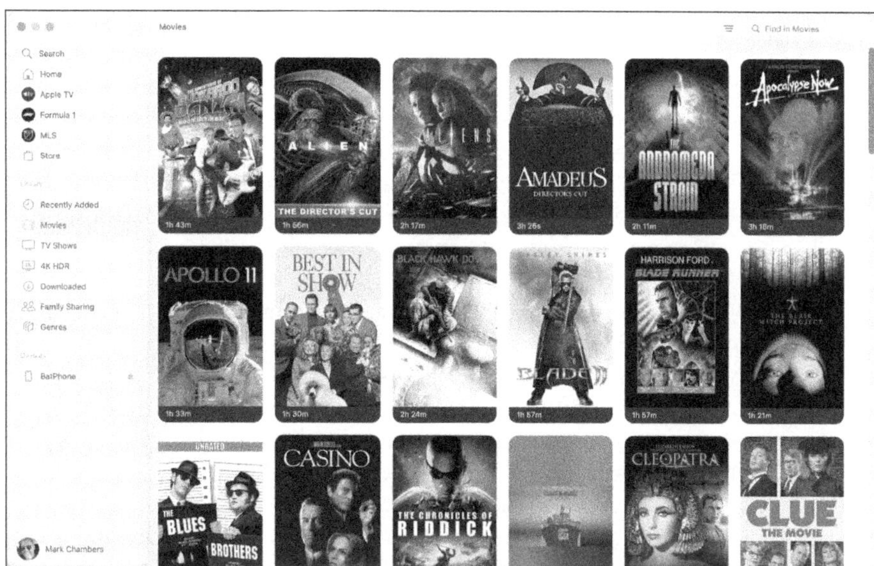

FIGURE 12-4:
My collection of movies appears in TV.

Watching video in TV couldn't be simpler. Click the desired media (or category) in the sidebar. From your collection, you can do the following:

>> Double-click a video thumbnail. If you interrupted a video by quitting TV, the app continues the video at the point where the app was closed.

>> Drag a QuickTime–compatible video clip from the Finder window to the TV window. (These clips typically end in .mov, .mv4, or .mp4.)

TV plays video in full-screen mode. Move your pointer to display the onscreen controls, including a control strip at the bottom of the screen (which sports the standard slider bar that you can drag to move through the video). The volume control occupies the top-right corner, while the familiar Play/Pause, Fast Forward and Reverse buttons occupy the center). Icons at the bottom right allow you to select subtitles if desired. To exit the video, press Esc. Click the Exit Full Screen icon at the top-left corner of the screen to return to a windowed display. Films may display an Extras button, which you can click to view additional content.

Buying Digital Media the Apple Way

The hottest spot on the internet for buying music is the iTunes Store, which you can reach from the cozy confines of Music — that is, as long as you have an internet connection.

Looking to buy TV shows or movies? You'll find them within the TV app.

Click the iTunes Store entry in the Music sidebar, and after a few moments, you see the latest offerings. Click a link in the store list to browse according to media type. The Back button at the top of the iTunes Store window operates much the same as the Back button in Safari, moving you backward in sequence through pages you've already seen.

To display the details on a specific album or track, just click it. If you're interested in buying only certain tracks (for that perfect road-warrior mix), you get to listen to 90 seconds of any track — for free, no less, and at full sound quality. When you're ready to buy, click the Buy button. (At the time of this writing, tracks are usually $1.29 a pop, and an entire album is typically $9.99 to $11.99. What a bargain!)

The iTunes Store uses your Apple ID to identify you, and it keeps secure track of your payment information for future purchases. The tracks and files that you download are saved to a separate category in the sidebar called Recently Added. When the download is finished, you can play them or copy them to playlists, just like songs in your Music library.

Music will automatically download the media you purchase on another iCloud device using the same Apple ID (including another Mac, your iPhone, or your iPad). *Epic* convenience!

Chapter **13**

Focusing on Photos

or decades now, the Mac has been the choice of professional photographers for working with digital images — which is not surprising, considering the Mac's graphical nature (and the incredible quality of Apple displays)! Apple continues this tradition with *Photos,* its photography tool for the home user that can help you organize, edit, and even publish your photographs. After you shoot your best work, you can import your images and video clips into Photos, edit them, and organize them. You're not limited to photos and clips that you take yourself, either; you can use all kinds of digital image files. You can even create a slideshow and share it!

In this chapter, I walk you through an overview of what Photos can do. After that, I give you a brief tour of the controls in Photos so that you can see what features are available to you, including those for managing, printing, and sharing your photos.

Delving into Photos

Figure 13-1 shows most of the major controls Photos offers. (Other controls appear automatically when you enter different modes; I cover them in upcoming sections.)

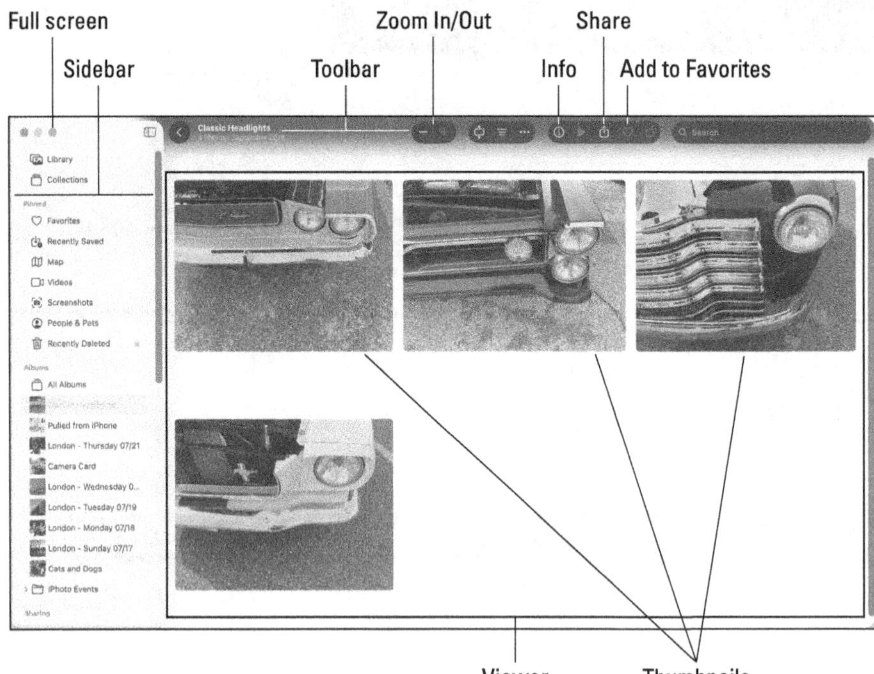

FIGURE 13-1: Photos greets you with an attractive window.

Here's a quick rundown of what you see when you launch Photos, click Library in the Photos window sidebar, and then click the All Photos mode button in the app's toolbar:

>> **Sidebar:** Like Music and Safari, Photos sports a sidebar that displays locations and groupings within the app — photos you've recently imported, for example, or specific photo albums, and slideshows you've created. Switching among your photo library, albums, and projects involves a single click!

>> **Toolbar:** This group of controls determines how many images the Viewer displays and enables you to perform several actions with selected photos. You can display photos by *years* or *months* (which group your photos by when they were taken) or *All Photos* in your library at one time. If the Back button is visible, you can click it to see more images. To zoom in on a specific photo, just double-click the desired thumbnail. To switch among these groupings, click one of the three view buttons on the toolbar or press ⌘+1 through ⌘+3.

>> **Viewer:** This pane displays the images from your Photos library. You can click and drag or ⌘+click to select multiple photos in the Viewer for further tricks, such as assigning keywords and editing images.

>> **Thumbnails:** If you're displaying a single image from your library, you can press Option+S to open and close the Thumbnails pane, where you can quickly switch to another image by clicking the desired thumbnail. (A helpful

feature when you're editing several images taken at around the same time.) Because you're viewing the contents of an album in Figure 13-1 instead of a single image, the Thumbnails pane is hidden.

>> **Full Screen:** Click the Full Screen/Maximize button in the top-left corner of the window (or press Control+⌘+F) to switch to full-screen display of your photos. In full-screen mode, you can double-click a thumbnail to view the image in your Mac's entire screen real estate. (The toolbar is still available at any time: Just move your pointer to the top of the screen to display it.) Press Esc to return to windowed mode.

Choose View ⇨ Always Show Toolbar and Sidebar in Full Screen to prevent the toolbar and sidebar from disappearing in full-screen mode.

>> **Zoom:** Depending on the mode you're using, you can either click the minus button or drag the slider to the left to reduce the size of the thumbnails in the Viewer, displaying more thumbnails at the same time. Click the plus button or drag the slider to the right to expand the size of the thumbnails, making it easier to differentiate details among similar photos. You can also use the Zoom slider when viewing a single image.

>> **Show Thumbnails as Square or Full Aspect Ratio:** This toolbar button bears a box icon with arrows pointing up and down – click it to toggle the thumbnail display between uniform squares (which may not show the entire image) and the full image in reduced size. Full-aspect-ratio format doesn't require any extra space, but some folks prefer uniform squares.

>> **Add To Favorites:** Click the Add to Favorites toolbar button (which bears a heart icon) to add the item(s) currently selected in the Viewer as Favorites. You can search for Favorite photos by using keywords, which are covered in "Organizing with keywords," later in this chapter.

>> **Info:** Click this button to display information on item(s) currently selected in the Viewer.

>> **Share:** Click this button to share the selected photos to your shared iCloud albums on your iPhone, iPad, or to another Mac. You can also add them to a note, attach the photos to a text message, email them, or share them via AirDrop.

>> **Edit:** Here's another button that's displayed on the toolbar only when you view a single image. Click this button to switch to the editing controls within Photos and make changes to the current image. (Note that the Edit button is disabled if you're viewing an image shared by someone else.) I cover editing in depth in "Edit mode: Removing and fixing stuff the right way," later in this chapter.

>> **Rotate Counterclockwise:** This one is pretty self-explanatory: A click rotates the selected image(s) counterclockwise. People find themselves clicking this button often, which is why Apple decided to park it here.

Working with Images in Photos

Even a superbly designed app such as Photos would be overwhelming if everything were jammed into one window. Thus, Apple provides operational modes such as editing and slideshow creation that you can use in Photos window. Each mode allows you to perform different tasks.

In this section, I discuss three of these modes: import, organize, and edit.

Import images 101

In *import* mode, you're ready to download images and video clips directly from your digital camera — and you're not limited to cameras, of course. You can also import items from a folder on your internal drive, a memory-card reader such as the SDXC card slot, an iOS device, a smartphone, or an external USB drive.

If your photos are stored on your iPhone or iPad, you don't need a physical cable connection to import your images — after you enable the iCloud Photos feature, those images are automatically available within Photos! I describe this shamelessly convenient importing at the end of this chapter.

REMEMBER

Follow these steps to import images directly from your camera or device:

1. **Connect your device to your Neo.**

   Plug one end of a USB cable into your device and the other end into your MacBook's USB-C port.

2. **Prepare your device to download files.**

   The procedure for downloading images and video varies by camera or device, but the process usually involves turning the device on and choosing a Download or PC mode. Check your device's user guide for more details.

3. **Launch Photos.**

   Your Neo may launch Photos automatically, but you can launch Photos manually by clicking the Photos icon on the Dock.

4. **Select the device in the sidebar.**

   Photos displays all the images and video clips currently stored on your device in the Viewer.

5. **Click the Album To drop-down menu and choose a destination for the imported files.**

   You can choose an existing album, create a new album, or simply add the imported photos to your library.

   To delete the original images from the device after you import them, click the Delete Items After Import check box to enable it.

6. **Click the Import All New Items button to import all new files from the device.**

   To select specific images to import, hold down the ⌘ key and click each desired photo; then click Import Selected instead of Import All New Photos.

   The images and clips initially appear within the Imports album in your Photos library, where you can organize them as you want.

Note that Photos automatically groups imported images and video by the year, month, and date when the files were created, if your device stores this information with each file. If you want to see photos from your graduation, for example, those photos appear in each view by that date.

IMPORTING IMAGES FROM YOUR DRIVE

Adding items stored on your internal drive, an external drive, or a USB flash drive is easy. If the images and clips are in a folder, just drag that folder from a Finder window and drop it into the Viewer. You can even drag items directly to the Photos icon on the Dock. Photos automatically creates a new album with the folder name, and you can sit back while the images are imported into that new album.

If you have individual images, you can drag them as well. Select the images in a Finder window and drag them into the desired album in the sidebar's Albums list. To add them to the album currently displayed in the Viewer, drag the selected photos and drop them in the Viewer instead.

If you'd rather import images by using the Open dialog, choose File ➪ Import. Simplicity strikes again!

Organize mode: Organizing and sorting your images

In the days of film prints, you could always stuff another shoebox with your latest photos or buy another sticky-backed album to expand your library. These days Photos can keep your entire collection of digital photographs and scanned images well-ordered and easy to retrieve!

A new kind of photo album

The most familiar method of organizing images in Photos is the *album.* Each album can represent any designation you like, be it your pets, a vacation, your daughter, or her ex-boyfriends. Follow these steps:

1. **Create a new album.**

   You can choose File ⇨ New Album or press ⌘+N. If you've selected any item thumbnails in the Viewer, they're added to the new album automatically.

2. **Type the name of your new photo album in the Untitled Album text box in the sidebar.**

3. **Press Return.**

You can copy selected items from the Viewer into any album you choose by dragging them from the Viewer to the desired album entry in the sidebar.

Memories are automated slideshows that Photos creates based on images taken on a specific day or at a specific location. You'll also see memories based on the type of photos, like Portraits. Click the Collections entry in the sidebar, and then double-click a Memories thumbnail to start the show! To exit a memory, press the Esc key.

Photos also offers a special type of album called a *Smart Album,* which you can create from the File menu. (For even faster action, press ⌘+Option+N.) If you're familiar with the Smart Folders that you can use within the Finder and the Smart Playlists within Music (see Chapter 12), you've figured this one out already. A *Smart Album* contains only photos that match certain criteria you choose, including the keywords you assign your images. Photos *automatically* builds and maintains Smart Albums for you. It adds new photos that match the criteria and deletes those you remove from your Photo Library. Smart Album icons carry a gear symbol in the Photos sidebar.

You can display (or edit) information about any photo or video clip by right-clicking the thumbnail and choosing Get Info from the shortcut menu. Click the Add a Title heading in the Info dialog to type a new value, or type a short description in the Add a Caption box.

To remove a photo or video clip that has fallen out of favor, right-click the offending thumbnail and choose Delete. You can remove an entire album by right-clicking the album in the sidebar and choosing Delete Album.

When you remove a photo or clip from an album, you don't remove the actual file from your collection (represented by the All Photos button on the toolbar or the Library entry at the top of the sidebar). An album is just a group of links to the images in your Photos library, just as a playlist in Music is a group of links to songs in your Music library. If you want to remove an offending photo, click the All Photos button at the top of the sidebar to display your entire library of photos and clips, and delete the item there. The item disappears from all albums with which it's associated.

To rename an album in the sidebar, click the entry below the Albums heading in the list to select it, and click again to display a text box. Type the new album name and press Return.

Change your mind? Photos comes with a handy-dandy Undo feature. Just press ⌘+Z, and it's as though your last action never happened.

Working with People & Pets

Photos includes a powerful organizational tool called People & Pets, which appears as a separate item within the sidebar.

People is a sophisticated recognition system that automatically recognizes human *and pet* faces within the photos you add to your Photos library. Naturally, you have to identify — or *tag* — faces before Photos can recognize them.

To tag a face, follow these steps:

1. **In the Viewer, double-click the photo with a person or pet you want to tag and click that person's face.**

   Note that Photos indicates each individual face in the photo with a circle. If a face has already been tagged, the label (which appears when you hover your pointer over the icon) matches the face. Images shared from others using the iCloud Sharing feature (which shows a tiny speech bubble icon in the lower-left corner) cannot be tagged.

To set Photos to always show labels in the Viewer — so that you don't have to click the Add Faces link — choose View ⇨ Show Face Names.

2. **Click the *unnamed* label below the face to open a text box.**

3. **Type the name of this person or pet and press Return.**

   If the name appears on a Contacts contact card — or is recognized as an existing People & Pets name or as one of your Facebook friends — you can click the matching entry that appears to confirm the identity.

Photos might not recognize the face if the subject is turned at an angle to the camera or is in a darker area of the photo. If so, display the Info dialog and click the Add Faces button (which bears a plus sign) to display a "floating" circular outline. Click the outline and drag the circle over the face. You can resize the box by dragging the handle on the right side of the circle. Finally, click the *Click to Name* label and type the person's name.

After you tag an image, it appears in your People & Pets collection, which you can view by clicking the People & Pets entry in the sidebar. You can double-click a portrait in your People & Pets collection to see all the images that contain that person or pet.

Organizing with keywords

"Okay, Mark, albums and People & Pets are great ideas, but there has to be a way to search my library by category!" you say. Never fear, good Neo owner. You can also assign descriptive *keywords* to items to help organize your library and locate certain pictures and video clips fast. Photos comes with several standard keywords, and you can create your own as well.

To illustrate, suppose you'd like to identify your images according to special events in your family. Birthday photos have their own keyword — by assigning that keyword, you can search for photos from Elsie's birthday party (no matter what collection or album they're in)!

Photos includes these keywords:

>> Favorite

>> Family

>> Kids

>> Vacation

>> Birthday

>> Flagged

>> Check mark

TIP

What's the check mark about, you ask? It's a special case: The check-mark keyword comes in handy for temporarily identifying specific items, because you can search for only your check-marked photos and clips.

To assign keywords to images (or to remove keywords that have already been assigned), select one or more photos in the Viewer. Then choose Window⇨ Keyword Manager or press ⌘+K to display the Keyword Manager window, shown in Figure 13-2.

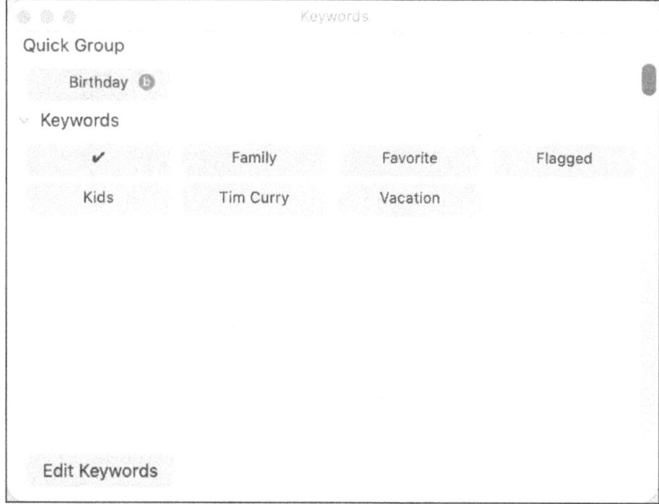

FIGURE 13-2:
Add keywords to
selected images.

TIP

Drag the keyword buttons that you use most to the Quick Group section of the Keyword Manager window, and Photos automatically creates a keyboard shortcut for each keyword in the Quick Group. Now you don't even need to display the Keywords window to get business done!

Click the buttons for the keywords you want to attach to selected images to mark them, or click the highlighted buttons for the keywords you want to remove from the selected items.

YOU NEED YOUR OWN KEYWORDS

I bet you take photos and video clips of things other than kids and vacations. That's why Photos allows you to create your own keywords. Display the Photos Keyword Manager window by pressing ⌘+K, clicking the Edit Keywords button, and then clicking Add (the button with the plus sign). Photos adds a new, unnamed keyword to the list as an edit box, ready for you to type its name.

You can rename an existing keyword in this same window, too. Click a keyword to select it and then click Rename. Remember, however, that renaming a keyword affects *all the images that were tagged with that keyword.* To be safe, I recommend applying a new keyword and deleting the old one.

To change the keyboard shortcut assigned to a keyword as well, click the keyword to select it and then click the Shortcut button. While you're editing keywords, you can also remove an existing keyword from the list by clicking the keyword to select it and then clicking the Delete button (which bears a minus sign). When your keywords are picture-perfect (pun grudgingly intended), click OK to save them and return to the Keyword Manager window.

Digging through your library with keywords

Behold the power of keywords! To sift through your entire Library of images by using keywords, click the Search button on the toolbar in the top-right section of the Photos window and type one or more keywords. To see all the items you've flagged as Favorites that include kids, for example, type **Favorite Kids**.

The images that remain in the Viewer after a search must have *all* the keywords you specified. If an image is identified by only three of four keywords you chose, for example, it isn't a match and doesn't appear in the Viewer.

To search for a photo by words in its caption, just click the search box and start typing. You can search your images by date and rating as well.

Searching by locations where photos were taken

Photos can also track the location where photos were taken automatically, but this feature requires a digital camera or device that includes GPS tracking information in the image metadata for Photos to do so without your help. (Naturally, today's iPhones and iPads support this feature.) You don't have to turn anything on to view photos by location.

When you're viewing photos by Memories, you'll notice that Photos often includes the location name to identify where the photos were taken. To search for all images taken at a specific location, type the location name in the Search field.

If you right-click a specific photo (that includes location information) to select it and then choose Get Info from the shortcut menu, you see a close-up map of the location where the photo was taken.

Edit mode: Removing and fixing stuff the right way

Not every digital image is perfect; just look at my collection if you need proof. For shots that need a pixel massage, Photos includes editing tools that can correct common problems.

The first step in any editing job is selecting the image you want to fix. (Double-click a thumbnail in the Viewer so that it fills the screen.) Then click the Edit button on the Photos toolbar to display the Edit-mode controls on the right side of the window, as shown in Figure 13-3. Now you can fix problems using the tools I discuss in the rest of this section.

FIGURE 13-3:
Photos is now in Edit mode. Watch out, image problems!

REMEMBER

If you display a video clip in the Viewer, you can play it by hovering your pointer over the clip and clicking the Play button that appears, and a subset of video-editing controls appear when you enter Edit mode.

TIP

While you're editing, you can click the thumbnail images in the strip at the bottom of the window to move between images. If you prefer to edit images while using more of your screen real estate, click the Full Screen/Maximize button in the top-left corner of the Photos window. To switch back to the standard window arrangement, simply press the Esc key.

Finished editing? Click the Done button again to return to the Viewer.

Rotating tipped-over shots

If an image is in the wrong orientation and needs to be turned to display correctly, click the Rotate button to turn it once counterclockwise. Hold down the Option key while you click the Rotate button to rotate clockwise.

Crop 'til you drop (and a whole lot more)

Does that photo have an intruder hovering around the edges of the subject? You can remove some of the border by *cropping* an item, removing unwanted portions from the edges of an image or video. (A great way to get Uncle Milton's stray head out of an otherwise-perfect holiday snapshot.)

From Edit mode, follow these steps to crop, flip, and straighten an item:

1. **Click the Crop button at the top of the window.**

2. **Select the portion of the image that you want to keep.**

   In the Viewer, click and drag the right-angle handles at the corners of the rectangle to outline the part of the image you want. Whatever is outside this rectangle disappears when the crop is complete.

TIP

   When you drag a corner or edge of the outline, a semi-opaque grid appears to help you visualize what you're claiming.

   You can expand the outline to the image's full dimensions at any time by clicking the Reset button in the bottom-right corner.

   See that attractive-looking Auto button that appears in the bottom-right corner of the Photos window when you're in Crop mode? A single click of the Auto button causes Photos to take its best shot at producing the ideal cropping and straightening job for you! If you don't like the results, use the Undo feature (⌘+Z) to return the image to its original state.

REMEMBER

   Photos features multiple Undo levels, so you can press ⌘+Z several times to travel back through your past several changes. Alternatively, you can return the image to its original form (before you did any editing at all) by clicking the Reset Adjustments button.

3. **(Optional) Choose a preset aspect ratio.**

   You might want to force your cropped selection to a specific aspect ratio, such as 4x3 or 16x9 for a widescreen desktop background, or 4x6 or 5x7 to match the dimensions of photo paper. If so, choose the desired aspect ratio on the right side of the window, under the Aspect heading (available only while cropping). Pick the Square selection for the perfect Facebook profile image or the Freeform selection to allow any aspect ratio.

4. **(Optional) Flip your photo or video horizontally.**

   Text on your T-shirt reversed? Not in Photos! A click of the Flip item gives you the mirror image of your original photo.

5. **(Optional) Straightening what's crooked.**

   Was your camera slightly tilted when you took the perfect shot? Click Straighten, Vertical, or Horizontal and drag in the desired direction. (Try some truly wild camera angles, just like in the '60s *Batman* TV series!)

6. **Click the Done button.**

Enhancing images to add pizzazz

If a photo looks washed out, click the Auto Enhance button to increase (or decrease) the color saturation and improve the contrast. (The toolbar button sports a magic-wand icon.) Auto Enhance is automatic, so you don't have to set anything — but be prepared to use Undo if necessary!

Removing rampant red eye

Unfortunately, today's digital cameras and devices can still produce the same "zombies with red eyeballs" as traditional film cameras did. *Red eye* can occur with both humans and animals.

Photos can remove that red eye (or green eye) and turn frightening zombies back into your family and friends. In Edit mode, click the Adjust button at the top of the window and click the Auto button next to the Red-Eye item on the right side of the screen. Photos automatically attempts to remove any red-eye effect that it detects in the photo, and a check mark appears next to the Red-Eye item to indicate that a change was made.

Retouching like the pros

The Photos Retouch feature is perfect for removing minor flecks or lines in an image (especially those you've scanned from prints). Click the Clean Up button in the toolbar, and then drag the Size slider under the Retouch header to specify the size of the retouch tool. Now hover your pointer over the photo to display the circular retouch tool. Drag the pointer across the imperfection and click Done when you finish touching up.

Using filters and adjustments to add a mood

Wonder whether a particular photo or video in your library would look better in black and white *(grayscale)*? Click the Filters button at the top of the window to display a list of effects that you can apply to the item, including black-and-white effects, enhanced color levels, and subtle shading. Click any thumbnail in the strip to apply the filter.

If you'd like more precise manual control of your image attributes — including sharpness, color levels, shadows, definition, and white balance — click the Adjust button at the top of the window and explore the lengthy array of options. Note that each of the adjustments offers an Auto button, and you can click the disclosure triangle to the left of each entry to display additional controls that create a different look.

I REALLY NEED A SLIDESHOW

You can use Photos to create slideshows by following these steps:

1. **Right-click the desired album in the sidebar and choose Create ⇨ Slideshow ⇨ Photos from the shortcut menu.**

2. **Type the name of the slideshow in the text box and press Return.**

   Photos adds a new entry below Projects in the sidebar, and a scrolling thumbnail strip appears at the bottom of the Viewer, displaying the images in the album.

3. **Click and drag the thumbnails to appear in the desired order.**

After arranging your images, you can customize your slideshow with the three controls on the right side of the Photos window:

- **Themes:** Click the Theme Picker button to choose the theme for your slideshow. The theme you choose controls the animation, transition type, and screen layout that Photos uses — everything from the classic Ken Burns "moving photo" animation to a nifty Sliding Panels layout.

- **Music:** Click the Music button to display Apple's theme music as well as the tracks from your Music library. To choose a standard theme, click the drop-down list box under the Music Library heading and choose Theme Songs; then click that perfect song to select it. To choose songs from your Music library, click the drop-down list box and choose Music, then click the songs you want in the order in which you want them.

- **Duration:** Click the Duration Settings button and you can choose to fit the display of images to the length of the music you've chosen or set individual timings for the selected slide thumbnails. If you want your slideshow to loop when it finishes, click the Loop icon near the bottom-right corner of the Viewer (which carries two curved arrows) to toggle it on.

To display a preview of your slideshow without leaving the Photos window, click the Preview button at the bottom-left corner of the Viewer. This button is a handy way to determine whether the theme and music you've selected are really what you want. When you're ready to play your slideshow, click the Play button that appears below the Viewer; Photos switches to full-screen mode. To create a movie file from your completed slideshow, click Export on the Photos toolbar.

Note that you can also play the contents of an album immediately in a slideshow by right-clicking the desired album and choosing Play Sideshow. However, you can't save one of these "quick and dirty" slideshows as a project, and you can't set durations or timings.

Exploring iCloud Photos

Yes, Apple has decided that everything except the kitchen sink should be stored online in iCloud, including your photographs and video clips! To turn the iCloud Photos feature on, choose Photos ⇨ Settings, click the iCloud tab, and click the iCloud Photos check box to enable it.

With iCloud Photos, your *entire* Photos library is stored online, and everything in your library is accessible from other Macs and iOS devices. (Think "central storage for everything visual that you can reach from anywhere with an internet connection.") If you take a photo with your iPhone, for example, it appears automatically within Photos. And if you recently edited a photo to perfection with Photos, you'll be able to retrieve that edited photo on any of your iOS devices or another Mac.

On the same iCloud pane in the Settings dialog, you can choose to:

>> Download copies of the full-resolution images and videos on your Neo's drive, which allows you to edit or view the originals even when you're not connected to the internet.

>> Store smaller images and smaller-resolution videos on your Neo (with the capability to retrieve the originals from the iCloud at any time when you're connected to the internet).

Naturally, if you're a photographer who needs constant, instant access to your original images, choose the Download Originals to this Mac option. If your Neo's drive is nearly full, however, and you'd like to conserve space, choose the Optimize Mac Storage option on the iCloud tab.

All this goodness is handled automatically, but there's a catch: Your *entire* Photos library needs to fit within your free 5GB of iCloud storage; otherwise, you'll have to pay a monthly subscription to get additional elbow room! (Storage subscriptions range from 99 cents a month for 50GB of space to $59.99 a month for a whopping 12TB of space.) If you have only 3GB of photos, you may be able to use iCloud Photos without spending any extra, but because my Photos Library is nearing 10GB, I needed to subscribe to take advantage of the feature. The choice is yours, dear reader.

Putting iCloud Shared Albums to Work

You can choose to share specific photos by using iCloud Shared Albums. Choose Photos ⇨ Settings, click the iCloud tab on the toolbar of the Settings dialog, and select the Shared Albums check box.

To subscribe to a shared-album invitation from another person, right-click the desired shared album in the sidebar and choose Accept.

To create your own shared album, select the images you want to share, click the Share button on the toolbar, select the Shared Albums item, and click the New Shared Album button. Photos prompts you for the album name and the email addresses of the folks you want to invite to your shared album. After you enter each email address, click the Create button at the bottom of the sheet to start the ball rolling. You can also add or delete items from your shared album in the same way that you would with a regular Photos album. Apple, you absolutely *rock!*

Creating an iCloud Link on the Web

If you're using iCloud Photos and you've enabled web access to iCloud, macOS Tahoe provides you with yet another way to share your images and video with others: the iCloud Link feature.

In order to use iCloud.com with Safari, you must enable the Access iCloud Data on the Web switch, which you'll find on the iCloud pane in System Settings. (Visit Chapter 4 for coverage of your iCloud settings.)

After you've connected to iCloud.com, sign in to your iCloud account and click the Photos tile. The online version of Photos shares many of the same sidebar entries as the Photos app, including Favorites and Albums. Click the desired entry in the sidebar and select the items you want to share, holding down the ⌘ key while clicking to select multiple items. Once you're finished, hover your pointer over any selected thumbnail and click the icon with the three dots that appears; then click Share.

There are two methods of sending an iCloud Link:

>> **Choose Email Link to send the link via an email message.** If you've set up an iCloud email account, iCloud.com opens the online version of Mail and

creates a new message for you, complete with a title and the link embedded in the text of the message! All you have to do is enter one or more recipients, using either the person's full email address or any names you select from your Contacts. After you've addressed the message, you can add more text if you like, or just click the bold blue arrow!

>> **Click Copy Link to display the link in a dialog.** Click Copy Link and you're ready to paste the link text anywhere you like that accepts text (perhaps a Message, or even a Pages or Numbers document).

For security, your iCloud Link will automatically expire after 30 days.

5

Getting Productive and Maintaining Your Neo

Chapter **14**

Desktop Publishing with Pages

What's the difference between word processing and desktop publishing? In a nutshell, it's in how you design your document. Most folks use a word processor like an old-fashioned typewriter, much like I'm using the Mac version of Microsoft Word right now. (Yawn.)

A *desktop publishing application* allows far more creativity in choosing where to place text, how to align graphics, and how to format all the elements in your document. I think desktop publishing is more visual and intuitive, allowing your imagination a free hand in creating a document.

In this chapter, I show you how to use your Neo to set your inner designer free from the tedious constraints of word processing. Whether you need a simple letter or a stunning brochure, Pages can handle the job easily, and you'll be surprised by how simple it is to use. Plus, Pages is a *free* download for your Neo (and free Apple software is always A Good Thing).

Creating a New Pages Document

To create a new Pages document, follow these steps:

1. **Click the Pages icon on the Dock.**

   If the Pages icon doesn't appear on your Dock, press ⌘+spacebar to display the Spotlight search box; then type *Pages* and press Return. If your Neo doesn't currently have the three Apple productivity applications installed — Pages, Numbers, and Keynote — click the App Store icon on your Dock and download them for free!

2. **Click the New Document button in the Open dialog.**

   Pages displays the Choose a Template window.

   You can also create a new Pages document at any time. Just choose File ➪ New to display the Choose a Template window.

3. **In the sidebar on the left, click the type of document to create.**

   The thumbnails on the right are updated with templates that match your choice. Note that templates in the Premium category require a monthly subscription to Apple's Creator Studio.

4. **Click the template that most closely matches your needs.**

   To start with a blank page, choose the Blank template.

5. **Click the Create button to open a new document that uses the template you selected.**

Opening an Existing Pages Document

You can always open a Pages document from a Finder window, of course. Just double-click the document icon. You can also open a Pages document from within the program. Follow these steps:

1. **Launch Pages as described in the preceding section.**

2. **Press ⌘+O to display the Open dialog.**

   To open a document you've already saved in your iCloud Drive, click the Pages item below the iCloud heading in the sidebar and double-click the desired document thumbnail. To open a document on your drive or network, click the desired location in the Open dialog sidebar.

3. **Click the desired drive under the Locations heading in the sidebar and click folders and subfolders until you locate the Pages document.**

   You can also click the search box in the top-right corner of the Open dialog and type a portion of the document's name or its contents.

4. **Double-click the thumbnail (or filename) to load it.**

   If you want to open a Pages document you've edited in the recent past, choose File ⇨ Open Recent and click the document.

REMEMBER

Pages can open documents created in Microsoft Word — however, documents created using some of the advanced formatting capabilities of Word (like macros) may not import properly into Pages. If this occurs, Pages displays a message alerting you that some content has changed.

Saving Your Work

Pages fully supports Tahoe's Auto-Save feature, but you may feel the need to save your work manually after you finish a significant edit (or if you need to take a break). If you're editing a document that's already been saved at least once, press ⌘+S. A new version of the document is saved in its current location and you can continue with your work.

If you're working on a new document that hasn't been saved, follow these steps to save it:

1. **With the Pages document open, press ⌘+S.**

2. **Type a filename for your new document.**

3. **Open the Where pop-up menu and choose a location in which to save the document.**

   Note that Pages defaults to your iCloud Drive as the target location. This way, you can open and edit your Pages document on any Mac or iOS device that uses the same Apple ID.

4. **Click Save.**

REMEMBER

To revert the current document to an older version, choose File ⇨ Revert To. Pages gives you the option of reverting to the last saved version, or click Browse All Versions to choose among multiple versions.

Touring the Pages Window

Before you dive into any real work, let me show you around the Pages window. You'll find the following major components and controls, as shown in Figure 14-1:

- » **Pages list:** This thumbnail sidebar displays all the pages you've created within your document. You can switch instantly among different pages in your document by clicking the desired thumbnail in the list. If the sidebar isn't visible, click the View button at the left end of the Pages toolbar and then click Page Thumbnails.

- » **Layout pane:** This section takes up most of the Pages window. It's where you design and edit each page in your document.

- » **Toolbar:** Yep, Pages has its own toolbar. It keeps all the most common application controls within easy, one-click reach.

- » **Inspector:** This extension allows you to quickly switch the appearance of selected paragraphs, characters, and lists (in Format mode) or to specify settings that affect the entire document (in Document mode). You can hide and display the Inspector from the View menu.

FIGURE 14-1:
The major points of interest in the Pages window.

Entering and Editing Text

If you've used a modern word processing program, you'll feel right at home typing within Pages. The bar-shaped text pointer, which looks like a capital letter *I*, indicates where the text you enter will appear in a Pages document. To enter text, simply begin typing. To edit existing text in your Pages document, select and highlight the text. As you type, Pages replaces the existing text. You can delete text by clicking and dragging across the characters to highlight them and then pressing Delete.

Using Text, Shapes, and Graphics Boxes

Within Pages, you'll quickly learn that text, shapes, and graphics appear in *boxes*, which you can resize by clicking and dragging one of the handles that appear around the edges of the box. (Click the box to select it and then hover the pointer over one of the square handles. The handle changes to a double-headed arrow, indicating that Pages is ready to resize the box.)

You can also move a box, including all the stuff it contains, to another location within the Layout pane. Click in the center of the box and then drag the box to the desired spot. Pages displays yellow alignment lines to help you align the box with other elements around it (or with regular divisions of the page, such as the vertical center of a flyer).

To select text or graphics within a box, you must first click the box to select it and then double-click the desired line of text or the graphic.

REMEMBER

The Three Amigos: Cut, Copy, and Paste

"Hang on, Mark. You've covered moving stuff, but what if you want to *copy* a block of text or a photo to a second location? Or how about cutting something from a document that's open in another app?" Good questions. That's when you can call on the power of the cut, copy, and paste features within Pages. The next few sections explain these actions.

Cutting stuff

Cutting selected text, shapes, or graphics removes them from your Pages document and places that material on your Clipboard. (The *Clipboard* is a holding area for sections of existing text and graphics you want to manipulate.) To cut, select some material and then choose Edit ➪ Cut or press ⌘+X.

Copying text and images

When you *copy* text, shapes, or graphics, the original selection remains untouched and a copy is placed on the Clipboard. Select some material and choose Edit ➪ Copy or press ⌘+C. You can also hold down the Option key while you drag the items to their destination.

If you cut or copy a new selection to the Clipboard, it erases what was there. (The Clipboard holds only the latest material you cut or copied.)

Pasting from the Clipboard

Wondering what you can do with the stuff that's stored on the Clipboard? *Pasting* the contents of the Clipboard places the material at the current location of the insertion pointer. You must paste the contents before you cut or copy again to avoid losing what's on the Clipboard.

To paste the Clipboard contents, click the insertion pointer at the location you want and choose Edit ➪ Paste or press ⌘+V.

Formatting Text the Easy Way

If you feel that some (or all) of the text in your Pages document needs a facelift, you can format that text any way you like. Formatting lets you change the color, font family, character size, and attributes as necessary.

After the text is selected, you can apply basic formatting in two ways:

>> **Use the Inspector.** The Inspector appears on the right side of the Pages window (refer to Figure14-1) — click the Format button on the right end of the toolbar, which looks like a tiny paintbrush, to display and hide the Inspector. The controls it displays vary according to the selection you've made, as well as which of the three tabs you've selected at the top of the Inspector. After you've selected the desired text, click the Text tab at the top of the Inspector; then click to select a font control and click your choice from the pop-up menu that appears. You can select characteristics, such as the text's paragraph style, or choose italic or bold. In addition, the Text tab provides buttons for vertical and horizontal text alignment.

>> **Use the Format menu.** Most controls displayed within the Format section of the Inspector are also available from the Format menu. Click Format and hover the pointer over the Font menu item to apply boldface, italics, and underlining to the selected text, or make the text bigger or smaller.

Adding a Spiffy Table

In the world of word processing, a *table* is a grid that holds text, shapes, and graphics for easy comparison. You can create a custom table layout within Pages with a few simple clicks.

Follow these steps:

1. **Click the insertion pointer at the location where you want the table to appear.**

2. **Click the Table button on the Pages toolbar.**

   Pages displays thumbnail images of table styles, some including colors and highlights. Click the left and right arrow icons to display different thumbnails until you find the one that's closest to the table you need.

   You can tweak the layout by selecting the table and displaying the Format Inspector, where you can fine-tune font, color, grid, and border options.

3. **Click the style thumbnail to insert the table.**

   To add or delete rows or columns directly from the table, select it and then click the row and column buttons that appear. (Each button bears two horizontal or vertical lines.) You can change the number by clicking the up or down arrows that appear.

4. **Click within a cell in the table to enter text.**

   The table cell automatically resizes and wraps the text you enter to fit.

   You can paste material from the Clipboard into a table. See the earlier section "Pasting from the Clipboard" for details.

REMEMBER

Here are a few pointers on dressing up your table and making its data more attractive and readable:

>> **Change the borders on a selected cell.** Click the Format icon on the toolbar, click the Cell tab, and then click the desired Border button.

Select a range of cells in a table by holding down Shift as you click. Hold down ⌘ and click to select multiple cells that aren't contiguous.

>> **Add a background color or image to selected cells.** Click the Cell tab, click the Fill section in the Inspector, and choose a type of background.

Adding Alluring Photos

You can choose one of two methods of adding a picture within your Pages document:

>> **As a floating object:** You place the image in a particular spot, and it doesn't move even if you make changes to the text. To add a floating object, drag an image file from a Finder window and place it at the spot you want within your document. (Alternatively, if you're an Apple Creator Studio subscriber, you can click the Content button on the toolbar, click Photos, and select a high-quality stock image from the Content Hub.)

Note that a floating object (such as a shape or image) can be sent to the background, where text doesn't wrap around it. To bring back a background object as a regular floating object, click the object to select it and then choose Arrange ⇨ Bring to Front. (More about background shapes in the next section.)

>> **As an inline object:** The image flows with the surrounding text as you make layout changes. To add an inline object, hold down the ⌘ key as you drag an image file from a Finder window and place it where you want within your document, or use the Content Hub if you're a subscriber.

To resize an image object, click the image to select it and drag one of the selection handles that appear along its border. (The handles look like tiny squares.) The side-selection handles drag only that edge of the frame. The corner-selection handles resize both adjoining edges of the selection frame. Hold down the Shift key to keep the image proportions fixed.

You can even create your own original images using Apple Intelligence, but it requires a subscription to Apple Creator Studio. From within the Content Hub window, click the Generate Image button (or click the Create an Image button). You can define the new image based on a text description, or you can use an existing image. You can also open the Image Playground app directly from the Insert menu! (More on Image Playground in Chapter 13.)

Adding a Background Shape

To add a shape (such as a rectangle or circle) as a background for your text, follow these steps:

1. **Click the insertion pointer in the location you want.**

2. **Click the Shape button on the Pages toolbar and choose a shape.**

   The shape appears in your document.

3. **Click the center of the shape and drag it to a new spot.**

   Shapes can be resized or moved in the same manner as image boxes. See the preceding section.

You can type over a shape set as a background. Before you do, though, select the shape and then choose Arrange ⇨ Send to Back.

If you've created a shape that you'd like to reuse in other documents, you can right-click that shape and choose Save to My Shapes; then type a memorable name for the shape.

Adding 3D Objects

No, you won't need 3D glasses to see 3D objects (or *models*) in your document! If you have a file containing a 3D model in USDA, USDC, or USDZ format, you can simply drag the file from a Finder window and drop it in the desired location.

Have you noticed that snazzy Rotate button that appears in the center of a 3D object? (It looks like two intersecting circles.) Click and drag the Rotate button, and you can actually rotate the 3D object to the desired angle! Okay, this is just *neat.*

Some 3D objects even have animation! If your 3D model includes animation, you'll see the familiar Play button appear at the lower-right corner of the object box. Click it to play the animation.

Are You Sure about That Spelling?

Pages can check spelling as you type (the default setting) or after you complete your document. If you find automatic spell-checking to be distracting, you should pick the latter method.

As my editor reminds me, spell-checking only confirms that a word matches an entry in the Pages dictionary, *not* that it's the right word for the job! If you've ever "red" what someone else "rote," you understand.

To check spelling as you type, follow these steps:

1. **Click the Edit menu and hover the pointer over the Spelling and Grammar menu item.**

2. **Choose Check Spelling While Typing from the submenu that appears.**

   If a possible misspelling is found, Pages underlines the word with a red dashed line.

3. **Right-click the word to choose a possible correct spelling from the list, or choose Ignore Spelling if it's spelled correctly.**

   To turn off automatic spell-checking, click the Check Spelling While Typing menu item again to deselect it.

To check spelling manually, follow these steps:

1. **Click to place the insertion pointer where the check should begin.**

2. **Click Edit, hover the pointer over the Spelling and Grammar menu item, and choose Check Document Now.**

3. **Right-click any possible misspellings and choose the correct spelling or choose Ignore Spelling if the word is spelled correctly.**

Don't Forget Apple Intelligence

Pages allows you to tap into Apple Intelligence using Writing Tools! To display the toolbox, you need to first select the text you want to polish or rewrite, and then click the Edit menu and hover the pointer over the Writing Tools menu item. From this submenu, you can invoke the power of AI to proofread text, change the tone of your writing, summarize a block of text, or even turn it into a list.

As a starting point, choose Show Writing Tools from the submenu. In the sheet that appears, click in the Describe Your Change box and type a task you'd like Pages to perform, such as *Shorten This Paragraph* or *Add Facts and Dates,* and then press Return. Shazam! Pages produces a list of suggestions on improving your original text. To accept a suggestion, click it and watch the magic happen!

You'll notice that you can also access a number of specific tasks directly, either from the sheet or from the Writing Tools submenu. These include proofreading, changing the tone of selected text (Friendly, Professional, or Concise), summarizing text, or building a list from the selected text.

But what if you want to replace text completely? Choose Compose from the Writing Tools sheet and Pages will prompt you for a description of the message you want to express. Using your description, Pages displays suggestions outlining the text it will create. Click the suggestion that's closest to your idea to replace the selected text with new original text!

Printing Your Pages Documents

Ready to start the presses? You can print your Pages document on real paper, of course, but don't forget that you can also save a tree by creating an electronic PDF instead! You'll find the PDF drop-down menu at the bottom of the standard Tahoe Print dialog; click it and choose Save As PDF.

To print your Pages document on old-fashioned paper, follow these steps:

1. **Within Pages, choose File ⇨ Print.**

   Pages displays the Print sheet.

2. **Click the Copies field and enter the number of copies you need.**

3. **Select the pages to print:**

   - **To print the entire document,** select All Pages.

   - **To print selected pages,** select Selection and click the desired pages in the sidebar.

   - **To print a range of pages,** select the Range From radio button and enter the starting and ending pages.

4. **Click the Print button to send the document to your printer.**

Sharing That Poster with Others

Besides printing (which is, after all, so *very* passé these days), you can choose to share your Pages document electronically after you've saved it via the internet or your network:

>> **Send a Copy:** To send a copy of the actual document (which the recipient can open in Pages on their own Mac or iOS device), choose File ⇨ Share from the Pages menu (or click the Share button on the toolbar), click the pop-up menu at the top of the dialog, and click the Send Copy item. You can send the document via Mail, Notes, Messages or AirDrop.

If you decide to send your Pages document as an mail attachment, don't forget that most internet service providers have a maximum message size. If your document is too large, your mail server probably will reject it.

>> **Export:** You're not limited to sharing over that internet thing! Pages can also export your work directly to your drive in one of seven formats: a PDF file, a Word document, an ePub file (for use with electronic book apps such as Books), a series of images (one per page, in the format you select), a document that's compatible with the 2009 version of Pages, a Rich Text Format document, and even plain text. Choose File ⇨ Export To and pick your format; Pages displays any options you can set for that format. When you're ready, click Save and select the location where Pages should save the file. Click Export and then sit back!

If the recipient of your document doesn't need to edit your work, I recommend creating a PDF file, which keeps your document as close as possible to the way it appears in Pages.

IN THIS CHAPTER

» Navigating Numbers

» Opening and saving spreadsheets

» Selecting cells and editing data

» Creating simple calculations

» Adding charts to your spreadsheets

» Putting Apple Intelligence to work

» Printing a Numbers spreadsheet

Chapter **15**

Creating Spreadsheets with Numbers

Are you downright afraid of spreadsheets? Does the idea of building a budget with charts and all sorts of fancy graphics send you running for the safety of the hall closet? Well, Apple has again taken something most of us consider to be super complex and turned it into something for normal human beings! (Much as Apple did with video editing and songwriting.) And Numbers is a free download from the App Store, to boot!

In this chapter, I demonstrate how the Numbers spreadsheet program can help you organize and analyze data for your important decisions — everything from an auto comparison to your company's sales statistics!

Before You Launch Numbers . . .

Are you unfamiliar with apps such as Numbers and Microsoft Excel — and their documents? Let me provide you a little background information.

A *spreadsheet* organizes and calculates data by using a grid system of rows and columns. The intersection of each row and column is a box called a *cell*, which can hold text or numeric values. Cells can also hold calculations called *formulas*, which usually act upon the contents of surrounding cells.

Spreadsheets are wonderful tools for making decisions and comparisons because they let you plug in different numbers — such as interest rates or your monthly insurance premium — and instantly see the results.

REMEMBER

Numbers can open, edit, and save documents created with Excel, but spreadsheets created with some advanced Excel features will not import properly, and Numbers will alert you if this happens. (The simpler the Excel document, the more likely it will open properly.) Numbers can also open a CSV (or *comma-separated values*) data file, which uses plain text.

Creating a New Numbers Document

Numbers ships with a selection of templates you can modify quickly to create a new spreadsheet. After a few modifications, you can easily edit the Budget and Mortgage templates to create your own spreadsheets.

To create a spreadsheet project file, follow these steps:

1. **Press ⌘+spacebar to open the Spotlight search box.**

2. Type *Numbers* into the Search box and press Return.

3. **Click the New Document button in the bottom-left corner of the Open dialog.**

   Numbers displays the Choose a Template window. (Note that you must subscribe to Apple Creator Studio to use the Premium templates.)

4. **In the sidebar on the left, select the document type to create.**

   The thumbnails in the center are updated with matching templates.

5. **Click the template thumbnail that most closely matches your needs.**

6. **Click the Create button to open a new document using that template.**

Opening an Existing Spreadsheet File

If you see an existing Numbers document in a Finder window (or you find it by using Spotlight), double-click the document icon to open it. It's equally easy to open a Numbers document from within the app. Follow these steps:

1. **Open your Applications folder in a Finder window and double-click the Numbers icon to run the app.**

2. **Press ⌘+O to display the Open dialog.**

   As a MacBook Neo power user running macOS Tahoe, you can save and load Numbers documents directly to and from your iCloud Drive. If the spreadsheet is stored in your iCloud Drive, click the Numbers folder below the iCloud heading in the sidebar on the left side of the dialog and then double-click the desired document thumbnail.

3. **If the document is stored in your Neo's drive, on your network, or in a Favorites location, click the drive or folder in the sidebar.**

4. **Drill down through folders and subfolders until you locate the desired Numbers document.**

   If you're unsure where the document is, click the search box at the top of the Open dialog and type a portion of the document name or even a word or two of text that it contains.

5. **Double-click the spreadsheet icon or filename to load it.**

If you want to open a spreadsheet you've been working on, choose File ➪ Open Recent to display documents that you've saved recently.

Save Those Spreadsheets!

Thanks to the Auto-Save feature in Tahoe, you need not fear losing work because of a power failure. But if you're not a huge fan of retyping data, *period*, you can always save your documents manually. Follow these steps to save your spreadsheet to your iCloud drive or your internal drive:

1. **Press ⌘+S.**

   If the document hasn't yet been saved, the Save As sheet appears.

2. **Type a filename for your new spreadsheet.**

3. **Open the Where pop-up menu and choose a location for the file.**

   Common locations are your iCloud Drive, Desktop, and Documents folder.

   If the location you want isn't listed in the Where pop-up menu, click the down-arrow button next to the Save As text box to display the full Save As dialog. Alternatively, type the folder name in the Spotlight search box in the top-right corner, and double-click the desired folder.

4. **Click Save.**

After you save a Numbers document for the first time, you can create a version of that document by choosing File ➪ Save. To revert to an older version of the current document, choose File ➪ Revert To. You can revert to the last saved version or click Browse All Versions to look through multiple versions of the document.

Exploring the Numbers Window

Apple has done a great job of minimizing the complexity of the Numbers window. Figure 15-1 illustrates these major points of interest:

>> **Sheets tabs:** Because a Numbers project can contain multiple spreadsheets, they're displayed in the Sheets tabbed bar at the top of the window. To switch among spreadsheets in a project, click the desired tab.

>> **Sheet canvas:** Numbers displays the rows and columns of your spreadsheet in this section of the window; you enter and edit cell values within the sheet canvas.

>> **Toolbar:** The Numbers toolbar sports the most common commands.

>> **Inspector:** Located on the right side of the Numbers window, the Inspector displays editing controls for the object that's currently selected. (If you enter an equal sign [=] in a cell to create a formula, the Inspector displays the Function list, where you specify a calculation for the cell.)

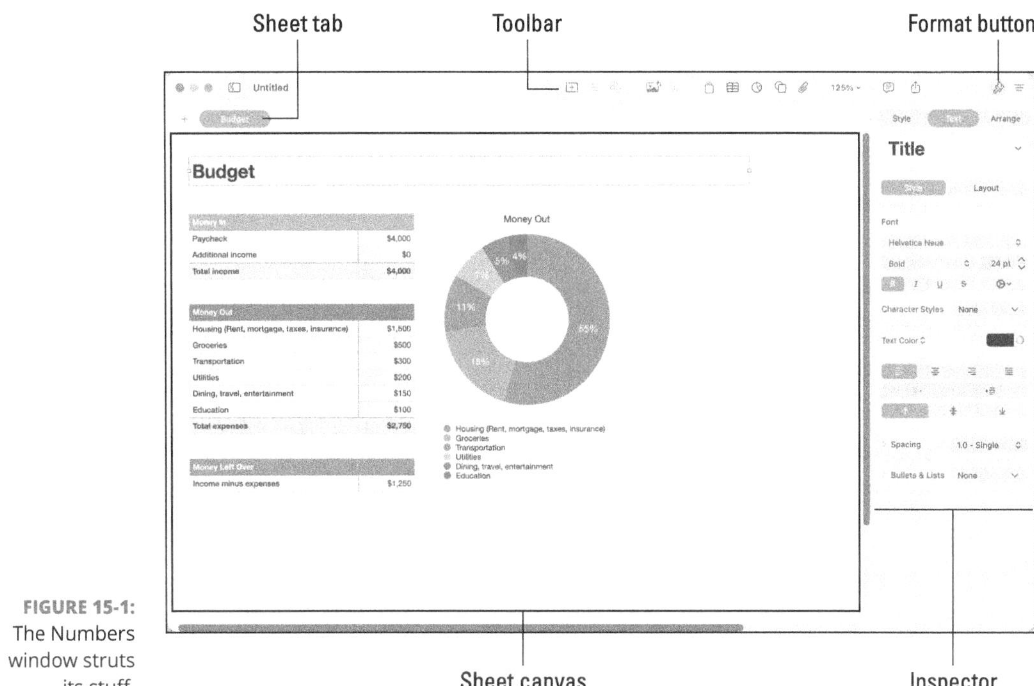

FIGURE 15-1:
The Numbers
window struts
its stuff.

Sheet canvas

Inspector

Navigating and Selecting Cells in a Spreadsheet

You can use the scroll bars to move around in your spreadsheet, but when you enter cell data, moving your fingers from the keyboard is a hassle. Numbers has various handy shortcut keys, as shown in Table 15-1. Commit these keys to memory and your productivity will shoot straight to the top!

You can also use the mouse or trackpad to select cells in a spreadsheet:

>> To select a *single* cell, click it.

>> To select a *range* of adjacent cells, click a cell in any corner of the range you want and drag in the direction you want.

>> To select a *column* of cells, click the alphabetic heading button at the top of the column.

>> To select a *row* of cells, click the numeric heading button at the far-left end of the row.

Movement Shortcut Keys in Numbers

Key or Key Combination	Where the Pointer Moves
Left arrow (←)	One cell to the left
Right arrow (→)	One cell to the right
Up arrow (↑)	One cell up
Down arrow (↓)	One cell down
Return	One cell down (also works within a selection)
Tab	One cell to the right (also works within a selection)
Shift+Return	One cell up (also works within a selection)
Shift+Tab	One cell to the left (also works within a selection)

Entering and Editing Data

After you navigate to the cell in which you want to enter data, you're ready to type. Follow these steps to enter That Important Stuff:

1. **Click the cell or press the spacebar.**

   A pointer appears, indicating that the cell is ready to hold the data.

2. **Type your data.**

   Spreadsheets can use both numbers and alphabetic characters within a cell; either type of information is considered to be data.

   REMEMBER

3. **When you're ready to move on, press Return (to move one cell down) or press Tab (to move one cell to the right).**

Made a mistake? No big deal:

>> **To edit data:** Click the cell that contains the error to select the cell, then click the cell again to display the insertion pointer. Drag the insertion pointer across the characters to highlight them, and type the correct data.

>> **To delete characters:** Select the cell, highlight the characters, and press Delete.

You can quickly step backward through changes you've made by using the Undo command. Press ⌘+Z or choose Edit ⇨ Undo.

Selecting a Number Format

After you enter your data in a cell, row, or column, you may need to format it so that it appears correctly — you may want certain cells to display a specific *type* of number, such as a dollar amount, percentage, or date. Numbers gives you a healthy selection of number-formatting choices.

If your spreadsheet contains units of currency, such as dollars, format it as such. When you enter the numbers, the currency formatting is applied automatically. To specify a number format, follow these steps:

1. **Select the cells, rows, or columns you want to format.**

2. **Click the Format button at the right of the toolbar to display the Inspector. (Refer to Figure 15-1.)**

3. **Click the Cell tab in the Inspector.**

4. **From the Data Format pop-up menu, choose the type of formatting you want to apply, as shown in Figure 15-2.**

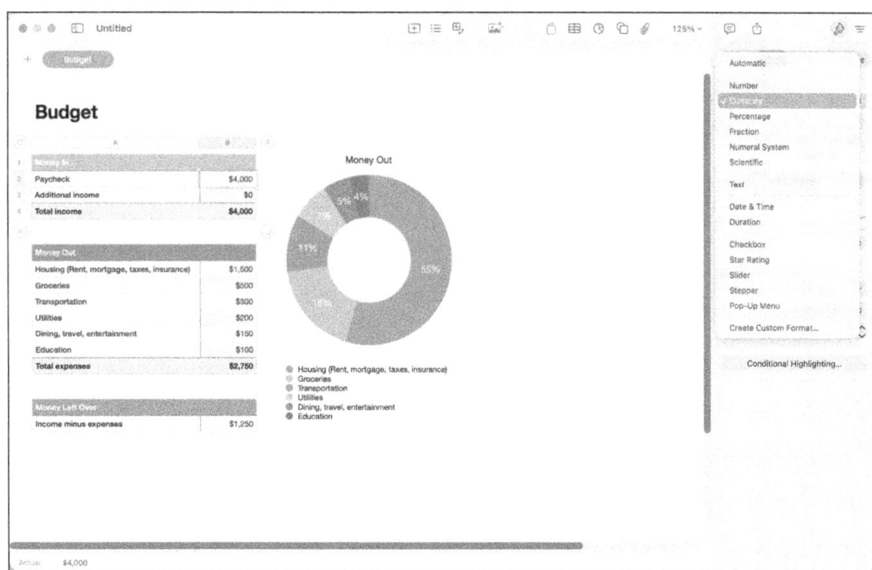

FIGURE 15-2:
In the Inspector, you can format the data you've entered.

Aligning Cell Text Just So

You can also change the alignment of text in the selected cells, which can make a big difference in readability for titles and "crowded" data that's packed into close columns. The default alignments are flush left for text and flush right for numeric data. Follow these steps:

1. **Select the cells, rows, or columns you want to format.**

   See the earlier section "Navigating and Selecting Cells in a Spreadsheet" for tips on selecting stuff.

2. **Click the Format toolbar button.**

3. **Click the Text tab of the Inspector.**

4. **Click the corresponding Alignment button to choose the type of formatting you want to apply.**

   You can choose left, right, center, and justified text under the Text Color section. Click the buttons in the second strip to specify the left and right indent levels for text. Text can be aligned at the top, center, or bottom of a cell using the third strip of buttons.

Do you need to set apart the contents of some cells, perhaps to create text headings or to highlight totals? Select the cells, rows, or columns you want to format; then click the Font Family, Font Size, or Font Color button on the Text tab.

Formatting with Shading

Shading the contents of a cell, row, or column is helpful when your spreadsheet contains subtotals or logical divisions. Follow these steps to shade cells, rows, or columns:

1. **Select the cells, rows, or columns you want to format.**

2. **Click the Format toolbar button.**

3. **Click the Cell tab of the Inspector.**

4. **Click the arrow next to the Fill heading and choose a shading option.**

5. **Click the color box to select a color for your shading.**

   Numbers displays a color picker wheel.

6. **Click at the desired spot within the wheel to select a color.**

7. **Once you've made your choice, click the color box again.**

You can add a custom border to selected cells, rows, and columns from the Cell tab. Use the fields under the Border heading to select the right border.

Inserting and Deleting Rows and Columns

What's that? You forgot to add a row, and now you're three pages into your data entry? No problem. You can easily add — or delete — rows and columns. First, select the row or column adjacent to where you want to insert (or delete) a row or column, and do one of the following:

» **For a row:** Right-click a row header and choose Add Row Above, Add Row Below, or Delete Row from the shortcut menu that appears.

» **For a column:** Right-click a column header and choose Add Column Before, Add Column After, or Delete Column from the shortcut menu that appears.

The Formula Is Your Friend

It's time to talk *formulas*, which are equations that calculate values based on the contents of cells you specify in your spreadsheet. If you designate cell A1 (the cell in column A at row 1) to hold your yearly salary and cell B1 to hold the number 12, you can divide the contents of cell A1 by cell B1 (to calculate your monthly salary) by typing this formula in any other cell:

    = A1/B1

Formulas in Numbers always start with an equal sign and may include one or more functions as well. A *function* is a preset calculation that will be performed, such as figuring the sum or average of a series of cells.

"So what's the big deal, Mark? Why not use a calculator?" Sure, you could. But maybe you want to calculate your *weekly* salary. You can simply change the contents of cell B1 to 52, and — boom! — the spreadsheet is updated to display your weekly salary.

That's a simple example, of course, but it demonstrates the basics of formulas (and the reason that spreadsheets are *the* app for predicting and forecasting). It's the what-if tool for those who work with numeric data.

To add a simple formula within a spreadsheet, follow these steps:

1. **Select the cell that will hold the result of your calculation.**

2. **Type = (the equal sign).**

   The Formula box appears within the confines of the cell.

3. **Click the Format button on the Numbers toolbar to display the available functions in the Inspector.**

4. **Click the category of calculation you want from the list at the top.**

   Instead of scrolling through the entire library, it's easier to choose a category — such as Financial for your budget spreadsheet — to filter the selections. (Alternatively, click the search box and type a function name.)

   To display more information about a specific function, click it in the list.

5. **After you select the perfect function in the right column, click the Insert Function button.**

   The function appears in the Formula box, along with any arguments it requires. The term *argument* refers to a value specified in a cell that a formula uses. The SUM formula, for example, adds the contents of each cell you specify to produce a total; each of those cell values is an argument.

6. **Click an argument button in the formula and click the cell that contains the corresponding data.**

   Numbers automatically adds the cell you indicated to the formula.

7. **Repeat Step 6 for each argument in the formula.**

8. **When you finish, click the Accept button — the green check mark — to add the formula to the cell.**

That's it! Your formula is ready to work behind the scenes, doing math for you so that the correct numbers appear in the cell you specified.

Adding Visual Punch with a Chart

Sometimes you just have to see something to believe it, so it can help to use the data you've added to a spreadsheet to generate a professional-looking chart. After you've entered the data you want to chart, follow these steps:

TIP

1. **Select the adjacent cells you want to chart by dragging.**

   For cells that *aren't* adjacent, hold down the ⌘ key as you click.

2. **Click the Chart button on the Numbers toolbar.**

   The Chart button bears the symbol of a pie chart.

   Numbers displays a thumbnail menu illustrating the different types of charts you can add. To display the different categories of charts, click one of the three tabs at the top (2D/3D/Interactive). You can scroll the menu to reveal more thumbnails by clicking the left- and right-arrow buttons.

3. **Click the thumbnail for the chart type you want.**

   Numbers inserts the chart as an object within your spreadsheet so that you can move the chart. You can drag by using the handles that appear on the outside of the object box to resize your chart.

   With your chart selected, click the Format button to display the Inspector and the controls you can use to customize your chart's appearance. You can change colors and add (or remove) the title and legend, for example.

4. **To change the default title, click the title box to select it; click it again to edit the text.**

Adding Images and 3D Objects

The first rudimentary spreadsheet programs I used — back in the early '90s — had no option to include images, much less 3D graphics! After all, why would you want an *image* in that businesslike spreadsheet?

Today's spreadsheets, of course, have evolved to feature all sorts of graphic finery, and Numbers is ready to accommodate your image, from a company logo to a video clip, or even a 3D animated model. Simply drag an image file from a Finder window and drop it into your worksheet.

If you subscribe to the Apple Creator Studio, use the Content Hub to select from a collection of images, clip art, backgrounds, and shapes.

You can also insert an image from your Photos library. Follow these steps:

1. **Click the insertion pointer in the cell you want.**

2. **Click the Insert button on the Numbers toolbar (it bears a paper clip icon) and click Choose Photos or Videos.**

3. **Numbers displays the contents of your Photos library. Double-click the desired thumbnail.**

Need to relocate the image within the worksheet? Click the center of the image object and drag it to a new spot. To resize an image, click the image to select it and drag one of the square selection handles that appear along its border. If you want to maintain the original proportions of the image, hold down the Shift key while you resize.

Typically, you'll want to move the image to the background so that the contents of your cells are visible. Select the shape and then choose Arrange ⇨ Send to Back.

You add 3D objects in a similar fashion by dragging the object file from a Finder window. Rotate 3D objects to the desired angle by clicking and dragging the Rotate button in the center of the object. (You can't miss it; it looks like two intersecting circles.) If your 3D model includes animation, click the Play button at the corner of the object to set things in motion!

Using the Writing Tools

The Numbers Edit menu includes a Writing Tools submenu that takes advantage of Apple Intelligence to help you refine, summarize, and proofread text in your Numbers document. To get started, select the desired text, and then click Edit ⇨ Writing Tools ⇨ Show Writing Tools to display the sheet you see in Figure 15-3.

Click in the Describe Your Change box and type the task you'd like to accomplish, like **Make it easier to see** or **Summarize this to a shorter length**; then press Return. Numbers calls on the ChatGPT engine that's built in to macOS Tahoe to provide you with suggestions on what to do. Click a suggestion to implement it! (Note that you generally don't need an active connection to the internet to use Writing Tools.)

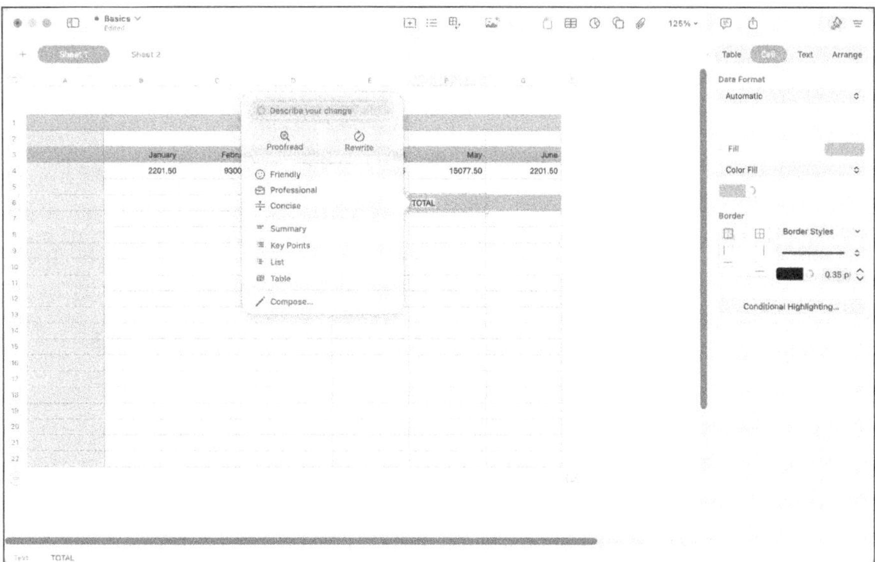

FIGURE 15-3:
Use Apple
Intelligence to
improve text in
your Numbers
document.

TIP

If you have a specific Writing Tools chore in mind, you can choose many functions directly from the sheet, like proofreading text, rewriting text in a specific tone (Friendly, Professional or Concise), summarizing the selected text, or creating a list from the selected text. You can also choose these functions from the Writing Tools submenu to save time.

If you choose Compose, ChatGPT will prompt you for a description of the information you want to convey, and it will provide suggestions for the format and content of the new text. Click the suggestion you prefer, and watch as your Neo replaces the selected text with the new wording!

Printing Your Spreadsheet

You can easily send a Numbers spreadsheet to a USB or shared network printer. Follow these steps:

1. **Choose File ⇨ Print from the Numbers menu bar.**

   Because a Numbers document can contain multiple spreadsheets, you can select a specific spreadsheet to print (click it in the grid and then select the Print This Sheet radio button), or you can print all spreadsheets in the document (select the Print All Sheets radio button).

<ol start="2">
<li>Click the desired page orientation.</li>
</ol>

Spreadsheets with a large number of columns are usually printed in landscape orientation. You can also scale the spreadsheet so that it fits on the page by clicking the Fit button (next to the Content Scale slider).

<ol start="3">
<li>Click Print at the bottom of the window.</li>
</ol>

Numbers displays the Print dialog. (If you'd rather create an electronic copy of the document as an Adobe PDF file, you can click the PDF button.)

<ol start="4">
<li>Click the Copies field and enter the number of copies you need.</li>
<li>Select the pages to print:</li>
</ol>

- **To print the entire spreadsheet,** select All.

- **To print a range of selected pages,** select the From radio button and enter the starting and ending pages.

<ol start="6">
<li>Click the Print button to send the document to your printer.</li>
</ol>

Would you rather share your Numbers document electronically? Click the Share button on the toolbar and choose Send Copy from the drop-down menu to share your spreadsheet masterpiece. You can choose to send the copy via Mail, Messages, Notes, or AirDrop.

IN THIS CHAPTER

» Creating, opening, and saving a presentation

» Navigating Keynote

» Working with slides

» Using Apple Intelligence

» Adding notes, media, and shapes

» Putting together a slideshow

» Printing slides and notes

Chapter **16**

Building Presentations with Keynote

It seems like only yesterday that I was giving business presentations with a clunky overhead projector and black-and-white acetate transparencies. Fancy color gradients and animation were unheard-of, and the only sound my presentations made was the droning of the projector's fan. I might as well have been using tree bark and chalk.

Thank goodness those "cave painting" days are gone. Keynote is the app Steve Jobs once used for his *Macworld* keynote addresses. So much visual candy is available that you'll never need to shout to wake your audience. Even better, this jewel of an app is a free download from the App Store!

In this chapter, I first demonstrate how simple it is to build a stunning Keynote presentation. Then I show you how to start and control your slide display from your Neo's keyboard (or even your iPhone or iPad). And don't forget that you can print your slides and notes so that your audience can keep a copy of your brilliant work.

Creating a New Keynote Project

Keynote begins the document-creation process with a Theme Chooser window. To create a new presentation project, follow these steps:

1. **Double-click your drive icon on your Desktop and double-click the Applications folder.**

2. **Double-click the Keynote icon, which looks like a lectern.**

3. **Click the New Document button.**

   The Choose a Theme window appears. (I have to say that these stylish templates are probably the most stunning visual building blocks I've ever seen in a presentation application.)

4. **Choose the aspect ratio, using either the Standard or Wide drop-down list box at the top of the window.**

   Although you don't necessarily need to select an exact match for your Neo's screen resolution, it's a good idea to select the value closest to your projector's maximum resolution. If someone else is providing the projector, Standard size is the more compatible choice. If you'll present on a typical high-resolution computer monitor (or a 16:9 format projector), Widescreen provides a better display.

   Nothing's stopping you from creating *two* documents of the same presentation: one in Standard and one in Wide. Be prepared!

5. **Click the theme thumbnail that most closely matches your needs.**

6. **Click the Create button to open a new document with that theme.**

Opening a Keynote Presentation

If an existing Keynote presentation appears in a Finder window, you can double-click the document icon to open the project. If Keynote is already running, follow these steps to load a project from within the application:

1. **Press ⌘+O to display the Open dialog.**

2. **Click the desired location in the sidebar; then click folders and subfolders until you locate the Keynote project.**

   If the project is stored in your iCloud Drive, click the iCloud item in the sidebar on the left side of the dialog and double-click the Keynote folder; then double-click the desired project thumbnail.

   Oh, and don't forget that you can use the search box at the top of the Open dialog to locate the document by name or by its contents.

3. **Double-click the filename to load it.**

If you want to open a Keynote document you've edited in the recent past, things get even easier! Just choose File ⇨ Open Recent, and you can open the document with a single click on the submenu that appears.

Keynote can open, edit, and save documents created with PowerPoint. However, PowerPoint includes advanced features not found in Keynote, so not everything will import properly. If changes have to be made to a PowerPoint presentation in order to open it, Keynote will alert you.

Saving Your Presentation

Keynote supports Auto-Save in macOS, so saving your work often isn't as critical as it used to be. If you're cautious, though, follow these steps:

1. **Press ⌘+S.**

   If you're saving a document that hasn't yet been saved, the familiar Save As sheet appears.

2. **Type a filename for your new document.**

3. **From the Where pop-up menu, choose a location.**

   By default, Keynote saves the project directly to your iCloud Drive (iCloud appears on the Where pop-up menu), making it available to other Macs and iOS devices that use the same Apple ID.

4. **Click Save.**

You can create a version of a Keynote presentation by choosing File ➪ Save. To revert the current presentation to an older version, choose File ➪ Revert To. Keynote gives you the option of reverting to the last saved version, or click Browse All Versions to revert to any saved version.

Putting Keynote to Work

Ready for the 5-cent tour of the Keynote window? Launch the app and create or load a project to see the tourist attractions shown in Figure 16-1:

>> **Slides list:** Use this thumbnail list of all the slides in your project to navigate quickly. Click a thumbnail to switch instantly to that slide.

   The Slides list can also display your project in outline format, allowing you to check all your discussion points. To display the outline, choose View ➪ Outline. While you're in outline mode, you can jump directly to any slide by clicking the slide's title in the outline. Switch back to the default Slides list view by choosing View ➪ Navigator.

>> **Layout pane:** Your slide appears in its entirety in this pane. You can add elements and edit the content of the slide from the Layout pane.

>> **Toolbar:** The Keynote toolbar makes it easy to find the most common controls you'll use while designing and editing your slides. Clicking an icon on the toolbar performs an action, just as choosing a menu item does.

>> **Presenter Notes pane:** Add notes to slides for your own use or to print as additional information for your audience! Choose View ➪ Show Presenter Notes to open the Notes pane at the bottom of the window.

>> **Inspector:** Keynote displays this pane on the right side of the window when you click the Format button (shown in Figure 16-1), allowing you to format the current slide, selected text, or a selected image.

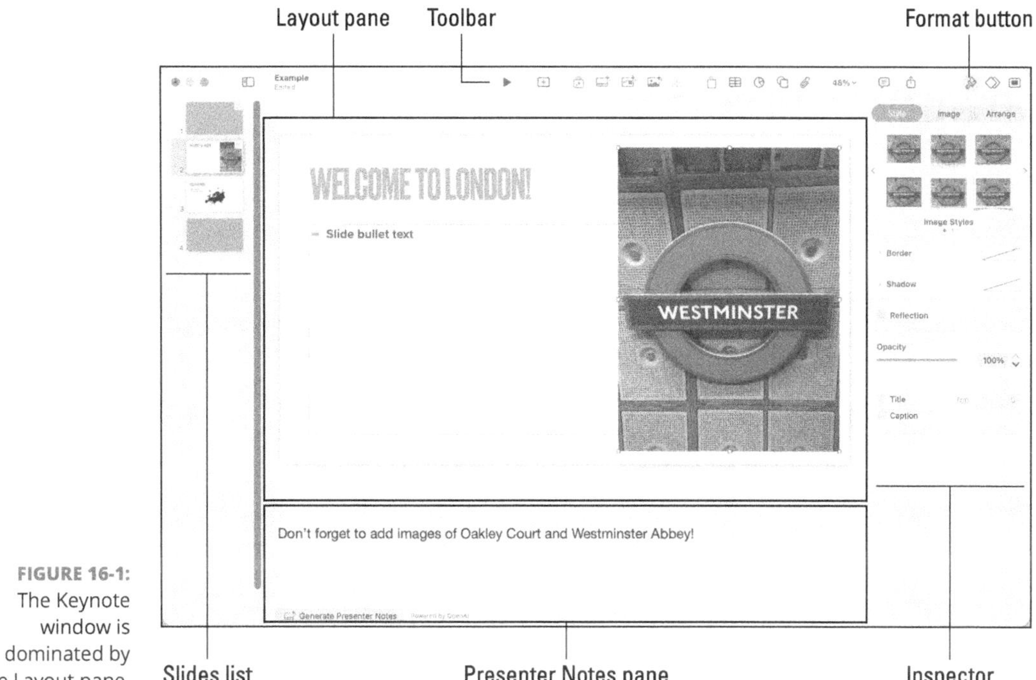

FIGURE 16-1:
The Keynote window is dominated by the Layout pane.

Adding Slides

Keynote creates a single title slide when you create a project. But not many presentations are complete with just a single slide! To add more slides to your project, click the Add Slide button on the toolbar. (Alternatively, you can Choose Slide ⇨ New Slide or press ⌘+Shift+N.) Keynote adds the new slide to your Slides list and automatically switches to the new slide in the Layout pane.

Need a slide that's very similar to a slide you've already designed? Right-click the existing slide and choose Duplicate to create a new slide just like it. (Consider this procedure to be cloning without the science.)

TIP

To move slides to different positions in the Slides list (changing their order in the presentation), drag a thumbnail to the desired spot in the list.

Working with Text, Shapes, and Graphics Boxes

All the text, shapes, and graphics placeholders on a slide appear within *boxes*. Keynote uses these boxes to control text, shapes, and graphics. You can resize a box and its contents by clicking the box and dragging one of the handles that appear around the edges. (The pointer turns into a double-sided arrow when you're "in the zone" — the right spot on the screen, that is, although you might be feeling in the zone yourself!) Side selection handles drag only the edge of the frame, whereas corner selection handles resize both adjoining edges of the selection frame.

Boxes make it easy to move text, shapes, and graphics together (as a single unit) to another location within the Layout pane. Click the center of the box and drag the box to the desired spot. Keynote displays alignment lines to help you align the box with other elements around it (or with regular divisions of the slide, such as horizontal center).

Click a box to select a box. To select the contents of a box (see the next section, "Adding and Editing Slide Text"), double-click the box.

When you resize a photo in a box, hold down the Shift key while you drag to preserve the image's aspect ratio so that the vertical and horizontal proportions remain fixed (to avoid it looking "squished" or "stretched"). To delete an image, click it to select it and then press the Delete key.

Adding and Editing Slide Text

You can add or edit text in Keynote with ease. Suppose that you have a box with the placeholder text `Double-click to edit`. Just double-click that box, and the placeholder text disappears, leaving the field ready for new text. Any new text you type appears at the blinking pointer within the box.

Here are some additional ways to work with slide text:

>> **Add a new text box.** Click the Text button in the Keynote toolbar, and click one of the sample styles. Your new text box appears in the slide.

» **Edit existing text.** Click — using the bar-shaped pointer to select just the right spot in the text — and drag the insertion pointer across the characters to highlight them. Then type the replacement text. Keynote obligingly replaces the old text with the new text.

» **Delete text.** Click and drag across the characters to highlight them; then press Delete. You can also delete an entire box and all its contents: Right-click the offending box, and choose Delete from the shortcut menu.

When a box's contents are just right, and you're finished with the text, click anywhere outside the box. You can click the text again to display the box later.

Perfecting Your Text with Writing Tools

Apple has included a suite of functions called Writing Tools that use artificial intelligence to assist you with the text in your slides. You can effortlessly change the tone of text on a slide, proofread or summarize the existing text, or turn text into a list of key points. (If you use short lists as much as I do in my presentations, that's welcome news!)

The first step is to select the text you want to tweak, and then click the Edit menu and hover the pointer over the Writing Tools submenu. If you're new to Writing Tools, choose Show Writing Tools. Click in the Describe Your Change box and type a task you'd like the app to perform, such as **Create a bulleted list** or **Summarize in a single sentence**; then press Return. Keynote displays a number of suggestions to accomplish the task. To accept a suggestion, click it. Talk about easy!

If you're familiar with Writing Tools, you can save time by using one of the specific tasks available from either the sheet or the Writing Tools submenu. You can focus on summarizing, proofreading, changing the tone of selected text (Friendly, Professional, or Concise) or building a list or table using the selected text.

To throw caution completely to the wind and allow Apple Intelligence to rewrite the selected text, choose Compose from the Writing Tools sheet or the Writing Tools submenu. Keynote requests a description of the text it will compose. After you've entered the description, Keynote displays suggestions on the content and format of the text it will create. Click a suggestion to replace the selected text!

Formatting Slide Text to Perfection

Keynote doesn't restrict you to the default fonts for the theme you chose. You can format the text in your slides using a different font family, font color, text alignment, and text attributes (such as **boldface** and *italics*).

Select the desired text by double-clicking a box and dragging the pointer to highlight the characters. Then apply formatting using one of two methods:

>> **The Inspector:** Click the Format button in the Keynote toolbar to display the Inspector pane. After you've selected text, format it using the buttons and pop-up menu choices (opening the Typeface pop-up menu, for example, displays a range of different formatting for the selected text). You can also create bullets and lists from the Text tab.

>> **The Format menu:** When you've selected text, the controls on the Keynote Format menu generally mirror those in the Inspector. To change the alignment, click Format and hover the pointer over the Text submenu item to display the alignment choices. To change text attributes, click Format and hover the pointer over the Font submenu.

Using Presenter's Notes

As I mention earlier, you can type presenter's text notes in the Notes pane. I use them to display related topic points while presenting my slideshow. You can also print the notes along with the slides. Handouts, anyone?

To type your notes, click within the Notes pane. If that pane is hidden, choose View ⇨ Show Presenter Notes. When you're finished adding notes, click the Slides list or the Layout pane to return to editing mode.

To display your notes while practicing, use the Keynote Rehearsal feature. Choose Play ⇨ Rehearse Slideshow, click the Tools icon in the top-right corner of the window, and select the Presenter Notes check box to enable it. Now you can scroll through the notes while the slideshow runs! (More on slideshows in a second.)

Every Good Presentation Needs Media

Adding audio, photos, and movies to a slide is drag-and-drop easy in Keynote! Simply drag an image, audio, or movie file from a Finder window and place it at the spot where you want it within your presentation.

If you subscribe to the Apple Creator Studio, you can also use the Content Hub to select from stock images, video, backgrounds, and shapes. You can display the Content Hub window using the Browse Content button on the toolbar.

Adding a Background Shape

Text often stands out on a slide when it sits on top of a background shape. To add a shape (such as a circle) as a background, follow these steps:

1. **Click the insertion pointer in the location you want.**

2. **Click the Shape button on the Keynote toolbar and choose a shape from the menu that appears.**

   The shape appears in your document.

3. **Click the center of the shape, and drag it to a new spot.**

   As you can with image boxes, you can resize or move shapes. You can read how to do that in "Working with Text, Shapes, and Graphics Boxes," earlier in this chapter.

4. **When the shape is properly positioned and sized, select it and choose Arrange ⇨ Send to Back.**

   You want to "send the shape to the back" so that any text you enter is sitting in front of the shape, not hidden behind it.

You're not limited to creating shapes and graphics within Keynote; consider using an application such as Adobe Photoshop or Illustrator to create graphics for your slides! As I mention earlier, you can easily drag and drop your new graphic into a slide from a Finder window.

Adding 3D Objects

How cool would it be to have 3D models appear on your slides? They'd grab the attention of your audience and add a unique touch to your presentation! If you have a 3D object file saved to your Neo's drive, you can easily add it to the current slide by dragging the file from a Finder window and dropping it into the Layout pane.

You can rotate your image during your presentation by clicking the icon that appears in the center of a 3D object. (It looks like two intersecting circles.) Click and drag the Rotate button to the desired angle.

If your 3D model includes animation, click the Play button that appears at the lower-right corner of the object box to start the animation.

Creating Your Keynote Slideshow

The heart of a Keynote presentation is the slideshow you build from your project. A Keynote slideshow is typically presented full-screen, with slides appearing in linear order as they're sorted in the Slides list.

You run a Keynote slideshow by clicking the Play button on the toolbar or by choosing Play ⇨ Play Slideshow. You can advance to the next slide by clicking or by pressing the right-arrow key.

Are you running a presentation along with a videoconferencing app? You can play a Keynote presentation in a window instead. To use this feature, choose Play ⇨ In Window.

If you connect an external monitor to your Neo and run a Keynote slideshow, the presentation will appear in full screen on the MacBook itself, with a preview display on the external monitor. You even get an onscreen clock to monitor the time!

Other controls are available besides the ones that advance to the next slide. Table 16-1 lists the shortcuts you'll use most often during a slideshow.

Keynote offers several settings that you can tweak to fine-tune your slideshow. To display these settings, choose Keynote ⇨ Settings and click the Slideshow button.

Key	Action
Right arrow	Move to the next slide.
Left arrow	Return to the preceding slide.
Home	Jump to the first slide.
End	Jump to the last slide.
C	Show or hide the pointer.
number	Jump to the corresponding slide in the Slides list. (Click the Go button when it appears.)
H	Hide the slideshow and display the last application used.
B	Pause the slideshow and display a black screen. (Press any key to resume the slideshow.)
Esc	Quit.

TIP

If you have an iPhone or iPad handy, and you've installed the iOS version of Keynote on your device, choose Keynote ⇨ Settings and click the Remote tab. Click the Enable check box to link your device to Keynote. Now you can use your device as a remote during your slideshow! *Sweet!*

TIP

Are you creating a Keynote slideshow for an unattended kiosk? Choose Keynote ⇨ Settings and click the Slideshow tab. Deselect the Exit Presentation After Last Slide check box, and select the Require Password to Exit Slideshows check box. Now your slideshow will run continuously (a password you set is required to exit), and your audience can move backward and forward with the left- and right-arrow keys.

Printing Your Slides and Notes

If you're presenting a lengthy slideshow with information that you want your audience to remember, nothing beats handouts that include scaled-down images of your slides (and, optionally, your presenter's notes).

You're not limited to paper. You can also use Keynote to create an electronic PDF (Portable Document Format) file instead of a printed handout, which your audience members can download from your website.

To print your slides and notes, follow these steps:

1. **Within Keynote, choose File ⇨ Print or press ⌘+P.**

   Keynote displays the Print sheet. If necessary, expand the Print sheet to show all the settings by clicking the arrow at the left of each heading.

2. **Choose one of the following formats (each of which displays a different set of layout options) under the Keynote heading:**

   - **Slide:** Print each slide on a separate page at full size. You can choose to print the presenter notes for each slide as well.

   - **Grid:** Print multiple slides on a page at a reduced size. Choose how many slides Keynote should print on each page from the Slides per Page pop-up menu.

   - **Handout:** Print a handout with multiple slides per page (and, optionally, with presenter's notes). Again, you choose how many slides appear on each page.

   - **Outline:** Print the contents of your Slides list in Outline view.

3. **Select the pages to print:**

   - **To print the entire document,** select the All Pages radio button.

   - **To print a range of selected slides,** select the Range radio button and then enter the starting and ending pages.

4. **Click the Print button to send the job to your printer.**

You can also send a copy of your finished presentation as an attachment with Mail or Messages. Click Share on the Keynote toolbar and choose Send Copy from the drop-down list to explore your options.

IN THIS CHAPTER

» **Avoiding the blame (righteously)**

» **Putting basic troubleshooting precepts to work**

» **Using Mark's Troubleshooting Tree**

» **Getting help**

Chapter **17**

When Good Mac Laptops Go Bad

wish you weren't reading this chapter.

Because you are, I can only surmise that you're having trouble with your Neo, and that it needs fixing. (The other possibility — that you truly enjoy reading about solving computer problems — is more attractive but much more problematic.)

Consider this chapter a crash course in the logical puzzle that is computer *trouble-shooting:* the art of finding out What Needs Fixing. I provide you with tricks that may fix the problem when you just can't solve it yourself.

Not surprisingly, you're going to encounter a lot of Tips and Mark's Maxims in this chapter. I learned all of them the hard way, so I recommend committing them to memory.

Repeat after Me: Yes, I Am a Tech!

Anyone can troubleshoot. Believe it, and put these common troubleshooting myths to rest:

» **It takes a college degree in computer science to troubleshoot.** Tell that to my readers all over the world. They'll think it's a hoot, because those other MacBook owners fix minor problems all the time. You can follow all the steps in this chapter without any special training.

» **I'm to blame.** Ever heard of viruses? Failing hardware? Buggy software? Any of those things can cause the problem. It's Mark's Maxim time:

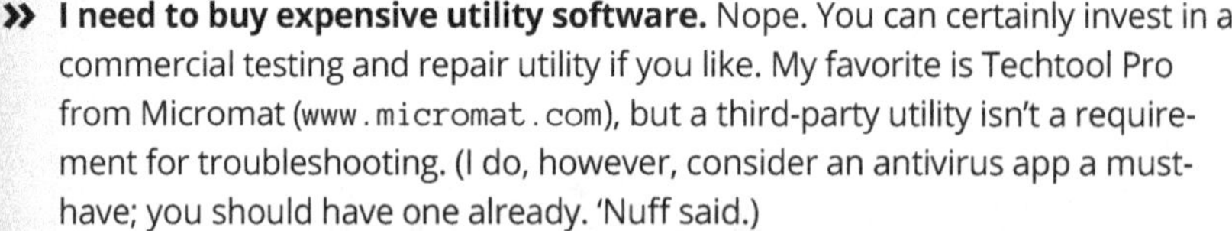

Don't beat yourself up! Your Neo *can* be fixed.

» **I need to buy expensive utility software.** Nope. You can certainly invest in a commercial testing and repair utility if you like. My favorite is Techtool Pro from Micromat (`www.micromat.com`), but a third-party utility isn't a requirement for troubleshooting. (I do, however, consider an antivirus app a must-have; you should have one already. 'Nuff said.)

» **There's no hope if I can't fix it.** Sure, parts fail and computers crash, but your Apple Service Center can repair just about any problem. And (ahem) *if you backed up your computer* (as I preach throughout this book), you'll keep that important data (even if a new drive is in your future).

» **It takes forever.** Wait until you read the number-one rule in the next section; the first step takes but 10 seconds and often solves the problem. Naturally, not all problems can be fixed so quickly. But if you follow the procedures in this chapter, you should fix your Neo (or at least know that the problem requires outside help) in an afternoon.

With those myths banished, you can get fixing and start feeling better!

Step-by-Step Laptop Troubleshooting

In the following sections, I walk you through my should-be-patented Troubleshooting Tree, as well as the macOS built-in troubleshooting application, Disk Utility. I also introduce you to several keystrokes that can make your Neo jump through hoops.

The number-one rule: Reboot!

The simple fact is that rebooting your Neo can often solve many problems. If you're encountering these types of strange behavior with your MacBook, a reboot might be all you need:

>> Intermittent problems communicating over a network

>> A garbled screen, strange colors, or screwed-up fonts

>> The swirling Beach Ball of Doom that won't go away after several minutes

>> An application that locks up

>> An external device that seems to disappear or can't be opened

To put it succinctly, here's a modest Mark's Maxim:

Always try a reboot before beginning to worry. *Always.*

MARK'S
MAXIM

If you're using an app, try to save all your open documents before you reboot. That might be impossible, but try to save what you can.

As your first (and best) option for shutting down, click the Apple () menu and choose Shut Down. If you need to force a *locked* application (one that's not responding) to quit so that you can reboot, follow these steps to quash that locked app:

1. **Click the Apple () menu and choose Force Quit.**

    The dialog shown in Figure 17-1 appears.

2. **Click the offending application and then click the Force Quit button.**

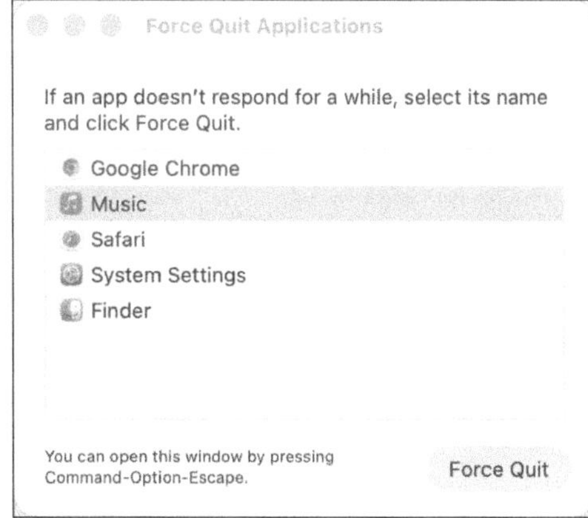

FIGURE 17-1:
Force a
recalcitrant
application
to take off.

When you get everything to quit, you should be able to click the Apple menu and choose Shut Down (*not* Restart) without a problem.

If your Neo simply won't shut down (or you can't get the offending application to quit), do what must be done:

1. **Press and hold your Neo's Touch ID until it shuts itself off.**

   (On a Neo with a Lock button, hold that button down instead.) You have to wait about 3 seconds for your Neo to turn itself off.

   If holding the Touch ID/Lock button down on your MacBook doesn't do the trick, press the Touch ID/Lock button *and* the Left Option+Left Shift+Left Control keyboard shortcut at the same time for about 10 seconds; then release them all at the same time. (This method also resets some of your MacBook's internal hardware settings, which is often A Good Thing.)

2. **Wait about 10 seconds after your Neo has shut down.**

3. **Press the Touch ID/Lock button again to start the laptop.**

After everything is backed up, check whether the problem is still apparent. If the problem doesn't reoccur in an hour or two, you likely fixed it!

Using Safe mode

You can use Safe mode to force macOS to run a directory check of your boot drive and disable any login items that might be interfering with your system. For the Neo, follow these steps:

1. **Choose the Shut Down menu item from the Apple () menu to turn off your MacBook.**

2. **Press and *continue to hold* the Touch ID/Lock button to start the Neo.**

3. **When you see the Loading Startup Options message displayed, you can release the Touch ID/Lock button.**

4. **Click the disk you want to boot with and then hold down the Shift key while you click Continue in Safe mode.**

5. **After macOS boots, you're in Safe mode. (You should see the words *Safe Boot* displayed in the Finder menu bar.) Check the operation of your Neo by using Disk Utility (or a commercial utility app).**

6. **When you're ready to return to normal operation, restart your Neo again.**

All hail Disk Utility, the troubleshooter's friend

The macOS *Disk Utility* is a handy tool for troubleshooting and repairing your Neo's drive — you can use it to check the format and health of both drives and volumes (and automatically correct any problems). You can find Disk Utility in the Utilities category in Apps.

Fire up Disk Utility to open the rather powerful-looking window shown in Figure 17-2.

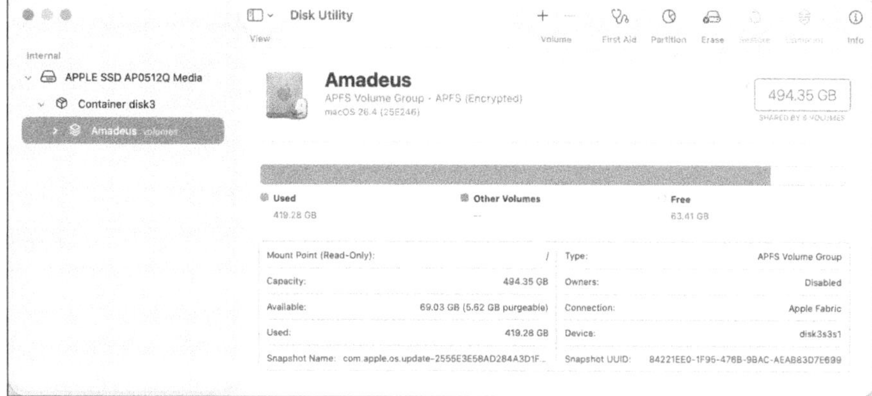

FIGURE 17-2: The physician of drives: the Tahoe Disk Utility.

In the left column of the Disk Utility window, you can now see:

>> The *physical* drives in your system (the actual hardware).

>> The *containers* (the formatted portions of the drives on your system).

>> The *snapshots* (used if you need to restore).

>> The *volumes* (the data stored on the drives).

You can always tell a volume, because it's indented below the Container entry. (If you don't see physical drives and containers as well as volumes, press ⌘+2 to show all devices.)

>> Any CD or DVD loaded on your Neo (if you have an external optical drive connected).

>> USB external drives.

Figure 17-2 shows that I have one internal drive (the Apple SSD entry) that has one volume (Amadeus).

The information in the bottom-right section of the Disk Utility window is the specifications for the selected drive or volume. This info includes capacity and available space for a volume, the connection type, and the total capacity for a drive.

Disk repair made easy

Disk Utility can check the format and health of both drives and volumes, and you can correct any problems it finds by clicking the First Aid button.

To check and repair problems using First Aid, follow these steps:

1. **Click the Go menu and choose Utilities; then double-click the Disk Utility icon.**

2. **In the list at the left side of the Disk Utility window, click the drive, snapshot, or volume you want to check.**

3. **Click the First Aid button, and click the Run button that appears.**

4. **Click Done to exit First Aid.**

   If changes were made, Disk Utility may prompt you to reboot after repairs have been made.

Figure 17-3 illustrates the details you see if you click Show Details to expand the display. Although some of the messages might include cryptic details, you can still tell from the final text that the operation is successful (and you get that snazzy green check mark). All is well!

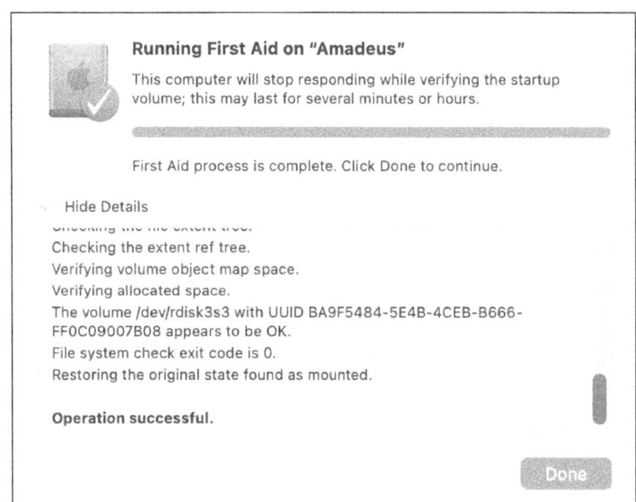

FIGURE 17-3: First Aid reports that this drive is error free.

TECHNICAL STUFF

Using Disk Utility to repair your system drive(s) carries a couple of caveats:

>> **You may not be able to immediately repair problems on your boot drive or boot volume.** This limitation actually makes sense, because you're actually using that drive and volume right now.

If First Aid finds a problem on your Neo's boot drive but reports that it can't fix that error, choose Shut Down from the Apple (&) menu to turn off your MacBook; then press *and hold* the Touch ID/Lock button to start the computer. (When you see the Loading Startup Options message displayed, you can release the Touch ID/Lock button.) Now click the Options icon, click Continue, and click the Disk Utility entry. Click your startup volume from the sidebar, and click First Aid to repair the problems. When you're done, click the Apple menu and choose Restart.

>> **You can't repair CDs and DVDs.** If you have an external optical drive and a CD or DVD is giving you problems, remember that CDs and DVDs are read-only media and thus can't be repaired by Disk Utility.

Mark's MacBook Troubleshooting Tree

As hip-hop artists say, "All right, kick it." And that's what my MacBook Neo Troubleshooting Tree is here for. If rebooting your supercomputer didn't solve the problem, follow these steps in order until you either find the solution or run out of steps (more on that in the next section).

If you're not sure quite what's producing the error, this process is designed to be *linear* — followed in order — but if you already know that the problem lies with one specific peripheral or one specific application, feel free to jump to the steps that concern only hardware or software.

Step 1: Investigate recent changes

The first step is a simple one that many novice MacBook owners forget. Retrace your steps and consider what changes you made to your system recently. Here are the most common culprits:

» **Did you just finish installing a new application?** Try uninstalling it by removing the application directory and any support files it might have added to your system. (And keep your apps current with the most recent patches and updates from the developers' websites.)

» **Did you just apply an update or patch to an app?** Uninstall the app, and reinstall it without applying the patch. If your Neo suddenly works fine again, contact the app's technical support to report the problem.

» **Did you just update macOS?** Updating Tahoe can introduce problems in your applications that depend on specific routines and system files. Contact the developer of the app, and look for updated patches that bring your software in line with the latest Tahoe updates.

» **Did you just make a change in System Settings?** Return the options you changed to their original settings; then consult Chapter 4 for information on what might have gone wrong. (If the setting isn't listed in Chapter 4, consider searching the macOS Help system or the Apple support website.)

» **Did you just connect (or reconnect) an external device?** Try unplugging the device and then rebooting to see if the problem disappears. Remember that some peripherals need software drivers to run, such as printers; without those drivers installed, they don't work correctly. Check the device's manual or visit the company's website to search for software.

If you didn't make any significant changes to your system before you encountered the problem, proceed to the next step.

Step 2: Run Disk Utility

The next step is to run Disk Utility and use First Aid. The earlier section "Disk repair made easy" shows how to complete this task on your drive.

Step 3: Check your cables

Cables can work themselves loose, and sometimes they fail. Check all the cables to your external devices — make sure that they're snug — and verify that everything's plugged in and turned on. (Oh, and don't forget to check for crimps in your cables or even Fluffy's teeth marks.) You can also swap cables to determine whether you have a bad one.

Step 4: Check your Trash

Check the contents of the Trash to see whether you recently deleted files or folders by accident. Click the Trash icon on the Dock to display the contents. If you deleted something by mistake, right-click the item in the Trash and choose Put Back from the contextual menu.

I know this one from personal experience. A slight miscalculation while selecting files to delete made an application freeze every time I launched it.

Step 5: Check your internet and network connections

Now that always-on broadband connections to the internet are the norm, don't forget an obvious problem: Your MacBook Neo can't reach the internet if your ISP is down or your network is no longer working!

When you're at home, a quick visual check of your modem usually indicates whether a connection problem exists between your modem and your ISP. My fiber modem has a set of activity lights that I always glance at first. If you can't check the modem visually, you can still check your internet connection by launching Safari and visiting `www.apple.com`.

If you can't reach your network at all, the problem lies in your network hardware or configuration. (In an office environment, your network system administrator will be happy to help you at this point, especially if you're blood relatives.)

Step 6: Think virus

If you've made it to this point, it's time to run a full virus scan. Make sure that your antivirus application has the latest updated data files. My antivirus application of choice is Avast Security for Mac from Avast Software (`www.avast.com`). It's both excellent and free!

Step 7: Check your login items

Tahoe might encounter problems with apps you've marked as login items in System Settings. Your account's login items are applications that run automatically every time you log in to your Neo. If one of these login items is to blame for your problems, your MacBook will encounter some type of trouble every time you log in. (This is usually the case when you receive an application error message each time you start your Neo.)

To check the boot process, it's time to use that fancy Safe Boot mode I discussed earlier in the chapter. Login items are disabled when you're running in Safe mode, so if your MacBook starts up without any errors, you know that one or more login items are probably to blame.

If your computer starts without problems in Safe mode, the next step is to check your login items. Restart your Neo and then follow this procedure for each item in the login list:

1. **Open System Settings, click General in the sidebar, and then click the Login Items & Extensions entry.**

   Jot down the entries in the Open at Login list on a handy notepad (or save a screenshot of the list items to your Desktop with the Shift+⌘+5 shortcut).

2. **Select the first item from the Open at Login list and remove it.**

   Delete the selected item by clicking the Delete button under the list, which bears a minus sign. (If a recurring error message mentions a specific app that appears in the Open at Login list, start by deleting that item.)

3. **Click the Close button to close System Settings.**

4. **Restart your Neo.**

5. **If your MacBook is still misbehaving, repeat Steps 1 through 4 and disable a new login item.**

   When your Mac starts up normally, you have discovered the perpetrator.

6. **Delete that application and reinstall it.**

   Don't forget to add back each of the *working* login items to the Open at Login list using the Add button (which carries a plus sign)! (Hence the notes or screenshot you created in the first step.)

Step 8: Turn off your screen saver

The next step is to turn off your screen saver. This remedy is a long shot, but it isn't unheard of to discover that a faulty, bug-ridden screen saver has locked up your Neo. If you are running a screen saver other than one from Apple, and your computer never wakes up from Sleep mode or hangs while displaying the screen saver, you've found your prime suspect.

Reboot your Neo (if necessary), open System Settings, click Wallpaper in the sidebar, click the Screen Saver button, and switch to an Apple screen saver. To disable the screen saver entirely from the same dialog, click the Start Screen Saver pop-up menu and choose Never.

Step 9: Run System Information

Ouch. You've reached the final step, and you still haven't uncovered the culprit. You've narrowed the possibilities to a serious problem, such as bad hardware or corrupted system files. Fortunately, macOS includes the System Information app, which displays real-time information on your hardware. To start System Information, follow these steps:

1. **Click anywhere on your Desktop and press ⌘+spacebar to display the Spotlight search box.**

2. **Type System Information and press Return to open the System Information window.**

3. **Click each of the Hardware categories in the sidebar in turn, double-checking to make sure everything looks okay.**

You don't have to understand the technical hieroglyphics, but if a Hardware category doesn't return what you expect or displays an error message, that's suspicious.

The Diagnostics category shows any errors encountered by your Neo during the last Power On self-test.

Okay, I Kicked It and It Still Won't Work

Don't worry, friendly reader. Just because you've reached the end of my spiffy MacBook Neo Troubleshooting Tree doesn't mean you're out of luck. In the following sections, I discuss the online help available in macOS Tahoe and on the Apple website, as well as local help in your own town.

Local service, at your service

In case you need to take in your Neo for service, an Apple Store or Apple Authorized Service Provider is probably in your area. To find the closest service, visit the

Apple website Support page (`www.apple.com/support`); then click the Start a Repair link.

Always call your Apple Authorized Service Provider before you take your Neo to the shop. Jot down your MacBook's serial number (displayed in System Information) and which version of macOS Tahoe you're using.

The macOS Help Center

Although most MacBook owners tend to blow off the Help Center when the troubleshooting gets tough, that's **never** the best course of action. Always take a few moments to search the contents of the Help Center by choosing Help on the Finder menu bar to see whether any mention is made of the problem you've encountered.

Apple Help Online

If you haven't visited the Apple MacBook Support site yet, run, don't walk, to that same Apple website I mention earlier in "Local service, at your service." Click Mac; then click Laptops. There, you find:

» The latest patches, updates, and tutorials for the MacBook line

» MacBook and macOS discussion boards, moderated by Apple

» Tools for ordering spare parts, checking on your remaining warranty coverage, and searching the Apple knowledge base

» Do-it-yourself instructions for troubleshooting and repairing your Neo

Chapter **18**

Tackling the Housekeeping

Nothing runs better than a well-oiled machine, and your cherished Neo is no exception. (But please, don't *ever* oil your MacBook; that's just a figure of speech.) In this chapter, I demonstrate how you can make good use of every byte of storage space provided by your internal drive.

With a little macOS maintenance, such as *Time Machine* (for backing up and restoring your data) and frequent scans of your drive for disk errors, you can ensure that your Neo is performing as efficiently as possible. In addition, configuring Software Update to run automatically allows you to live life free and easy.

Cleaning Unseemly Data Deposits

Criminy! Where does all this stuff *come* from? Suddenly, that spacious 512GB solid-state drive has 19GB left, and you start feeling downright pinched.

Before you consider buying a new external drive, take the smart step: Sweep your drive clean of unnecessary and space-hogging software.

Managing your storage in macOS (or cleaning the elegant way)

Apple includes the Manage Storage feature within macOS to help identify and delete those huge files that are taking up so much of your drive's real estate. Right-click the Desktop icon for the drive to clean, and choose Manage Storage to display the Storage settings shown in Figure 18-1.

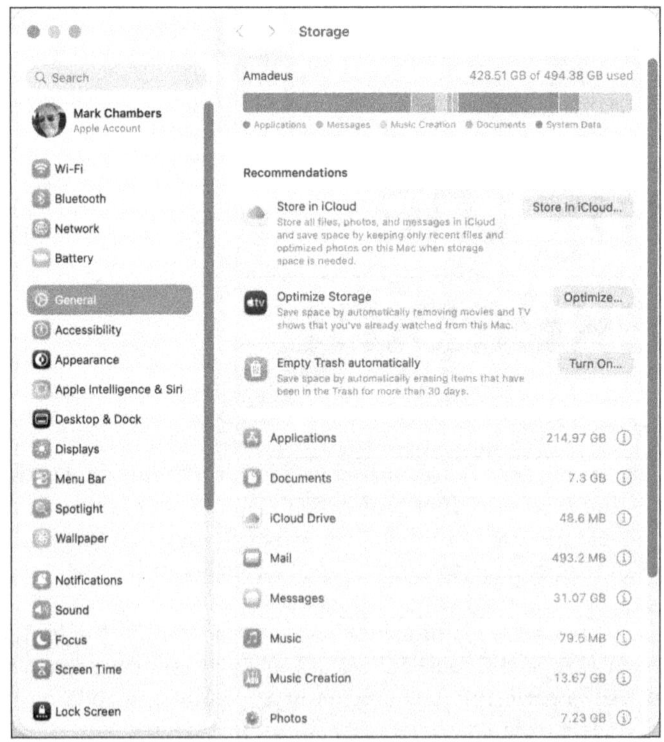

FIGURE 18-1:
Manage your storage to reclaim drive space.

Note the categories in the list at the right side — from here, you can see the approximate amount of space taken up by notoriously prodigious items like your documents and apps. Click the Info icon (the lowercase *i* inside the circle) next to a category to display the worst offenders, sorted by size. If you see an unneeded item (like that 2GB cat video you downloaded years ago), click the item to display options to remove it, such as uninstalling it or simply deleting it. If only cleaning your house were this easy!

The Recommendations section is unique because it suggests space-saving features that macOS offers rather than displaying files. You can also choose to empty your Trash automatically from here.

Getting dirty (or cleaning things the manual way)

If you're willing to dig into your data a little, you can dive elbow-deep into your drive to hunt down *every* unnecessary file. All you really need is the willpower to announce, "I simply don't need this particular item any longer." (Sometimes, as with physical stuff around your home, that decision is tougher than it may seem.)

Unnecessary files and unneeded folders

Consider all the stuff that you probably don't really need: game demos and shareware that you no longer play, old videos, temporary files that you created and promptly forgot and downloads that have long since passed into obscurity. How hard is it to actually clean this stuff off your drive? Easier than you might think!

>> You can quickly delete unnecessary files and apps. Don't forget to delete an app's folder that was created during the installation process to save even more territory.

If you created any documents in the app folder that you want to keep, don't forget to move them before you trash the folder! (Some apps come with their own uninstall utility, so check the app's documentation first.)

>> You can delete apps purchased from the App Store. Again, these applications can be reinstalled at any time (although deleting an application will likely also delete any setting changes you may have made).

>> You can remove items from your Music and TV media library (especially movies, which take up several gigabytes of space *each*). If you've purchased an item from the iTunes Store, don't forget that you can always download that item again in the future for free — perhaps when you've added an external drive to hold some of your stuff.

>> You can move seldom-used files and folders to external storage (such as a USB flash drive).

Removing an application or file from your drive usually takes two simple steps:

1. **Display the file or application folder in a Finder window.**

2. **Delete the file or folder by dragging the icon or filename to the Trash, or by right-clicking the icon or filename and choosing Move to Trash.**

Truly, no big whoop.

Don't forget to actually *empty* the Trash, or you'll wonder why you aren't regaining any drive space. (macOS works hard to store the contents of the Trash until you manually delete it, just in case you want to undelete something.) To get rid of that stuff permanently and reclaim the space, do the following:

1. **Right-click the Trash icon on the Dock.**

2. **Choose Empty Trash from the pop-up menu.**

As I mention earlier in the chapter, if you use the Manage Storage feature, you can elect to set your Trash to empty automatically.

Associated files in other folders

Some applications install files in different locations across your drive. (Apps in this category include the Microsoft Office suite and Adobe Photoshop.) How can you discard these orphan files after you delete the app folder?

The process is a little more involved than deleting a single folder, but it's still no big whoop. Here's the procedure:

1. **Click the Search icon (which looks like a magnifying glass) in a Finder window.**

   You can read more about Finder windows in Chapter 3.

2. **Type the name of the application in the Search text box and choose Name Contains from the pop-up menu.**

   Figure 18-2 shows a typical search. I wanted to remove orphan files associated with an app called Parallels Desktop; I had already deleted the application itself. By searching for the word *Parallels* with the Name Contains option, I found support documents and data files that are now no longer needed and could also be deleted. This trick displays files created in other folders that include your search word in their names, such as project and PDF files.

3. **Decide which of these files belong to the to-be-deleted application.**

   Be sure that the files you choose to delete are part of the deleted app. If necessary, right-click the file and choose Get Info from the shortcut menu to display more information.

   Many associated files either have the same icon as the parent application or are in the Preferences, Caches, or Application Support folders.

4. **In the Search Results window, click the associated file(s) that you want to delete and just drag them to the Trash.**

   Don't empty the Trash immediately after you delete these files. Wait a day or two. That way, if you realize that you deleted a file you truly need, you can easily restore it from the Trash.

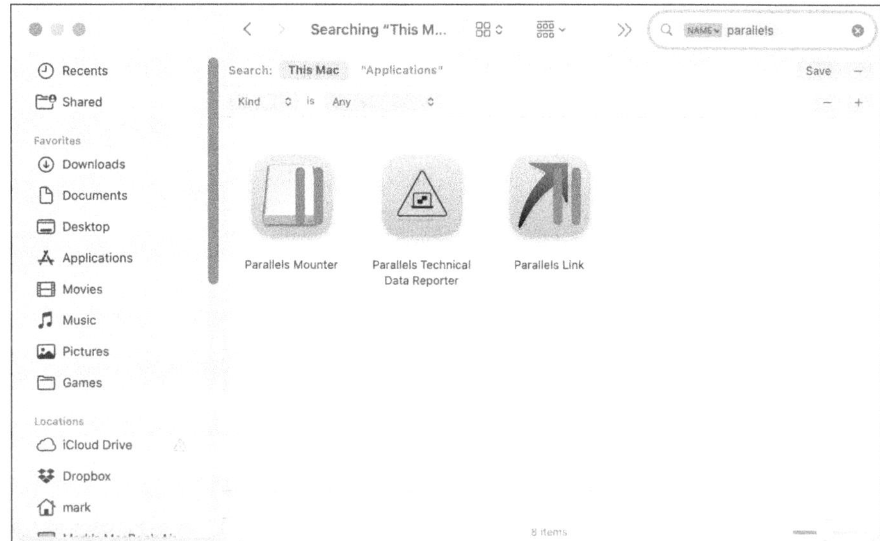

FIGURE 18-2: Mine your drive for additional files to delete.

Using a commercial cleanup tool

If you'd rather use a commercial application to help you clean up your drive, several apps are available — sadly, most are shareware apps that perform only one task. For a good all-around cleanup utility, I recommend CCleaner for Mac, from Piriform (`www.ccleaner.com/ccleaner-mac`). This great utility can clean everything from internet crud in your browser to those macOS system caches that can grow so doggone huge. The utility can also uninstall many applications with a single click. Oh, and did I mention that the basic edition is free? I *really* like free!

Backing Up Your Treasure

Do it.

I'm not going to lecture you about backing up your Neo's drive . . . well, perhaps just for a moment. Imagine what it feels like to lose *everything:* names, numbers, letters, reports, presentations, saved games, photographs, video, and music. Then ask yourself, "Self, isn't all that irreplaceable stuff worth safeguarding?"

Time for a Mark's Maxim:

Back up. **On a regular basis.**

Take my word for it; you *will* thank me someday!

You can back up your files either by saving them to external media or — as I strongly recommend — by using the awesome Time Machine feature included with Tahoe. Read more about Time Machine in the "Putting Things Right with Time Machine" section, later in this chapter.

Saving Files

The simplest method of backing up files is simply to copy the files and folders to an external drive. Nothing fancy — I call this procedure the "quick-and-dirty backup" — but it *works.* If you have an external drive or USB flash drive on your Neo, you can easily drag backup files to it from your internal drive:

1. **Open separate Finder windows for:**

   - The external drive

   - The internal drive

   Because you're using macOS, you can also open a Finder tab within a single Finder window to accomplish the same task — from the keyboard, press ⌘+T.

2. **Select the desired files that you want to back up from your internal drive.**

3. **Drag the selected files to the external drive window (or tab).**

Putting Things Right with Time Machine

If you enable backups via the macOS Time Machine feature, you can literally move backward through the contents of your Neo's drive, selecting and restoring all sorts of data. Files and folders are ridiculously easy to restore — and I mean easier than *any* restore you've ever performed, no matter what the operating system or backup app. To sum it up, Time Machine should be an important and integral part of every Mac owner's existence.

Before you can use Time Machine, you must have it enabled within the Time Machine pane in System Settings. I cover the Time Machine configuration settings (and how to turn the feature on) in more detail in Chapter 4. You'll also need a USB 3.0 external drive that provides considerably more storage capacity than the drive you're backing up. I recommend that your external Time Machine backup drive be at least twice the capacity of your Neo's drive; for example, if your internal drive has a capacity of 512MB, shop for a 1TB external drive. Make sure to leave your external Time Machine drive plugged in to your Neo whenever possible.

Here's how you can turn back time to restore a deleted file:

1. **Open a Finder window and navigate to the folder that contained the file you want to restore.**

2. **Click the Time Machine icon on the Finder menu bar (which bears a clock with a counterclockwise arrow) and click Browse Time Machine Backups.**

   The oh-so-ultra-cool Time Machine background appears behind your folder, complete with its own set of buttons at the bottom of the screen. On the right, you see a timeline that corresponds to the different days and months included in the backups that macOS has made.

3. **Click any segment within the timeline to jump directly to a date (displaying the folder's contents on that date).**

   Alternatively, use the Forward and Back arrows at the right to move through the folder's contents through time. (You should see the envious faces of Windows users when you riffle through your folders to locate something you deleted several weeks ago!) The backup date of the items you're viewing appears between the Forward and Back buttons.

4. **After you locate the file you want to restore, click it to select it.**

5. **Click the Restore button at the bottom of the screen.**

   Time Machine returns you to the Finder, with the newly restored file(s) now appearing in the original folder. *Outstanding!*

As I mention earlier, you can easily restore the *entire* contents of your Neo's internal drive from your Time Machine backup, too. Shut down your Neo; then press and hold down the Touch ID/Lock button. Choose Options and click Continue to boot using the macOS Recovery HD volume; then use the Restore from Time Machine function. (In some cases, a full restore may not be possible, but you can still use Migration Assistant to restore your data.)

For robust backup and restore protection, Time Machine is all that a typical Mac owner at home is likely to ever need. Therefore, here's a very easy Mark's Maxim to predict:

Get an external drive, connect it, and turn on Time Machine. *Do it now.* Don't make a humongous mistake.

Maintaining Drive Health

There are shifty-eyed, sneaky, irritating little problems that can bother both your internal and external drives: *permissions errors.* Incorrect disk and file permissions can make your Neo lock up or make apps act screwy (or refuse to run at all). Problems with your drive can also result in corrupted data and files that won't open.

To keep macOS Tahoe running at its best, I recommend that you fix disk errors at least once per week. Follow these steps:

1. **Press ⌘+spacebar to display the Spotlight search box.**

2. **Type the words** disk utility.

3. **Double-click the Disk Utility entry in the results list.**

4. **Click the volume or named partition to check in the sidebar.**

5. **Click the First Aid button and then click Run.**

   Disk Utility does the rest and then displays a message about whatever it has to fix, if anything. (When do we get a *car* with a Repair Me button?)

   Note that running First Aid on your internal drive may cause your Neo to stop responding for several minutes.

Updating macOS Automatically

I prefer my Neo to take care of cleaning up after itself whenever possible, so updating macOS should be automatic as well. In Tahoe, macOS updates are controlled by the Software Update settings within the System Settings General pane. (Note that Software Update requires an internet connection.)

To set Software Update to check for critical system updates and install them automatically, click the Software Update item in the System Settings General pane and then click the Info button next to the Automatic Updates button. Make sure that the following three switches on the Automatically dialog are turned on: Download New Updates When Available; Install macOS Updates; and Install System Data Files and Security Updates. Then click Done. Now your Neo is an automated update champion!

The Part of Tens

Chapter **19**

Ten Neo Rules to Follow

h, the sedentary life of a desktop Mac. It sits there like a bump on a log, comfortable and immobile. As long as you have a stable surface and an uninterrupted power supply, your desktop Mac is a happy puppy.

But you, good reader, are *mobile!* Whether you're on campus or attending a convention, your Neo is rarely running in the same spot, so it's susceptible to all sorts of road-warrior pitfalls. In this chapter, I remind you of ten of the most important rules every laptop owner should follow.

Keep Your Neo in a Bag

Using a laptop case or bag sounds like common sense. But MacBooks are so doggone sexy that you'd be surprised how many people carry them around without any protection. These Mac owners hear phrases like "unibody construction" and "solid-state drive" and figure that their laptop can survive a construction site, college campus, or hotel room.

Part of that is true. MacBooks *are* some of the toughest laptops ever made, but they're not immune to bumps, scratches, and the rare fall. If you carry your Neo without protection, soon it'll look like a boxer after a bad fight.

If you're like me, you're proud that your computers remain in pristine condition, so use a laptop bag or case that offers ample padding and a shoulder strap or carry handle. (My laptop bag even converts to a backpack. It includes plenty of extra space for stuff like power supplies, my wireless trackball and keyboard, and a snack or two.) Spend an extra $30 on a laptop bag, and your $700 MacBook Neo can weather the worst.

Using a traditional laptop bag comes with a caveat, however. Some folks think a bag draws too much attention to its expensive cargo. (To some extent, I agree. Few people tote an obvious 15-by-7-inch bag with a hardware manufacturer's logo emblazoned on it these days.) Consider a *well-padded* laptop sleeve (with corner protectors) that allows you to carry your Neo in your backpack. (The laptop always goes on top of those heavy books, of course.) Remember, though, that the padding is the important thing; without that extra cushion, you might as well just toss your unprotected Neo in with the rest of your books and must-have equipment.

Oh, and if you use your MacBook Neo for a longer period, and it's warm to the touch, don't pack it immediately. Allow it to cool for a few minutes before stowing it to help prevent damage to your Neo's hardware.

Opt for That Larger Drive

If you haven't actually bought your Neo yet, let me make a heartfelt recommendation: *Spend the extra 100 clams and pick the Neo model with Touch ID and the larger 512GB drive!*

Why spend the extra cash? If you make full use of your new laptop friend, I can pretty much *guarantee* that you'll end up needing that extra space. Each new version of macOS requires more space than the previous version, and if you decide to install a productivity suite like Microsoft Office or a larger app like The Sims 4, you'll quickly learn how fast 256GB can fill up!

I should also say that I prefer using the Touch ID sensor on the upgraded model because it eliminates most password entry and simplifies all sorts of actions you perform every day (like logging on to your Neo and verifying your identity when making a purchase).

Keep Tabs on Your Neo

Suppose the unthinkable happens: Your Neo is stolen while you're on vacation, and you know that the chances it will be returned are next to nil. You've resigned yourself to replacing it (and all your data). But wait! What if I told you that you might just be able to display your MacBook's current location, as well as wipe the data that's on it (if necessary)?

If this scenario sounds a little like a James Bond movie, you'll be surprised to discover that a *tracker application* can turn your Neo into a transmitting beacon, broadcasting to you its current location and all the internet information it can get. Then you can alert the police, who will apprehend the crook (who may be in the middle of creating a new album in Photos).

In fact, the Find My Mac feature built into Tahoe is a tracker application in disguise! (Note that you must set up your iCloud account in the Apple Account pane in System Settings before you can use Find My Mac, as I cover in Chapter 8.) If your MacBook Neo is lost or stolen, and someone uses it to connect to the internet, you can visit `https://www.icloud.com`, sign in with the same Apple ID, and click the Find My icon; then click the entry for your Neo in the All Devices sidebar to display its current location. From the dialog that appears, you can choose to mark it as Lost (which locks the Neo) or Erase the drive completely.

Invest in an Apple AirTag for your bag to add another layer of tracking!

Keepeth Thy Drive Encrypted

In Chapter 4, I discuss the Privacy & Security pane — it's particularly important because it allows you to *encrypt* your drive. Encryption prevents just about anyone from accessing any of the files you've stored on your Neo. This robust encryption will certainly stymie just about anyone but the National Security Administration. (I won't even go there.)

In System Settings, click Privacy & Security, click the FileVault entry under the Security heading, and then click Turn on FileVault. You can use your Apple ID to unlock your Neo's drive, or you can choose a unique recovery key just in case. (Your login account password is your primary password.) Tahoe takes care of automatically encrypting and decrypting files as necessary. You won't even know that it's working.

To take full advantage of an encrypted drive, you need the proper login mode (as I discuss in Chapter 9). Think about this possible security back door: From the Users & Groups pane, you've set your laptop to log you in automatically every time you boot your Neo. This scenario is the very definition of Not Secure, because your login account password automatically bypasses FileVault encryption! Therefore, play it smart and *make sure that you actually have to log in to access your account.* For the full scoop, see Chapter 9.

Brand Your Neo

Put your brand on your MacBook! Whether you use an engraving tool on the bottom of the machine (my personal favorite) or a permanent metal tag, your Neo deserves some sort of identifying information. After all, most people are honest, so you might not need to use the Find My Mac feature that I mentioned in the previous section. You might have left your Neo behind by accident, and someone would like to return it to you. (Don't forget to offer a reward!) Note that engraving or affixing certain types of tags may void your warranty or AppleCare coverage, however, so it's a good idea to contact Apple Support to verify that everything is copacetic.

Some laptop owners want to include their name, address, and other contact information. (I've even seen business cards taped to the bottom of MacBooks.) Other road warriors feel more comfortable with just their name and email address. Whatever information you choose to provide, branding your Neo is as important as backing it up — and avoids any confusion when going through airport security!

Disable Your Wireless

Funny how we don't think about it, but wireless communications take juice, and that power comes straight from your Neo's battery! Because your MacBook comes with built-in Wi-Fi and Bluetooth hardware, you're constantly broadcasting — or at least *trying* to exchange data with others.

Therein lies the rub: If you're not connected to a wireless network or Bluetooth device, you're wasting precious battery power. That's why Tahoe lets you turn off your Wi-Fi and Bluetooth hardware to save energy. When you're sitting in a crowded auditorium without access to an AC socket or a wireless network, the energy savings you reap when you disable your wireless hardware can be significant.

In fact, you might *have to* disable your wireless connectivity in situations where smartphones aren't allowed, such as during airplane flight takeoffs or in certain areas of a hospital. And because I'm a security-conscious guy, I **always** disable my wireless hardware whenever I'm not using it. Call me overly careful, but none of my shared files have ever been sucked out of my MacBooks (without my permission)!

To turn off your Wi-Fi hardware from the Finder menu bar, click the Wi-Fi icon and then click the "master switch" at the top of the Wi-Fi menu. To turn off your Bluetooth hardware from the Control Center, click the Control Center icon in the Finder menu bar and click the Bluetooth tile.

Take a Surge Protector with You

Many locales around the world offer a less-than-perfect power grid, which sometimes translates into a sudden loss of power — usually at exactly the wrong moment. (Think *Great American Novel Takes a Nosedive.*) Unlike a desktop, however, your Neo is smart enough to immediately switch from AC current to its battery in case of a power failure. So why am I suggesting a surge protector for your laptop, especially seeing as how it adds bulk and weight to your laptop bag or luggage?

>> **The risk of a power spike:** A surge protector is good protection from a massive power spike, such as an overload or lightning strike.

>> **Extra sockets on tap:** Don't forget that you might need several more AC sockets for external devices, such as a DVD drive or projector. A surge protector can provide extra access to power even when your host can't.

Don't Consider an Internal Drive Upgrade!

If you've been thinking about upgrading your internal drive, in a word: *don't.* The solid-state drive used in the Neo has been soldered directly onto the motherboard — so, like your MacBook's memory modules, they can't be upgraded. (As I said earlier in the chapter, it's always best to buy a MacBook with as much internal storage as you can afford.)

If you're short on drive space, first clean up your existing drive by deleting all the crud you don't need, including game and app demos, duplicate copies of images and documents, files that you downloaded from the internet, and the contents of the Trash. You can read how in Chapter 18.

WARNING

Perhaps you won't be truly satisfied with your life until you upgrade your Neo's "hardwired" internal drive. I'm sure that you can find magazine articles or You-Tube videos purporting to show you how, with instructions that claim to lead you down a rosy path to an internal Neo drive upgrade. Here's my take on those instructions: You're walking into a minefield with someone else's map, so you'd better have *complete* faith in your technical skills (and a darn good backup). My recommendation? *Don't.*

Add Storage Space Externally

"So how do I add more storage space if I can't upgrade my internal drive?" A great question, dear reader, and one that I can easily answer: Use an external drive! Use your Neo's faster USB-C port to connect a second drive the quick and easy way. You can move your external drive between Macs with a minimum of fuss and bother. A typical external USB-C solid-state drive that holds 1TB costs less than $100!

An external drive can do anything that your internal drive can do. You can boot from it, for example, or install a different version of macOS (great for beta testers like me). External optical drives work the same way.

TECHNICAL STUFF

Since data typically transfers more slowly over a cable connection than via an internal drive, most Mac owners use their external drives to store lesser-used documents and apps or Time Machine backups. Their favorite apps and often-used documents are housed on the faster internal drive.

Putting a port to work

A MacBook Neo carries two USB-C ports for connecting external devices. The USB standard is popular because it's just as common in the PC world as it is in the Mac world. The USB port closest to the back of the laptop supports the faster USB 3.0 standard. I use the second USB port almost exclusively for charging my Neo, since the USB 2.0 standard is far slower.

REMEMBER

Naturally, USB 3.0 offers faster data transfer speeds than the "creaky" older USB 2.0 standard. You should buy only USB-C external drives, DVD recorders, or flash drives that support USB 3.0 speeds, and connect them to the port closest to the back of the Neo. 'Nuff said.

Connecting an external drive

With USB, it's simple to install an external drive! With your MacBook turned on, follow these steps:

1. **Connect the USB cable between the drive and your Neo.**

2. **Plug the external drive into a convenient surge protector or uninterruptible power supply (if necessary).**

   Note that some external devices are *bus-powered,* meaning that they don't need a separate power supply. These devices draw their power directly from the port — but will also drain your Neo's battery faster.

3. **Switch on the external drive.**

4. **If the drive is unformatted or formatted for use in Windows, partition and format the external drive.**

   The drive comes with instructions or software for you to do this. Don't worry — you won't damage anything by formatting it. Partitioning divides the new drive into one or more volumes.

   If the drive comes preformatted for use with a Windows PC, I **strongly** suggest reformatting it for use with macOS. Doing so will result in faster performance and more efficient use of space.

After the drive is formatted and partitioned, the volumes you've created immediately appear on the Desktop. Shazam!

Not Again! What Is It with You and Backing Up?

Yes, this is one of the Top Ten Neo Rules as well. I'm not kidding: If you think you don't need to back up on a regular basis, *you'll eventually lose every byte of data you have.* **Period.** It's only a matter of time. Even if you have incredible luck and don't do something you regret with a Finder window, your MacBook Neo is just a machine, and it'll wear out in the long run — especially with the mobile life of a road warrior, with all the bumps and bruises of travel.

Backing up your drive with Time Machine isn't difficult and doesn't take long, and it does indeed protect *every* file and folder. Also, you can restore all your data files on your Neo's entire internal drive with ease. Chapter 18 explains everything you need to know. After you finish your first full backup, sit back and celebrate your Neo Peace of Mind!

Chapter **20**

Ten Things to Avoid Like the Plague

f you've read my other books in the *For Dummies* series, you might recognize the title of this chapter. It's my favorite Part of Tens subject. I don't like to see *any* computer owner fall prey to pitfalls. Some pitfalls are minor (such as not keeping your Neo clean), and others are catastrophic (such as providing information over the internet to persons unknown).

All these potential mistakes, however, have one thing in common: They're *easy to prevent* with a little common sense, once you're aware of them. And making you aware is my favorite job. In this chapter, I fill in what you need to know. Consider these pages to be valuable knowledge gained easily!

USB 2.0 Storage Devices

Man, a USB 2.0 storage device is the very *definition* of sluggish. Only a creaking USB 2.0 external device such as a hard drive, USB hub, or CD-ROM drive could be as slow as a turtle on narcotics. Unfortunately, you still find countless examples of USB 2.0 hardware hanging around, ready to ensnare unsuspecting MacBook owners. eBay is stuffed to the gills with USB 2.0 equipment, and your family might try to gift that old 8x CD-RW drive to you. (This present, like your Aunt Harriet's fruitcake, is one you should politely refuse.) These drives were considered speedy in the past — but today, a USB 2.0 external drive is simply a slow-as-maple-syrup-in-January *embarrassment*. Since your trendy Neo offers a USB-C port operating at USB 3.0 speed, **use it whenever possible for external devices!** I use my USB 2.0 port almost exclusively for charging. (Don't forget, you'll also need a adapter to use a USB 2.0 device with any USB-C port.)

I do admit that plenty of great USB 2.0 devices are still around these days, such as joysticks, keyboards, mice, and other controllers, along with printers that work just fine with slower transfer rates. But if a peripheral's job is to store or move data quickly — including external drives, network connections, USB hubs, DVD or Blu-ray drives, and USB flash drives — take my heartfelt advice and give a USB 2.0 device a wide berth. Opt instead for a USB-C device that supports the USB 3.0 standard!

Phishing Operations

Phishing is no phun. No, the first word is not misspelled. In internet lingo, *phishing* refers to an attempt by unsavory characters to illegally obtain your personal data. If that sounds like an invitation to identity theft, it is. Thousands of sites have defrauded individuals like you and me (along with banks and credit card companies) out of billions of dollars. Unfortunately, the phishing industry has grown like a weed, and more innocent folks are being ripped off every day. (The lowlifes running phishing operations are pond scum. I'm being polite because this will appear in print.)

A phishing scam works like this: You get an email purporting to be from a major company or business, such as eBay, a government agency, or a credit card company. The message looks genuine, with all the proper graphics and company information. It warns you that you must "update" your login or financial information to keep it current or that you must "validate" your information. It even provides a convenient link to an official-looking web page. After you enter your oh-so-personal information on that bogus page, the info is piped directly to the bad guys, and they're off to the races.

Here's a Mark's Maxim that every internet user should take to heart:

No *legitimate* company or agency will *ever* solicit your personal information through an email or text message!

Never respond to these messages. If you smell a scam, open your browser, visit the company's site (the *real* one) directly and contact the company's customer-support personnel. They'll certainly want to know about the phishing, and you can provide them the scam email and web addresses. If you respond to a phishing email, the perpetrators know that your email address is "live" and you may be deluged by a flood of spam (and worse).

In fact, sending *any* valuable information (including passwords) through unencrypted email — even to those you trust — is a bad idea. Email messages can be read from any email server that stores your messages.

The Twin Terrors: Viruses and Malware

It's a common misconception that all Macs are safe from viral attack. I've talked to many a Mac power user who assures me that "macOS is simply not a target for malicious programs, because Windows is more popular and easier to hack." And they're right, if you happen to be living in the 1990s . . . . Believe me, those halcyon days are **long** gone.

Dear friend, I'm here to tell you that your MacBook Neo is *indeed* a target for viruses and *malware* (apps that can slow down your Neo or even capture your personal data and send it to who-knows-where). In fact, Macs can be attacked with the extremely nasty *ransomware* virus strain, which encrypts your entire drive, preventing you from accessing any of your data unless you pay a "ransom" in digital currency. Other virus strains remain hidden, turning your Neo into a mindless zombie that spews spam to everyone in your Contacts list, all while you're innocently using your laptop.

As I mention elsewhere in this tome, there are a number of free antivirus apps to install, or you can invest in a commercial app with additional features and technical support. Do what I do: Use an antivirus app, and keep it updated to maintain your defenses!

Submerged Keyboards

Do you *really* want a submerged keyboard? Your answer should be an unequivocal no! And that's why you should make it a rule to keep all beverages well out of range of keyboards, trackpads, and external devices — especially when kids or cats are in close proximity to your Neo.

If soda gets spilled on your Neo, you're likely to be visited with intermittent keyboard problems (or, in the worst case, a short in your MacBook's motherboard). Remember, 12 inches of open space can make the difference between a simple cleanup and an expensive replacement!

Antiquated Utility Software

Everyone plays the upgrade game. If you're using Tahoe, you must upgrade your older macOS utility programs — such as an older copy of TechTool Pro from Micromat (`https://www.micromat.com/`) written for macOS Sonoma. I know you spent good money on 'em, but these older disk-utility applications can do more harm than good to an internal drive under Tahoe. If you use an older utility application, you could find yourself with corrupted data. (Of course, the macOS Disk Utility app is perfectly safe!)

Software Piracy

Avoiding pirated software is a no-brainer. **Don't endorse software piracy.** Remember, Apple's overall market share among worldwide computer users currently weighs in at around 10 percent. Software developers know this, and they have to expect (and *receive*) a return on their investment; otherwise, they'll find something more lucrative to do with their time. As a shareware author, I can attest to this fact firsthand.

Pirated software may seem attractive. The price is right, no doubt about it. But if you use an app without buying it, you're cheating the developer, who'll eventually find that doing Mac programming is no longer worth the time. Believe me, the MacBook Neo is a great machine, and Tahoe is a great operating system, but the sexiest laptop on the planet won't make up for an absence of good apps. Pay for what you use, and everyone benefits.

The Forbidden Account

You may never have encountered the *root,* or *System Administrator,* account in macOS — and that's A Good Thing. Note that I'm not talking about a standard Administrator (or Admin) account; every Mac needs at least one Admin account. (In fact, it may be the only account on your Neo.)

The *root account,* though, is a different beast altogether, and that's why it's disabled by default. Anyone who logs in with the root account can do *anything* to your system, including modifying system files (which no other account can normally access). Believe me — formatting your drive is about the only thing worse than screwing up your macOS Tahoe core files.

Luckily, no one can access the root/System Administrator account by accident. Unless an Apple support technician tells you to enable and use it, you should promptly forget that the root account even exists.

Unsecured Wireless Connections

I like free internet access as much as the next "groovy" technology author. It's cool, it's convenient, and public wireless networks are popping up all over the world. Many U.S. cities offer citywide free wireless internet access.

Just because something is *free,* however, doesn't mean that it's *safe.* (Impromptu and overly trusting bungee jumpers, take note.) Unfortunately, the free public wireless access you're likely to encounter is *not secure.* Anyone can join, and the data you transfer can be intercepted by any hacker worthy of the name. You have no guarantee that your email, your company's spreadsheets, and your Great American Novel aren't being intercepted while you're uploading and downloading them in the airport.

REMEMBER

If you *must* use your Neo on an unsecured public network, make sure that the connection itself is secure instead. Don't check your email by using a web browser, for example, unless your Internet service provider or email service offers an encrypted connection that begins with "https:". If you regularly need to establish a secure connection with your home or office network, use an SSL-enabled *virtual private network* (VPN) client, which allows you to transfer files and remotely operate a host computer with bulletproof security. (Your wireless router might have VPN functionality built in, so check your router's manual closely.)

Naturally, macOS includes a built-in basic VPN client, so you don't need additional software to connect. Open System Settings, click the Network entry and then click the . . . More button. Click the Add VPN Configuration entry from the pop-up menu to select the proper connection, and then enter the connection settings from your VPN provider and click Create.

Refurbished Hardware

Boy howdy, do I **hate** refurbished stuff. I always make it a point to dispel the myth that you're "saving" money when you buy a refurbished piece of hardware. As the saying goes, if it sounds too good to be true, *it probably is.*

Consider what you get when you buy a refurbished external drive. It's likely that the drive was returned as defective and then was sent back to the factory. There, the manufacturer probably performed the most cursory of repairs (just enough to fix the known problem), perhaps tested the unit for a few seconds, and then packed it up again. Legally, retailers can't resell the drive as a new item, so they cut the price so low that you're willing to take a chance on it.

Before you spend a dime on a so-called bargain that's *remanufactured* (I can't get over that term), make sure to find out how long a warranty you'll receive, if any. Consider that the device is likely to have crisscrossed the country at least once, picking up bumps and bruises during its travels. Also, there's no telling how well the repairs were tested or inspected.

I don't buy refurbished hardware. (The exception is the Apple online store, where you can buy a refurbished Mac with a one-year warranty. Even then, I would strongly recommend that you purchase AppleCare as well.)

Dirty Laptops

Clean your Neo. Every computer (and every piece of computer hardware) appreciates a weekly dusting. You should clean your screen every two or three days — unless you *like* peering through a layer of dust, fingerprints, and smudges. *Never* spray anything directly on your screen or your Neo's case. A wipe with a soft cloth will keep your Neo's case in spotless shape.

Index

Numerics

802.11ax wireless standard, 143

802.11b/a/g/n/ac standards, 146

A

access levels, 129

account name, 130

account's access settings, managing, 134–135

AC outlet, standard, 12

Action button, 58

active window, 41, 50, 186

Add a Caption box, 191

Add a Title heading, 191

Add Column After command, 225

Add Column Before command, 225

Add Controls button, 54

Add Faces button, 192

adding users, 129–131

Add List button, 90

Add Reminder button, 91

Address box, 108

Add Row Above command, 225

Add Row Below command, 225

Add Slide button, 235

Add To Favorites button, 187

Adjust button, 198

adjustments, filters and, 198

administrator account, 128, 129, 132, 134. *See also* user accounts

Advanced Audio Coding (AAC), 168

Advanced Data Protection, 76

AirDrop, 72, 83, 94, 99, 142, 148, 159, 187, 195. *See also* file sharing; network sharing

AirDrop & Continuity option, 72, 122

airline flight information, 84

AirPlay, 72, 142, 171, 172, 181

AirPods, 181

AirTag, 267

Album Artist field, 175

aliases, 42

Alignment buttons, 224

Allow Guests to Log In to This Computer, 133

Allow This User to Administer This Computer, 131, 134

All Photos button, 186, 191

App corner, 71

Appearance pane, 77–78

Apple A18 Pro CPU, 11

Apple Account pane, 267

Apple Authorized Service Provider, 253–254

AppleCare, 278

AppleCare & Warranty, 72

AppleCare Protection Plan, 23, 24

AppleCare toll-free number, 21

Apple Creator Studio, 212, 218, 228, 239

Apple Help Online, 254

Apple ID, 24, 89, 120, 121, 123, 124, 163, 171, 180, 184, 267

Apple Intelligence Writing Tools, 214–215. *See also* Writing Tools

Apple Lossless format, 168

Apple Mail, 16, 17, 23, 30, 49, 51, 133

Apple menu, 33, 246, 249

Apple Music, 168, 172, 177, 180

Apple Music Radio, 179–180. *See also* internet radio

Apple online store, 278

Apple Pencil, 123

Apple's digital lifestyle suite, 16

Apple's digital productivity suite, 16

Apple Support website, 60, 250, 268

Apple technician, 247

Apple TV, 142, 171

Application menu, 33

Application Support folders, 258

Application Windows corner, 71

App Store, 16, 20, 257

Arrange All command, 40

arrow keys, 38, 43

aspect ratios, 187, 197

associated files, 258–259

Audiobooks, 168

audio CDs, ripping, 177–178

audio chat, 160

audio equalizer, 178

audio features, 9

audio files, 172, 177, 178

Auto Enhance, 198

AutoFill, 108, 109

AutoFill & Passwords, 72

Auto Login, 137

Automatically Hide and Show the Dock, 68

Automatically Hide and Show the Menu Bar, 74

automatic macOS updates, 262

automatic song information, 176

Automatic Updates, 71

Auto-Save feature, 207, 219, 233
Avast Security for Mac, 251

B

Back and Forward icons, 64
Back button, 108, 184, 186
background shapes, 213
backups, 259–260, 271
base station, 145
battery, 10
  Battery pane, 21, 22, 73–74
  calibration, 22
  icon, 21, 22
  management, 21–22
  -monitoring system, 21
Beach Ball of Doom, 245
Birthday photos, 192
bit rate, 178
Blank template, 206
Bluetooth, 11, 148, 268–269
  mouse, 36
  networking, 123
  speaker systems, 9
Bookmarks, 107, 109, 111, 112
boot drive, 246, 249
boot volume, 249
branding your Neo, 268
Brightness slider, 66
broadband modem,
    144, 150, 152
Browse All Versions, 234
Browse Content button, 239
Browse Time Machine
    Backups, 261
bundled software, 15–16
bus-powered devices, 271

C

cables, 18, 251
  connecting, 14
    internet connection, 14
    power connection, 14

Caches folders, 258
Calendar, 17, 95
camera, external, 17
Caps Lock key, 20
Cat5/Cat5E/Cat6 Ethernet
    cables, 149
CCleaner for Mac, 259
CD audio, 168
cells, navigating and
    selecting, 221–222
cell shading, 224–225
Cell tab, 223–225
cell text alignment, 224
cellular connections, 159
Chart button, 227
charts, 227
ChatGPT, 228–229
Cheat Sheet pages, 4
checklists, 94
check-mark keyword, 193
Chess, 17
cleanup utilities, 259
Clipboard, 209–211
Close button, 40
Collections entry, 190
ColorSync profile, 66
Comments field, 175
commercial cleanup tool, 259
commercial utility app, 246
Completed list, 91
Compose feature, 215, 229, 237
Configure IPv4
    pop-up menu, 150
connecting cables, 14
  internet connection, 14
  power connection, 14
Contacts, 17, 83, 99, 160
Contacts Card, 131
Containers, 248
Content & Privacy
    settings, 181–182
Content Hub, 212, 228, 239
Content pane, 100–101, 107
contextual menu, 33, 36

Continuity Camera, 17, 163
Control Center icon, 21, 31–32,
    53–54, 74, 269
cookies, 116–117
Copy command, 210
copying items, 44–45
CPU, 11
Create button, 206
cropping and straightening
    images, 196–197
CSV (comma-separated values)
    files, 218
currency formatting, 223
custom Music Radio
    stations, 179–180
Cut command, 209–210

D

Data Access, 77
data entry and editing, 222–223
Data Format, 223
data migration
  from old Mac, 24–26
  from Windows, 26–27
Date & Time, 72
Delete Album command, 191
Delete button, 252
Delete Column command, 225
Deleted Users folder, 132
Delete Items After Import
    option, 189
Delete key, 173, 236
Delete Row command, 225
Desktop & Dock pane, 50,
    51, 56, 66
  Desktop & Stage Manager
    settings, 69
  Dock settings, 67–68
  Mission Control settings, 70–71
  widgets settings, 69–70
  Windows settings, 70
Desktop & Stage Manager
    settings, 69
desktop computers, 1

Desktop corner, 71

Desktop customization, 52–53

Desktop settings, 128

Desktop widgets, 55–56, 96

Details tab, 175–176

Device Management, 73

DHCP server, 150–151

Diagnostics category, 253

digital audio playback, 168

finding songs, 172

removing songs, 173

digital extraction, 177

digital lifestyle suite, Apple, 16

digital productivity suite, Apple, 16

disclosure triangle, 59

Disc Number field, 175

Disk Utility, 247–250, 262. *See also* First Aid; laptop troubleshooting

Display Calibrator, 66

Displays pane, 65–66

Dock, 30–31, 36, 56

customization, 54

adding applications and extras, 54–55

Desktop widgets, 55–56

resizing, 57

Stacks, 56–57

settings, 67–68

documents

creating, 206, 218

iCloud Drive, 121–122

opening, 206–207

saving, 207

sharing, 216

Word, 216

Download New Updates When Available, 262

Downloads folder, 57, 113

dragging, 43–44, 54

drive maintenance, 262

Driving mode, 97

DSL internet router, 14

Duplicate command, 235

duplicating items, 45–46

DVD drive, 12, 169, 171, 177–178

Dynamic Host Configuration Protocol (DHCP), 151

Dynamic Wallpaper, 75

Dynamic WEP encryption, 147

E

Edit button, 187, 195

editing song information, 176–177

Edit Keywords button, 194

Edit menu, 214

Edit Widgets button, 95

Eject icon, 58

email, 16, 23, 83, 109, 159, 201–202, 275, 277

emoji, 161

Empty Trash command, 258

ePub file, 216

equalizer, audio, 178

Equalizer window, 178

Esc key, 40, 190, 196

Ethernet adapter, 14

Ethernet cable, 14, 18, 149

Ethernet hub or switch, 14

Ethernet jack, nearby, 12

Ethernet LAN port, 146

Ethernet network, 11

Ethernet switch, 145, 149

explicit content, 181

Explore mode, 97

Export button, 199

Export To command, 216

external camera, 17

external devices, 245, 250–251

external drives, 37, 53, 142. *See also* Time Machine

external keyboard, 12, 13, 15

external monitors, 65, 66, 75

external optical drive, 177, 248, 249

external storage, 270

connecting external drives, 271

USB-C ports, 270

F

Facebook profile image, 197

FaceTime, 95, 96, 159–160, 163. *See also* video chat

FaceTime HD camera, 9–10, 131, 157

Fast Forward button, 183

Fast User Switching, 136–137

Favorites, 101, 106, 107, 111–112

file downloads, 113

File Open dialog, 49

files, saving, 260

file sharing, 87, 153. *See also* network sharing

FileVault, 138–139, 267–268

Fill heading, 224

filmstrip, 159

filters and adjustments, 198

Filters button, 198

Finder, 29

Finder and app shortcuts, 47–48

Finder menu bar, 10, 21, 22, 33, 73, 74, 77, 82, 246, 254

Finder Search window, 86–87

Finder tabs, 46, 260

Finder windows, 33, 38, 42, 168–169, 173, 180, 183, 189, 219, 227–228, 233, 239–240, 257–258, 260, 261

closing, 40–41

minimizing and restoring, 39

moving and zooming, 39–40

scrolling and resizing, 38–39

Find My icon, 267

Find My Mac, 125, 267

Find My Network, 125

fire sharing, 138

firewalls, 154–155. *See also* unsecured wireless networks

First Aid, 248–249, 262

flagged reminders, 91–92

floating objects, 212

Flyover Tour option, 97

folders and icons, 42. *See also* Finder windows

copying items, 44–45

duplicating items, 45–46

Finder Tabs, 46

icon types, 42–43

moving items, 45

selecting items, 43–44

folders sidebar, 93

Font Color button, 224

Font Family button, 224

Font Size button, 224

Force Quit dialog, 37, 245

Format button, 210, 223, 226, 227, 234, 238

Format Inspector, 211

Format menu, 211, 238

formulas and functions, 225–226

Forward button, 108

full-aspect-ratio thumbnails, 187

Full Name text box, 130

full-screen mode, 40, 108, 187, 199

Function list, 220

G

General pane, 71–73

Generate Image button, 212

Genius feature, 173

Genius playlists, 173

Get Info command, 191, 195, 258

Google Mail, 23

graphics, 212

grid display, 56–57

grocery lists, 92

Guest account, 132–133

guest users, 132–133

H

Handoff, 122–123. *See also* Continuity Camera; Sidecar

Hard Disks, 32

headphone jack, 9

healthy laptop checklist, 20–21

help resources, 60

Apple support website, 60

online resources, 60

Tahoe Help system, 60

hidden parts, 10–11

high-speed internet, 11, 14

History, 109, 114

Home button, 111

Home folder, 48–49, 128, 131, 132, 138

home page, 108–109

hot-corner settings, 71

https connections, 277

Hulu, 142

I

iCloud, 24, 119

account, 89, 92, 267

configuration, 124–125

connectivity, 92

Handoff, 122–123

how iCloud works, 120–121

iCloud Drive documents, 121–122

settings, 76–77

Sidecar, 123

storage management, 125

tab, 110, 200, 201

iCloud+ button, 76, 125

iCloud Drive, 125, 206, 207, 233–234

iCloud ID, 24

iCloud Keychain passwords, 117

iCloud Links, 201–202

iCloud Photos, 124–125, 200. *See also* Photos

iCloud Shared Albums, 201

icon types, 42–43

Image Playground, 195, 212

images, 188

editing, 195

Auto Enhance, 198

cropping and straightening, 196–197

filters and adjustments, 198

red-eye removal, 198

retouching, 198

rotating images, 196

importing, 188–189

organizing, 190

keywords, 192–193

keyword searches, 194

location searches, 194–195

People & Pets, 191–192

photo albums, 190–191

and 3D objects, 227–228

IMAP mail servers, 23

iMovie, 157, 163

Important Hidden Stuff (IHS), 10

Imports album, 189

Info dialog, 175–177

inline objects, 212

Insert button, 228

Insert menu, 212

Inspector, 210, 220, 238

instant messaging, 16

internal devices, 11

internal drives, larger, 266

internal drive upgrades, 269–270

Internet Accounts, 92, 94

internet and network connections, 251

internet connections, 14, 152

internet features, 16

internet, high-speed, 11, 14

internet radio, 178. *See also* Apple Music Radio

custom Music Radio stations, 179–180

radio playlists, 179

streaming stations, 179

internet router, 144–145, 149, 150, 152

internet service provider (ISP), 23, 251

internet-sharing device, 144–145, 149, 152

iOS devices, 120–123

IP address, 150

iPhone, 16, 17

iPhone and iPad, syncing with, 180–181

iTunes Store, 180, 183–184, 257

J

Journal entries, 159

K

keyboard and trackpad, 9

keyboard shortcuts, 46, 181

Finder and app shortcuts, 47–48

special keys, 47

keyboards, liquids near, 276

Keynote, 16, 231

background shape, 239

creating presentations, 232

media, 239

opening presentations, 233

Presenter Notes, 238

printing slides and notes, 241–242

saving presentations, 233–234

slides, 235

slideshows, 240–241

slide text, 236–237

text, shapes, and graphics boxes, 236

text formatting, 238

3D objects, 240

toolbar, 234, 236, 238, 239, 242

window, 234–235

Writing Tools, 237

Keyword Manager, 193, 194

keywords, 82, 192–193

searches, 194

L

Language & Region, 72

LAN (local-area network), 146

laptop bags and sleeves, 265–266

laptop cleaning, 278

laptop docking station, 18

laptop sleeve or case, 17

laptop troubleshooting, 243, 244

Disk Utility, 247–248

First Aid, 248–249

myths, 244

rebooting, 245–246

Safe mode, 246

steps, 249

cables, 251

Disk Utility checks, 250

internet and network connections, 251

login items, 252

recent changes, 250

screen savers, 252–253

System Information, 253

Trash, 251

virus scans, 251

technical support, 253

Apple Help Online, 254

local service, 253–254

macOS Help Center, 254

launching and quitting apps, 36–37

Layout pane, 209

LED display, 8

Left Option+Left Shift+Left Control shortcut, 246

links, 107

Liquid Glass, 77

List of Users login, 136

List view mode, 57

Live Updating, 174

Loading Startup Options message, 246, 249

local service, 253–254

location considerations, 12–13

location searches, 194–195

locked applications, 245

Lock Note, 95

logging out, 137

login items, 37, 133–134, 252

Login Items & Extensions, 72, 133

login options, 136–137

login password, 138–139

Loop icon, 199

Low Power Mode, 21, 74

Lyrics button, 177

M

MacBook Neo, 13

connecting cables, 14

internet connection, 14

power connection, 14

handling, 15

setup and unpacking, 13–14

Mac laptop, 8

hidden parts, 10–11

parts, 8

audio features, 9

battery, 10

FaceTime HD camera, 9–10

keyboard and trackpad, 9

power button, 9

power cable, 9

screen, 8

ports, 10

USB-C ports, 11–12

macOS Disk Utility, 247

macOS Help Center, 254
macOS Help system, 27
macOS Quick Look feature, 37
macOS Tahoe, 1, 2, 15, 29, 50
  applications, 17
  bundled software, 15–16
  Control Center
      customization, 53–54
  Desktop customization, 52–53
  Dock customization, 54
    adding applications and
        extras, 54–55
    Desktop widgets, 55–56
    resizing, 57
    Stacks, 56–57
  Finder windows, 38
    closing, 40–41
    minimizing and restoring, 39
    moving and zooming, 39–40
    scrolling and resizing, 38–39
  folders and icons, 42
    copying items, 44–45
    duplicating items, 45–46
    Finder Tabs, 46
    icon types, 42–43
    moving items, 45
    selecting items, 43–44
  help resources, 60
    Apple support website, 60
    online resources, 60
    Tahoe Help system, 60
  Home folder, 48–49
  internet features, 16
  keyboard shortcuts, 46
    Finder and app
        shortcuts, 47–48
    special keys, 47
  launching and quitting
      apps, 36–37
  Mission Control, 50
  operating system (OS), 30
  printing, 58–59

  setting up, 22–24
  Spaces desktops, 51–52
  Stage Manager, 50–51
  Tahoe Desktop, 30
    Control Center, 31–32
    Dock, 30–31
    Finder menu bar, 33
    Finder window, 33
    icons, 32
    menus, 32–33
    widgets, 34
  trackpad and mouse
      controls, 34–36
  Trash, 57–58
magnification, 67
Mail, 83, 95, 99
Mail button, 109
malware, 275
Manage Storage, 256, 258
manual cleanup, 257
  associated files, 258–259
  unneeded files and
      folders, 257–258
Maps, 96–97, 122
  directions, 99
  map views, 97–98
Memories, 190, 195
menu bar, 32–33
  background, 74
Menu Bar pane, 74
menu commands, 2
Messages, 9, 16, 83,
    142, 160–161
messaging, instant, 16
metadata, 84, 194
Migration Assistant, 25, 261
Minimize button, 39
minus sign button, 252
Mission Control, 50–52, 70–71.
    See also Spaces Desktops;
    Stage Manager
modems, 251
modules, 74

Mouse pane, 36
Move to Trash command, 257
moving items, 45
MP3 files, 168
multiplayer games, 142
Multi-Touch feature, 40
multiuser Neo, 127
  access fairy tale, 127–128
  FileVault encryption, 138–139
  fire sharing, 138
  logging out, 137
  login options, 136–137
  user accounts, 128–129
    access levels, 129
    access
        management, 134–135
    adding users, 129–131
    deleting user accounts, 132
    login items, 133–134
    modifying user
        accounts, 131–132
Music, 16
Music and TV, 167
  audio equalizer, 178
  digital audio playback, 168
    finding songs, 172
    removing songs, 173
  internet radio, 178
    custom Music Radio
        stations, 179–180
    radio playlists, 179
    streaming stations, 179
  iTunes Store, 183–184
  Music formats, 168
  parental controls, 181–182
  playlists, 173–174
  ripping audio CDs, 177–178
  song information, 175
    automatic song
        information, 176
    editing song information,
        176–177

syncing with iPhone and
iPad, 180–181

TV app, 182–183

Music controls, 171, 177, 181

Music Equalizer, 178

Music formats, 168

music for slideshows, 199

Music library, 128, 169–174,
176, 180, 184

Music Radio station, 179–180

Music sidebar, 169

Music Videos entry, 170

Music window, 169, 171

N

Name and Password login, 136

Neo rules, 265

backups, 271

branding your Neo, 268

external storage, 270

connecting external
drives, 271

USB-C ports, 270

FileVault encryption, 267–268

Find My Mac, 267

internal drive
upgrades, 269–270

laptop bags and
sleeves, 265–266

larger internal drives, 266

surge protectors, 269

wireless hardware,
disabling, 268–269

Netflix, 142

network connections, 145

wired connections, 148

joining wired Ethernet
network, 150–151

wired network
hardware, 149–150

wired network setup, 149

wireless connections, 145

connecting to existing
wireless networks, 145

joining wireless
networks, 147–148

wireless base
stations, 145–146

network printers, 153–154

networks, 141

advantages, 142

firewalls, 154–155

internet sharing, 144–145

wired vs wireless
networks, 143–144

network sharing, 151

file sharing, 153

internet connections, 152

printer sharing, 153–154

News, 100–101

favorites and channels, 101

window, 100

Next button, 169

Night Shift button, 66

Notes, 92–95, 159

Notification Center, 35,
55, 71, 95–96

Notifications settings, 78–79

number formatting, 223

Numbers, 16, 217

cell shading, 224–225

cell text alignment, 224

charts, 227

creating documents, 218

data entry and
editing, 222–223

formulas and
functions, 225–226

images and 3D
objects, 227–228

navigating and selecting
cells, 221–222

number formatting, 223

Numbers window, 220–221

opening spreadsheets, 219

printing spreadsheets,
229–230

rows and columns, 225

saving spreadsheets, 219–220

spreadsheets, 218

window, 220–221

Writing Tools, 228–229

Numbers Edit menu, 228

numeric heading buttons, 221

O

Open at Login list, 252

Open dialog, 206–207

Open in New Tab command, 46

Open Recent
command, 207, 219

operating system (OS), 30

optical drive, 9

Options icon, 249

Outline view, 242

P

Page Down key, 38

page orientation, 230

Pages, 16, 205. *See also*
Keynote; Numbers

Apple Intelligence Writing
Tools, 214–215

background shapes, 213

Copy command, 210

creating documents, 206

Cut command, 209–210

documents, 120

icon, 206

opening documents, 206–207

Paste command, 210

photos and graphics, 212

printing, 215

saving documents, 207

sharing documents, 216

spell-checking, 214

Pages *(continued)*

 tables, 211–212

 text, shapes, and graphics boxes, 209

 text editing, 209

 text formatting, 210–211

 3D objects, 213

 window, 208

Page Thumbnails, 208

Page Up key, 38

parental controls, 181–182

Partitioning function, 247

Password Hint text box, 130

Paste command, 210

Pause button, 169

PDF button, 230

PDF files, 216

People & Pets, 191–192

phishing scams, 274–275

photo albums, 190–191

Photo Booth, 10, 157–159. *See also* FaceTime HD camera

Photos, 16, 185

 and graphics, 212

 iCloud Links, 201–202

 iCloud Photos, 200

 iCloud Shared Albums, 201

 images, importing, 188–189

 images, organizing, 190

 keywords, 192–193

 keyword searches, 194

 location searches, 194–195

 People & Pets, 191–192

 photo albums, 190–191

 interface, 185–188

 library, 93, 228

 mode, editing, 195

 Auto Enhance, 198

 cropping and straightening, 196–197

 filters and adjustments, 198

 red-eye removal, 198

 retouching, 198

 rotating images, 196

 synchronization, 124–125

Photos Browser, 93

Photos Retouch feature, 198

picture-in-picture display, 160

pie chart icon, 227

pinned tabs, 107, 115

Play button, 169, 196, 199, 228, 240

playlists, 173–174. *See also* Music library

Playlists header, 169

Plexiglas, 13

plus sign button, 252

podcasts, 180, 182

pointer, 34

POP3 mail servers, 23

pop-up ads, 118

portable powerhouse, turning on, 19

 battery management, 21–22

 healthy laptop checklist, 20–21

 migrating data from old Mac, 24–26

 migrating data from Windows, 26–27

 powering on your Neo, 19–20

 setting up macOS Tahoe, 22–24

ports, 10

power button, 9

power cable, 9

power connection, 14

powering on your Neo, 19–20

Power On self-test, 253

power spikes, 269

Preferences folders, 258

Premium templates, 206

Preview thumbnails, 59

Previous button, 169, 176

Print All Sheets option, 229

Print button, 109

printer sharing, 153–154

printing, 58–59, 215

printing spreadsheets, 229–230

printing web pages, 115–116

Print sheet, 215

Print This Sheet option, 229

Privacy & Security pane, 267

privacy protection, 116

 cookies, 116–117

 iCloud Keychain passwords, 117

 pop-up ads, 118

 website notifications, 117–118

Privacy Report, 110

Profile, 110

Progress bar, 169

Public folder, 131, 138, 142, 153

Q

Quick Group, 193

Quick Look, 83, 86

Quick Note corner, 71

QuickTime video clips, 183

R

radio, internet, 178

 custom Music Radio stations, 179–180

 radio playlists, 179

 streaming stations, 179

radio playlists, 179

RAID Assistant, 247

ransomware, 275

Reader panel, 113

Reading List, 105, 107, 110, 112, 113

rebooting, 245–246

Recent Applications feature, 55

Recent Calls list, 160

recent documents, 74

Recent Items, 37

Recently Added category, 184

Recently Deleted folder, 94

Recommendations section, 256
red-eye correction, 198
red-eye removal, 198
refurbished hardware, 278
Rehearse Slideshow, 238
Reload icon, 109
Remember icon, 3
Reminders, 83, 90–92, 159. *See also* Notification Center
Remote tab, 241
Reset Adjustments button, 197
Restart command, 249
Restore button, 261
Restore from Time Machine function, 261
retouching, 198
Return key, 2, 222
Reverse button, 183
Revert To command, 207
right-click menu, 33, 35
ripping audio CDs, 177–178
root account, 277
root/System Administrator account, 277
Rotate button, 196, 213, 228, 240
rotating images, 196
rows and columns, 225

S

Safari, 16, 30, 37, 46, 49, 55, 57, 60, 83, 105
  bookmarks, 111–112
  browser, 4
  file downloads, 113
  History, 114
  printing web pages, 115–116
  privacy protection, 116
    cookies, 116–117
    iCloud Keychain passwords, 117
    pop-up ads, 118
    website notifications, 117–118
  profiles, organizing with, 110–111
  Reading list, 113
  Safari window, 105–107
  tabbed browsing, 114–115
  visiting websites, 107–108
  web navigation, 108–110
  window, 105–106
Safari Settings dialog, 117, 118
Safari Translation feature, 112
Safe Boot mode, 252
Safe mode, 246
Satellite mode, 98
Save As dialog, 220
Save As PDF, 215
Save to My Shapes, 213
saving files, 260
screen, 8
Screen Mirroring icon, 123
screen saver settings, 252–253
screen sharing, 161–162. *See also* FaceTime
Screen Time, 133–135
screen wipes, 18
scroll bars, 77, 78
SDXC card slot, 188
Search box, 90, 218
Search button, 194
search criteria bar, 86
search engines, 108
searching, Spotlight, 81
  basic Spotlight searching, 82–84
  customizing Spotlight, 88
  Finder Search window, 86–87
  Spotlight capabilities, 84–86
Search Privacy button, 88
Search Results window, 259
Secondary Click, 35
selecting items, 43–44
selection handles, 212
Send Copy option, 230, 242
Send to Back command, 213, 228, 239
serial number, 254
Settings dialog, 177, 182
setup and unpacking of MacBook Neo, 13–14
Setup Assistant, 26
Share button, 94, 101, 110, 159, 195, 201
Shared Albums, 201
sharing, 72
sharing documents, 216
sharing-only account, 129
Sheet canvas, 220
Sheets tabs, 220
Shift key, 212, 228, 236
shortcut menu, 57
Show/Exit Tab, 109
Show Indicators for Open Applications, 68
Show On All Spaces, 75
Show Suggested and Recent Apps in Dock, 68
Show Tab Overview button, 114
Sidebar, 45, 49, 100, 106, 109
Sidecar, 123. *See also* Handoff
Siri voice assistant, 161
sleep mode, 15, 21, 22
slideshows, 199, 241
Slides list, 234, 235, 238, 240, 242
Smart Albums, 190
Smart Playlists, 174
SMS text messaging, 160
SMTP mail servers, 23
software piracy, 276
software updates, 71
Software Update settings, 255, 262
solid-state drives, 11, 265, 269, 270
song information, 175
  automatic song information, 176
  editing song information, 176–177

songs
  finding, 172
  removing, 173
Songs entry, 169, 170, 179
Spacebar, 37
Spaces Desktops, 51–52
speakers, stereo, 9
spell-checking while typing, 214
Spotlight, 85, 87
Spotlight search box, 25, 65, 82, 86, 88, 151, 159, 162, 206, 218, 220, 253, 262
Spotlight search icon, 151, 188
Spotlight searching
  basic, 82–84
  customizing Spotlight, 88
  Finder Search window, 86–87
  Spotlight capabilities, 84–86
spreadsheets, 218
  opening, 219
  printing, 229–230
  saving, 219–220
SSL-enabled VPNs, 277
Stacks, 56–57
Stage Manager, 50–51, 69. *See also* Mission Control
standard account, 129, 134
Start Page, 107, 109–111
Startup Disk, 73
startup tone, 20
Status bar, 44, 107
stereo speakers, 9
Stop/Reload, 109
storage, 11
storage cleanup, 255
  cleanup utilities, 259
  Manage Storage, 256
  manual cleanup, 257
    associated files, 258–259
    unneeded files and folders, 257–258
Storage entry, 72
storage space, 255

automatic macOS updates, 262
  backups, 259–260
  drive maintenance, 262
  saving files, 260
  Time Machine, 260–262
straightening images, 196–197
streaming internet radio, 168
streaming stations, 179
SUM formula, 226
Summary pane, 180
surge protectors, 269
surge suppressor, 18
Switchers, 2, 149
synchronization pushing, 120
Sync Settings button, 180
System Data Files and Security Updates, 262
System Information window, 253
System Preferences, 25
System Settings, 21, 22, 25, 34–38, 50, 53–56, 63, 64, 83, 84, 87–88, 92, 94, 96, 129, 131–133, 136, 139, 250, 252–253, 261, 262, 278
  Appearance pane, 77–78
  Battery pane, 73–74
  Desktop & Dock pane, 66
    Desktop & Stage Manager settings, 69
    Dock settings, 67–68
    Mission Control settings, 70–71
    widgets settings, 69–70
    Windows settings, 70
  Displays pane, 65–66
  finding setting, 65
  General pane, 71–73
  iCloud settings, 76–77
  Menu Bar pane, 74
  Notifications settings, 78–79
  Wallpaper pane, 75–76

T

Tab bar, 106
tabbed browsing, 114–115. *See also* Safari
tables, 211–212
  in notes, 94
Tab Overview display, 114
tags, 91
Tahoe Desktop, 30
  Control Center, 31–32
  Dock, 30–31
  Finder menu bar, 33
  Finder window, 33
  icons, 32
  menus, 32–33
  widgets, 34
Tahoe Help system, 60
Tahoe Setup Assistant, 20
Tap to Click, 34
TCP/IP settings, 150
Technical Stuff icon, 3
technical support, 253
  Apple Help Online, 254
  local service, 253–254
  macOS Help Center, 254
Techtool Pro, 244
templates, 206
text alignment, 210
text editing, 209
text formatting, 210–211
text pointer, 209
text, shapes, and graphics boxes, 209
Theme Chooser window, 232
Themes, 199
things to avoid, 273
  laptop cleaning, 278
  liquids near keyboards, 276
  outdated utility software, 276
  phishing scams, 274–275
  refurbished hardware, 278
  root account, 277

software piracy, 276
unsecured wireless
    networks, 277–278
USB 2.0 storage devices, 274
viruses and malware, 275
3D objects, 213, 227–228
thumbnail icons, 86
Thumbnails pane, 186–187
Thunderbolt Bridge, 150
Time Machine, 73, 260–262
  backups, 270, 271
  external drive, 26
Tip icon, 3
toolbar, 41, 106, 208,
    210, 216, 234
Touch ID/Lock button, 19–20,
    94–95, 246, 266
trackball, 266
trackpad, 9, 276
  and mouse controls, 34–36
Trackpad pane, 34
Transfer or Reset, 73
Transit mode, 98
Translate icon, 112
Trash, 54, 57–58, 251, 258
troubleshooting,
    laptop, 243, 244
  Disk Utility, 247–248
  First Aid, 248–249
  myths, 244
  rebooting, 245–246
  Safe mode, 246
  steps, 249
    cables, 251
    Disk Utility checks, 250
    internet and network
      connections, 251
    login items, 252
    recent changes, 250
    screen savers, 252–253
    System Information, 253
    Trash, 251
    virus scans, 251

technical support, 253
  Apple Help Online, 254
  local service, 253–254
  macOS Help Center, 254
TV app, 182–183
TV shows, 167, 182, 184. *See also*
    Music and TV

U

Undo command, 223
Undo feature, 191, 197
uninterruptible power supplies
    (UPS), 271
Universal Clipboard, 123
unneeded files and
    folders, 257–258
unpacking of MacBook
    Neo, 13–14
unsecured wireless
    networks, 277–278
UPS (uninterruptible power
    supply), 18
Usage History display, 22
USB 2.0, 270, 274
USB 3.0, 270
USB-A ports, 10, 18
USB-C cable, 123, 163
USB-C device, 270, 274
USB-C ports, 9, 11–12, 18,
    188, 270, 274
USB-C-to-Ethernet
    connector, 148
USB flash drives, 27, 37,
    257, 260, 274
USB printers, 58, 146
user accounts, 128–129. *See also*
    administrator account
  access levels, 129
  access management, 134–135
  adding users, 129–131
  deleting, 132
  login items, 133–134
  modifying, 131–132
username, 136

users, adding, 129–131
Users & Groups pane, 129,
    131–133, 137
Utilities folder, 247
utility software, outdated, 276

V

video card, 11
video chat, 16, 157, 159, 160.
    See also FaceTime
video clips, 157, 159
videoconferencing, 9
Viewer pane, 196–197, 199
View menu, 208
virtual private network (VPN)
    client, 277–278
viruses and malware, 275
virus scans, 251
volume controls, 183
Volume slider, 169

W

Wallpaper pane, 75–76
WAN (wide-area
    network) port, 146
Warning icon, 3
web addresses, 3
web navigation, 108–110
web pages, printing, 115–116
website notifications, 117–118
Website Settings, 110
web surfing, 16
WEP encryption, 147
widgets, 69–70, 95–96
Wi-Fi connections, 159, 163
Wi-Fi hardware, 268–269
Wi-Fi status icon, 147
Wi-Fi tile, 54
Wi-Fi wireless networking, 21
window controls, 39, 41
Windows Migration Assistant, 26
Windows PCs, 2

Windows settings, 70

Windows-to-Mac Switcher, 26

window title bar actions, 67

wired connections, 148
  joining wired Ethernet
    network, 150–151
  wired network hardware, 149
    wired network
      components, 149
    wired network
      connections, 150
  wired network setup, 149

wired networks, 143

wired/wireless network
  connection between
  computers, 25–26

wireless communications
  devices, 11

wireless connections, 144, 145.
    See also networks
  connecting to existing wireless
    networks, 145
  joining wireless
    networks, 147–148
  wireless base
    stations, 145–146

Wireless Diagnostics, 151

wireless Ethernet, 11

wireless hardware,
  disabling, 268–269

wireless input devices, 20

wireless networking, 12

wireless networks,
  unsecured, 277–278

wireless printing, 11

Word documents, 216

WPA2 encryption, 147

WPA3 encryption, 147

wrist rest, 18

Writing Tools, 94, 214–215,
  228–229, 237

X

X button, 114, 159

Z

Zoom button, 41, 109

Zoom/Full Screen
  button, 40, 108

Zoom slider, 187

About the Author

Mark L. Chambers has been a technology author, computer consultant, BBS sysop, programmer, and hardware technician for almost 50 years, pushing computers far beyond "normal" performance limits for decades. His first love affair with a computer peripheral blossomed in 1984 when he bought a lightning-fast 300 bps modem for his Atari 400. Now he spends entirely too much time on the internet and drinks far too much caffeine-laden soda.

With a degree in journalism and creative writing from Louisiana State University, Mark took the logical career path: programming computers. However, after five years as a COBOL programmer for a hospital system, he decided there must be a better way to earn a living. So he became Documentation Manager for Datastorm Technologies, a well-known communications software developer. Somewhere in between writing software manuals, Mark began writing computer how-to books. His first book, *Running a Perfect BBS*, was published in 1994. After a short 30 years or so, Mark is a best-selling technology author (and very happy to boot)!

His pastimes include building scale models, watching St. Louis Cardinals baseball, playing his three pinball machines, enjoying both classic and cutting-edge computer games, supercharging computers, and rendering 3D flights of fancy. During these activities, he listens to just about every type of music imaginable, with a Music library of well over 300 GB.

Mark's expanding pantheon of books includes *MacBook For Dummies*, 10th Edition; *iMac For Dummies*, 11th Edition; *MacBook All-in-One For Dummies*, 2nd Edition; *Mac OS X Yosemite All-in-One For Dummies*; *Macs for Seniors For Dummies*, 5th Edition; *Build Your Own PC Do-It-Yourself For Dummies*; *Building a PC For Dummies*, 5th Edition; *Scanners For Dummies*, 2nd Edition; *CD & DVD Recording For Dummies*, 2nd Edition; *PCs All-in-One For Dummies*, 6th Edition; *Mac OS X Tiger: Top 100 Simplified Tips & Tricks*; *Microsoft Office v. X for Mac Power User's Guide*; *BURN IT! Creating Your Own Great DVDs and CDs*; *The Hewlett-Packard Official Printer Handbook*; *The Hewlett-Packard Official Recordable CD Handbook*; *The Hewlett-Packard Official Digital Photography Handbook*; *Computer Gamer's Bible*; *Recordable CD Bible*; *Teach Yourself VISUALLY iMac*; *Running a Perfect BBS*; *Official Netscape Guide to Web Animation*; and *Windows 98 Optimizing & Troubleshooting Little Black Book*.

His books have been translated into 15 languages; his favorites are German, Polish, Dutch, and French. Although he can't read them, he enjoys looking at the pictures a great deal.

Author's Acknowledgments

This project hit all the right notes for a technology author! It was challenging (because of the pace of writing and the scope of the material), it was fun to write, and it featured the revolutionary MacBook Neo (which hits a brand-new target for low-cost, high-value Apple hardware)! I am officially enamored with the Neo, and I know you will be, too.

But without the best and hardest-working folks in the technology publishing business working alongside me, you would never have seen this book! These folks made sure that what you read is accurate, instructive, and easy to understand.

Coincidence? I think not. That's the Wiley Way.

I need to send my heartfelt thanks to two wonderful editors at Wiley: my superb project manager and project editor, Susan Christophersen, and my first-class executive editor Lindsay Berg. These two folks provided the patience, guidance, and hard work necessary for any challenging project — and they're great friends as well. It's win-win!

Finally, as with every book I've ever written, I'd like to thank my wife, Anne, and my children, Erin, Chelsea, and Rose, for their support and love!

Dedication

This book is dedicated to the finest new additions to my growing family: James Joseph Skosky III and Violet Adelle Huntsman, my glorious grandchildren!

Publisher's Acknowledgments

Executive Editor: Lindsay Berg

Senior Editorial Assistant: Hanna Sytsma

Senior Managing Editor: Kristie Pyles

Project Manager: Susan Christophersen

Proofreader: Debbye Butler

Development and Copy Editor: Susan Christophersen

Production Editor: Tamilmani Varadharaj

Cover Images: Mark L. Chambers, Viktoriia Nigmatulina/Getty Images